D1627805

Archie's Lights

Archie's Lights

The Life and Times of a Scottish Lightkeeper

ARCHIE MacEACHERN
AND ANNE MacEACHERN

Whittles Publishing

Published by
Whittles Publishing Ltd.,
Dunbeath,
Caithness, KW6 6EG,
Scotland, UK

www.whittlespublishing.com

ISBN 978-184995-399-3

© 2019 Anne MacEachern
Illustrations by Duncan Baillie
Photographs from family albums unless otherwise attributed

All rights reserved.
No part of this publication may be reproduced,
stored in a retrieval system, or transmitted,
in any form or by any means, electronic,
mechanical, recording or otherwise
without prior permission of the publishers.

Cover illustrations: Archie's father
spying through a station telescope;
St Abbs Head lighthouse at dawn
(Ian Cowe); birds attracted to a
lighthouse lantern (Duncan Baillie)

Print and production managed by Jellyfish and CPI

Contents

To Kathleen, and in memory of her late brother, Angus

To Erik and Marianne

Acknowledgements

I would like to express my grateful thanks to Duncan Baillie for the generous contribution of his illustrations; Ian Cowe for his colour photographs of remote lighthouses; Hector Mackenzie for kindly agreeing to write the foreword; Kathleen for answering questions and providing some of the black and white photographs; Archie's nieces, Shona and the late Elizabeth, for more answers and for copies of old letters; my husband George for his patience and support with this project; the Northern Lighthouse Board with many of its staff, past and present, especially Lorna Hunter; Jean Reid for valuable advice; Michael Strachan at the Museum of Scottish Lighthouses, Fraserburgh; Keith Whittles for all his help and his team at Whittles Publishing. Much appreciation is also due to other family members and friends not mentioned individually.

To all – your encouragement and enthusiasm over many years have been invaluable. You've had a long wait for 'the book', but here we are at last!

Fair Isle

North Rona

Sula Sgeir

Orkney Isles

Stromness

Butt of Lewis

Flannan Isles   Breascleit

Covesea
Skerries   Kinnaird Head

Eilean Glas   Rattray Head

Chanonry   Buchan Ness

Monach   Inverness
Isles

Kyle of Lochalsh

Barra

Barra Head   Butterstone

Tiree   Mull   Oban

                                        Isle of May
Skerryvore   Erraid   Bass Rock

Dhuheartach   Granton   Barns Ness
                            Edinburgh

                                        St Abbs Head

Turnberry

Isle of Man

Chicken Rock

Preface

'Unwearying zeal' was expected of lightkeepers, according to a General Order book. In return, they received a tied house, free fuel and regular pay – security that was of particular value before the days of the welfare state. There were dangers and hardships to be faced; men in this line of work had to be strong, resourceful and disciplined. A liking for wild places, salt fish and dried figs would also have been an advantage! Wives needed to be self-sufficient; their men were absent for much of the time.

Having been born into a lighthouse family, Archie MacEachern was familiar with the demands of being a keeper. His grandfather, who came from a croft on Islay, was the first MacEachern to join the service of the Northern Lighthouse Board (NLB). Of this grandfather's six children, two sons became lightkeepers and two daughters married keepers. Other family members followed the same occupation, and some joined the Board's ships that tended the lights: Archie's brother became master of the *Hesperus* and finally of the *Fingal*. They grew up with the Board's traditions and aware of its ideal, 'For the Safety of All', conveyed by the official motto: *In Salutem Omnium*.

Archie was among those who fought for improved conditions – this was before the age of health and safety – often with his friend and colleague George Mackenzie. Archie served at many lighthouses, sometimes for short spells to provide emergency cover and some in wartime. After what he called the 'lonely years', Archie went to Covesea Skerries at Lossiemouth and then to Chanonry, from where he eventually retired. His first wife, Peggy, died there while he was still a keeper. Subsequently he and I met, and we married in 1973.

Archie retired as a full-time keeper in 1975, although he was asked to act as a relief welfare officer for the following six months. Soon after that he returned to work again, in part-time capacities, as the 'occasional' keeper at Chanonry and the attendant there when the light was automated in 1984. Altogether he served with the Northern Lighthouse Board for 66 years. He died in 2005 aged 95.

I was fortunate to become involved in this close-knit world of lighthouses and was fascinated by Archie's reminiscences and stories. When I told him that I would like

ix

Archie's father and uncle - in early days - with visitors at a pillar rock station.

to write a book about his life he did not show much enthusiasm at first. Lighthouse life, often in isolated places, was the only way of life he had known. As an outsider and much younger than Archie, I found it different. So I started to make notes from his recollections. Other snippets of background detail came my way that I checked carefully. Only later did Archie show real interest in this project. During our 31 years of marriage many retired and serving personnel visited us, including some of the characters in this book. They reminisced, swapping yarns, and those still working passed on the latest news. Of the old-timers, Jimmy Groat sometimes called when he drove north to his old home in Orkney; then tales of Dhuheartach and Erraid would come to life over a cup of tea. Meeting with Stewart and Annie from Fair Isle brought particular joy as did visits from Duncan of Turnberry days and his wife Kathryn. From further back, two of the Gibson brothers reappeared, to a great welcome.

As a boy Archie heard many stories from his father and the others around him. This is perhaps not surprising given the circumstances – he was only four when his mother died, so much time was spent in his father's company. Eventually he passed these stories on to his family, adding more from his own experiences. In recounting them, I have tried to convey the courageous spirit and humour of the man and his colleagues. They tell of a way of life that ended when all Scottish lighthouses were automated, the last being Fair Isle South in 1998.

During his later years, it became increasingly apparent how deeply Archie felt about the Flannan Isles tragedy. The 100th anniversary of the men's disappearance, in the year 2000, prompted a flurry of distorted stories in the press once more. He was keen then that his theory as to the probable cause should be aired. After all, his father had served at the lighthouse shortly before and after the disaster, so he knew the men who died – luckily he was not there

Grandfather and Grandmother MacEachern with Uncle Claude about 1880.

when it happened. Archie also worked at the Flannan Isles light for a spell many years after that. There he heard a startling piece of information from a local source. He was in a unique position to suggest the likely cause of the disaster and his first-hand knowledge could prove the most sensational stories to be ill-founded. Recalling other sad incidents, including the wartime death of a young German, brought him close to tears but there were many more that raised a smile.

For various reasons it has taken me a long time to complete this biography sprinkled with anecdotes. At the time of publication, nearly fourteen years have passed since Archie's death. The content of this book is factual but some people's names have been changed. It is as told to me over 30 years. It resembles a conversation with digressions, as memories were triggered, so is not necessarily always in strict order. It is written in the first person, in the hope you will be able to imagine Archie's voice with occasional Highland words of his day. Before I hand you over to Archie, here is a little about his parents' background:

Grandfather MacEachern (also called Archibald) was stationed at Skerryvore lighthouse when Archie's father, Angus, was born. His birth certificate stated: 'Angus MacEachern, son of Archibald MacEachern, Lightkeeper, and Catherine nee MacLeod was born in 1870 at Hynish Lighthouse in Tyree'. In those days, the Skerryvore families were housed at a shore station on Tiree.

During his lighthouse career Angus spent ten years at Dhuheartach lighthouse, 14 miles southwest of Mull. While stationed there, he met and married Jessie MacDonald, the assistant postmistress at Bunessan. Archie's parents' first home together was on the adjacent isle of Erraid where their eldest child, Katie, was born.

Archie's story opens at St Abbs Head.

Anne MacEachern

Foreword

by Lord Mackenzie of Culkein

Archie's Lights evokes so many memories for me. The freedom of a lighthouse childhood; shining copper and brass; sweeping light beams; fog signals. Then as a young adult the memory of a three-hour watch in an unheated lightroom immediately followed by three hours of trying to keep awake in a very hot engine room! For those of us born into lighthouse families and the disciplined way of life, I often think that training to be lightkeepers was inculcated from the time we could walk and talk. That would be as true for Archie and his brother as it was for my brother and me.

Like so many other lighthouse families, Archie's family and mine have a rich lighthouse tradition going back generations. Both families had lots of lightkeepers; both had Captains of Northern Lighthouse ships. Our families intermarried twice: my great uncle Hugh, a lightkeeper, married Mary MacEachern, an aunt of Archie. My Dad's sister, Jessie, married Archie's cousin, Finlay MacEachern, who was, of course, another keeper.

Archie MacEachern's illustrious career with the Northern Lighthouse Board (NLB) begins as a boy seaman in 1926. At the age of sixteen, he joined the flagship tender NLV *Pharos,* before transferring to train as a supernumerary lightkeeper six years later. His career follows the usual NLB pattern of transfers every few years with, in his case, as a senior assistant keeper, being frequently dispatched at short notice during wartime shortages to stations where his experience was needed.

For many workers the 1930s were difficult times. This was, to some extent, also true in the lighthouse service. In response, my father, together with a fellow keeper, John Scott, founded the Scottish Lightkeepers' Association. Archie was also active in this tiny trade union and was a regular part of the team who met with the Commissioners at No. 84 (as the HQ was always known). The Association maintained a good relationship with the Commissioners and secured many improvements over the years. In the little free time available, Archie was a skilled fisherman on sea, river or loch and a brilliant ornithologist, as well as working for the wellbeing of his colleagues.

It is interesting that by the 1960s experienced keepers, like Archie, forecast that there would be no manned stations by the end of the century and they were correct. Developing technology (for example telemetry, as evidenced in the early space programmes) and helicopter reliefs at rock lights would increase the pace of automation. It was the microchip that brought the end to this proud occupation which had so many compensations as well as inherent dangers and isolation for families at some stations.

One needs to ask whether there will be a need for lighthouses in the long term, with electronic charts and other sophisticated bridge instruments in use for shipboard navigation, and autonomous shipping now under development. Whatever happens in the long term the magnificent lighthouse structures need to be looked after. But is is also crucial that, while we can, we record the memories and stories of lightkeepers and their service to shipping.

A few books have been written by keepers who served in UK and Irish lighthouses, but there will not be many, if any more. That is why this book is so important. Its stories are a remarkable and significant addition to lighthouse service history and importantly, to the social history of Scotland and the Isle of Man.

Seaman, lightkeeper, acting welfare officer; then retirement aged 65 and reappointment as occasional keeper and attendant keeper at Chanonry lighthouse. After Archie finally retired his wife, Anne, continued the family tradition by serving a further eleven years as attendant keeper there. Archie's sixty six years of service to the Northern Lighthouse Board with Anne's eleven is a unique record that cannot be beaten.

Thanks are due to Anne for persuading Archie to recount this life story. He was a true servant of the mariner and a person of great wisdom, humour and kindness. Needless to say he was present on 31 March 1998 when the last Scottish lighthouse, Fair Isle South, was converted to automatic operation in the presence of the Board's Patron, the Princess Royal.

I am sure that all those who have an interest in lighthouses, their history and the lives of keepers will enjoy *Archie's Lights* as much as I have.

Hector MacKenzie, Lord MacKenzie of Culkein

1

First Lights

1910–C.1920

Father was an assistant keeper at St Abb's Head near the Scottish Border when I was born in 1910. My sister Katie, known to us as Kitty, was already two and our brother Bobbie arrived three years later. This was the only lighthouse in Scotland where you had to walk down steps to reach the tower, which sat on the edge of a cliff. With three small children, Mother had to watch constantly.

Archie in lace, with his sister Kitty.

My first memory of St Abb's Head is of a woman screaming, 'Norman's over the cliff! Norman's over the cliff!' Again and again she screamed. People rushed around, lightkeepers and coastguards were busy with ropes, then Father disappeared over the cliff edge, holding on to a rope with both hands. Quite quickly he found the son of his fellow assistant, but the three year old was already dead. I was taken away before he climbed back with Norman's body. At clifftop lighthouses children were sometimes tethered with a line around the waist to keep them from falling. We were never restrained like this, although we were often taken to play in safety at the Gibson's house in St Abbs (Captain Gibson at 'The Anchorage' was a friend of Father's who had four young sons, with whom we became great friends).

This was not the only rescue Father had to undertake. By the age of six, Kitty was already developing a passion for flowers and birds, and one day Father had to rescue her from a ledge on the cliff. Intent on picking a bunch of sea pinks, she was oblivious to the danger below and the long drop to the sea. While she was reaching for a bonny clump Father managed to find himself a foothold lower down the rock face. Then he spoke gently so she would not get a fright and gathered her safely into his arms.

Father gave us rubbery stalks of seaweed to bite on when we were teething; the hard fresh kelp eased our gums. He cut pieces from long stems which he gathered from the shore and scraped off the outer layer with his sharp penknife.

Early in 1914 Mother wrote from St Abbs to a cousin:

> *Kitty is five and a half now and getting helpful and we have had two babies, Archie aged three and a half and Robert aged five months. My hands are very full, baby is a very restless little fellow. He sleeps well at night but hardly ever closes his eyes till nine o'clock. You can understand how difficult it is even to get the most necessary things done; however Angus is always at home, the lighthouse is only a few yards from the house and he helps a lot.*

When Father was promoted to principal keeper we moved to Eilean Glas lighthouse, a fog signal station on Scalpay, Harris. Kitty's pet brown hen, Ruby, came too and soon hatched 13 chicks. However, there were many hoodie crows around, and one day when we were taken to feed the hens we saw a hoodie carry off a chick. With the baby still in its beak, it was hotly pursued by a furious Ruby, who took off clumsily from the top of the cliff. This time it was a mother hen that Father rescued from a ledge.

Our dreadful day came in September 1914. Father and his two assistants carried Mother on a stretcher down the steep road to the little harbour; I wondered why Kitty was crying while we walked beside them. A fishing boat was waiting at the pier and Mother was carried on board, but we had to stay behind. Soon the *White Heather* set off for Lewis, taking away our warm and gentle mother. She died in Stornoway hospital from peritonitis, following appendicitis. Father took me with him to her funeral in

Tobermory and I stood at his side in the churchyard. He held my hand and people kept coming to embrace us. I did not understand all these gestures and handshakes; most people were speaking Gaelic anyway. We sailed back from Mull to Scalpay on the *Plover*, with people making strange noises due, I was told, to seasickness.

After this, Kitty was sent to a lighthouse on Fair Isle to be looked after by an aunt and uncle; we did not see her again for five years. Bobbie was only a year old and Father cared for the two of us, assisted sometimes by housekeepers – someone from Scalpay came to help and later, a cousin from Oban. An old family friend visited from time to time and I did not like this at all; she was a nurse and very particular about washing. While she and Father chatted away in Gaelic, I ran outside and hid. She always managed to catch me though, and I girned at her efforts with soap and water.

When the First World War started Father became especially busy, as new wartime orders and regulations for the light were being issued all the time. A defence boom was laid across East Loch Tarbert in Harris and telephone instructions came to the lighthouse when naval ships needed access through the loch. These orders had to be relayed by the keepers to the boom defence vessel using semaphore by day and Morse lamp at night. Father gave the assistants some training in signalling and a succession of naval officers came to ensure that they were up to standard. There was a lot of activity on the sea off Eilean Glas and from the tower we saw warships passing. I remember vividly the day a fleet of big battleships and cruisers, escorted by a flotilla of destroyers, steamed past us at high speed. Clouds of thick black smoke belched from their funnels as they headed north towards Scapa Flow.

Although I often heard the keepers talk of the war, it did not mean much to me. I didn't realise what was involved in relaying the vitally important messages that came to the lighthouse – these enabled our ships to pass through the defence boom on Loch Tarbert without allowing German submarines in. Father was responsible for keeping the station in first class order through these difficult days while at the same time looking after us.

I often went up to the lightroom with Father although I was only allowed there in daylight. We walked around the balcony to see what we could see – mostly ships of

course, but there were occasional glimpses of huge herring whales (fin whales) out at sea. The engine room was my favourite place; it was always warm and welcoming, with its comforting oily smell. However, when the engines were running the doors were left open to prevent overheating and we were forbidden from entering, as the six-foot flywheels spun at high speed without protective guards. Father would only take me in briefly as a rare treat; it was exciting to see these throbbing monsters come to life. Fridays were the best, as that was when the men serviced the enormous engines and there was always plenty for us to watch. They polished the brass and copper too, until the mass of tubes, pipes and fittings gleamed brilliantly. Part of the Friday routine was to test the fog signal if it had been idle that week; each engine was run for ten minutes and the horn sounded loudly. We were so used to the rhythmic throaty boom that we were not woken by its blasting on a foggy night.

Father took me everywhere with him when he was not on watch, and I particularly loved it when we went fishing off the rocks, catching big pollock, saithe and rock cod from a wide ledge above the water. Climbing down the cliff to the ledge, I had no fear of falling, as there was always a strong hand clasping mine. One day Father found a dead porpoise on the shore. He thought it had been hit by a ship's propeller and had to dig a very large hole to bury it.

As soon as Bobbie was old enough he joined us to look for birds and animals, with Father gradually passing on his love of wildlife as we learnt about the creatures we saw. There were often curlew and oyster catcher nests to be seen; their eggs were big and blotchy, and their young ones well camouflaged among the rocks. We heard otters whistle in the gloaming and watched them dive and play on the loch that supplied water to the lighthouse. Father made little leaf boats which we floated down the burns. He would split a leaf from the segs (the Highland name for wild yellow irises) and thread the tip to make a billowing sail that fairly danced across the water.

We played with the assistants' children, though I do not remember having any toys apart from a ball. As we grew bigger, we amused ourselves by seeing how far we could throw stones. Hours were spent aiming at rabbits and trying to skite flat pebbles across the water at the shore. There was great entertainment when the men gathered the lighthouse sheep and we helped to chase them into the drystane fank (stone pen) as they had no dog. Two of us had a special hidey hole between the hen house and the stone dyke. Father never seemed worried when we disappeared; if we did not appear when expected, he knew he could find us there.

Very occasionally the keepers crossed to Tarbert, on Harris, in a fishing boat. Once or twice Father took me with him. In a big shed by the pier we watched women weaving Harris Tweed on clattering looms. They smiled cheerfully at us through the clacking frames that they pushed to and fro. Each time we went he bought me sweeties and we took a large piece of beef home from the butcher.

Provisions for the three lighthouse families came from Glasgow every month on the SS *Dunara Castle* or her sister ship. Father sent an order beforehand and three big wooden tea boxes of groceries arrived. The suppliers always included a tin of toffees, black striped balls, or occasionally chocolate for us children. Usually these were the only times we had such treats.

The keepers kept their own sheep on a large area of thick green grass. However, some of the crofters used to open our gate to let their own animals wander in for a fresh bite until a new latch put a stop to this. The sheep were our only regular source of meat and one day I watched Father and an assistant kill one at the shed. I rushed outside to be sick when I saw the slaughter. 'I know how it makes you feel, but we must have meat,' said Father. 'Just run away home for now.' I never watched that again.

After a sheep was butchered, a big black pot bubbled for ages on the stove; the 'marrachs' were cooking. These were black puddings, made from mutton fat and blood mixed with oatmeal, onion, and plenty of seasoning. White puddings were made too, without the blood. They were all hung on strings to be stored in the meat safe outside the house and were a great dinnertime treat. The sheep's fleeces were sent to Stornoway to be spun and returned as oiled knitting wool. Ours were sold after Mother died, although we had a wooden trunk that was always full of socks, given to Father by kind Scalpay women who knitted them for us.

All the keepers kept hens and grew their own vegetables in the big lighthouse gardens. Enough potatoes were grown to last the year. Everyone gathered gulls' eggs at nesting time and most people fed these to their hens as they were supposed to make them strong and healthy. Father set a clucking hen on eggs and showed me how to look after the chicks when they hatched. The assistants waited with a gun for the thieving hoodies; one day Father shot one.

We ate plenty of fish – fresh fish during the summer and salted fish with boiled potatoes at any time of the year – and all sorts were caught from the boat. I liked to watch the fish being taken off the lines, especially the long and athletic ling. There was always a bit of sport when a conger eel, sometimes several feet long, had to be tackled. By hooking their fingers through the gills, people could drag the slippery carcasses up from the boats. Our men threw congers away, but others took them home for eating. A great many large saithe (or coalfish) were caught – 'blackjacks' we called them. These were salted in a wooden barrel and then hung on a line to be dried by the sun in front of the house. Cod, ling, and haddock were preserved in the same way, but salt herring were kept in a barrel. A few sea trout were caught in a net at the slipway. When the men brought in John Dories they gave them away for lobster bait and occasionally fishermen provided us with crabs. The keepers had no time to set creels of their own; they all had extra duties during the war.

When we visited Scalpay houses the women were often knitting with long needles or working at a spinning wheel. Crotal was the lichen they used for dying wool, and among their cutlery there was sometimes a tablespoon with one side worn from scraping tough crotal off rocks. In our house they were dented because Father liked to play the spoons, tapping out a tune on his knee and humming along. He played the fiddle too and often gave us a few tunes in the evening. To amuse us before bedtime, now and again he would do a sword dance in stockinged feet, springing over crossed fire irons on the kitchen floor. He was quite light on his feet until he put on his thigh-length watch boots which were made of thick felt and tied at the top. He always saw us into bed before going up the tower to take a watch.

I slept in a box bed in the corner of our kitchen; its side was adorned with brass knobs that I liked to unscrew. Father would sit and rock Bobbie's cradle with his foot while I lay on the heavy mattress. Once Bobbie was big enough he shared the bed with me. An enamel dirler (chamber pot) sat underneath and I took great delight in pushing its handle to the back, causing panic if there was an urgent need in the night.

Bobbie and I were always pleased when the occasional keeper came on duty. John Kyles was always smiling and cheerful, and had a great fund of tales of exciting adventures at sea and fishermen's exploits. He sang Gaelic songs to us, and tossed Bobbie in the air to make him laugh. He often brought a bag of scones or oatcakes, treats baked for us by his mother.

Artificers visited for a fortnight every summer – these teams were sent to each lighthouse for maintenance and repairs. There was plenty to watch and they were great company as well as being different people to answer our questions. They never worked on Sundays out of respect for local customs. One year they stayed for longer than usual to lay lengths of big pipes to take fumes from the engine room out over the cliff. One day, while Father worked with the men on this project I was skiting stones to pass the time when one hit his bald head. This must have been very sore because he was not wearing a cap, but he just glared at me and shook his head. He was a man of great patience and kindness but I was certainly more careful where I threw stones after that!

Another exciting happening was the annual arrival of stores on the lighthouse tender *Pharos*. Essentials for the running of the lighthouse and three households for a year were delivered. The sailors joked with us as they carried big loads, and all sorts of surprises appeared; everything from building materials to crockery. Crates and bundles were unpacked and containers were returned to the ship. Everyone was very busy and seemed pleased with the things that had arrived. Every year a coaster delivered coal to the pier and a horse and cart brought it to our house. One morning though, I saw a coaster like the one that brought our coal lying on her side on one of the little islands to the south of us. She had approached at the wrong angle to hear the foghorn and had grounded during the night.

I started school when I was seven and big enough to undertake the walk. On Monday mornings Father, or John Kyles if Father was too busy, walked the several miles across the moor with me. I stayed in lodgings near the school during the week and came home by myself on a Friday afternoon. On my way I passed various crofts and was often asked in for milk and scones, or bannocks with crowdie. Sometimes I was so full that I could not take another drop or crumb and Father must have wondered why I arrived back so late. How kind the people were – they helped the miles pass – and their welcomes left a lasting impression.

The houses that lined the moorland route were traditional black houses. Ropes over their thatched roofs were weighted with stones as protection from gales. In summer I often saw a man on a ladder repairing the thatch. Inside a black house it was quite dark; windows were few and small and set deep into very thick stone walls. The mat inside the door was often a split tattie sack. In winter the smell of peat and cow greeted me and I could see a cow tied at the far end of the room. I warmed myself by the peat fire in the middle of the earthen floor; the smoke escaped through a hole in the roof. The women made bannocks as big as dinner plates over the burning peat. They flipped them skilfully on the girdle (griddle) and then stacked them on edge against the ring of dried peats that surrounded the fire. There seemed to be some magic in this finishing process. Big bowls of milk for making crowdie stood where it was warm; at every house there was lovely crowdie. Cream for making butter was skimmed from other, shallower, bowls.

I often saw women washing clothes outside in a wooden tub that sat on stones. They did a lot of the heavy outdoor work. In long dark clothes they carried home the peats in large wicker creels strapped to their backs. Their arms were folded and shoulders hunched to steady the load. They also milked the house cow and carried creels full of kelp from the shore. A large black pot hung on a chain over the fire and seaweed was boiled for cattle feed. The older women wore beanaigs – black shawls – over their heads and shoulders.

In the village there were white houses with chimneys; newer and larger, these were more substantial dwellings than the black houses. During the school week I lodged with Mrs Macdonald in a white house with a slate roof and dormer windows. She cooked on a kitchen range and her bowl of milk for crowdie stood on top beside the hotplate. Mrs Macdonald was a widow who ran the village post office and lived with Rachel, her sister, and their father. They were all very kind, though at first I was frightened of the father. He had a long white beard and sat silently in front of a large open Bible. Every morning and evening he said family prayers in Gaelic which we all had to attend.

There were often ceilidhs in their house, with Gaelic singing and storytelling. One evening Mrs Macdonald's brother, Norman, arrived home on leave from the Army. He had puttees on, rather strange things I thought. He was rosy-cheeked, full of fun and music, and wore his uniform proudly. He patted me on the head and smiled the day he left for Ypres. 'I'll see you again, next time I come back,' he said. But he never returned, and a terrible sadness settled on the village for a time.

Years later, when I was a sailor and the ship had put in to Scalpay, I went back to visit the Macdonalds. The father was bedridden and he clasped both my hands with delight. It was a touching moment when he blessed me in Gaelic and said, 'Thank you for coming to see an old man.'

Everyone in the Scalpay school spoke Gaelic. At first I could not understand a word they were saying; the other children had very little English. With help though, I soon picked up enough Gaelic to do my lessons and make myself understood. One of the games we played was a kind of shinty with homemade sticks. A good ball was made from a piece of fishing net bound tightly with string, or sometimes we used a cork fishing float. One summer evening my pals and I were trying to catch rabbits outside the village. This involved throwing stones, but our aim was not altogether accurate. In the excitement of a chase I was knocked out as I ran from an overhanging bank in the warren. I was carried back to the Macdonalds' and visited by the district nurse.

If there was a one-day holiday during the school week, I did not go home to the lighthouse. On these days the Macdonalds occasionally took me peat cutting with them – they had the peat rights on one of the small outlying islands. We crossed in an open fishing boat with a big brown sail. Food was carried aboard with plenty of good soup in a large black pot. I was fed on milk and scones at regular intervals during the day. While they were working I searched for bird nests, and once found a merganser's.

When I was eight I suddenly slipped while climbing aboard the lighthouse boat to go fishing with one of the assistants. I plunged straight into the depths and clutched at strands of seaweed before struggling to the surface. On the way up I saw a row of strange little creatures gazing at me (later identified as seahorses). Before I could wonder what they were, I was hauled back on board and carried straight home.

Just after the end of the First World War a large converted steam yacht, the *Iolaire*, was bringing serving soldiers and sailors home to the islands for New Year when she was wrecked as she approached Stornoway. There was heavy loss of life and several Scalpay men were among the victims; island families were devastated. Apparently, a naval officer among the *Iolaire* passengers had told the captain he was sailing dangerously close to the rocks known as the 'Beasts of Holm'. It was desperately tragic that men who had fought for their country and survived the carnage of war should subsequently die so near home. Many aboard were bringing presents for their families; toys to be treasured became sad pieces of flotsam. The *White Heather* brought men home to Scalpay for burial – I watched weeping relatives arrive at the pier to claim their loved ones from the row of bodies wrapped in canvas that lay on the deck. One young sailor aboard, from Port of Ness in Lewis, received a gallantry award for his outstanding conduct that day – he had swum ashore with a line and saved a number of the men.

When I was about ten, Father was transferred to Barns Ness lighthouse, near Dunbar. Kitty came back from Fair Isle to live with us and to help run the house. A cousin of Father's had come to Scalpay as our housekeeper and she moved with us to our new station. Sadly there was soon another family tragedy when she died suddenly.

At Barns Ness the light warned ships of hazards as they headed to the Firth of Forth. The water was full of craggy rocks that appeared at low water, but no steep cliffs surrounded us here, and we had plenty of freedom to play. We fished in pools and went beachcombing on the long beaches with Lachie, an assistant's son. At low tide a particularly deep pool appeared; from this we would catch crabs with a stick and line and take them home to be cooked. One day a huge lobster appeared from under a ledge; it was not interested in our bait, so I ran home for a large cod hook. This was straightened and fixed to the end of a stick. When the lobster came out again we speared it swiftly through the back. Lachie and I halved it, with help, and we all had lobster for tea.

Further along the beach there were holes in the rocks and the pools were edged with white deposits. Not far away, a disused lime kiln looked interesting, but when we went to investigate, there was an unshaven tramp in tattered clothes asleep in a dark corner. The wild-looking man awoke and chased us. We were terrified and ran for our lives, not stopping until we reached home. We were told to never go there again.

There was further excitement during a miners' strike when people filled sacks from a coal-filled hollow above the beach and took them away with horses and carts. One day a crowd of strikers turned up on bicycles and began to fight with the men who were digging coal.

Another time, Father had just put the light in when he saw a ship heading dangerously close to the rocks. He ran downstairs and told an assistant to get the rockets and start firing. While there was still a little daylight he hoisted the lighthouse flag as a warning. Then he hurried to wind the machine and keep the light revolving. We sat on the dyke outside, thrilled at seeing the rockets shoot into the air. When the first one exploded it was so loud that Lachie fell backwards off the wall! Suddenly, there was a grinding crash and the ship hit the rocks before our eyes. The SS *Malabar*, loaded with silver lead ore and esparto grass, had run aground close to the lighthouse.

The coastguard's telephone was out of order that day, so Father rang the coxswain of the Skateraw lifeboat a few miles away. Before long it was dark and the wind had risen to gale force. The lifeboat, which was powered only by sail and oar, capsized twice on the way to the wreck. But she was self-righting and none of her crew was lost. They rescued all the crew of the *Malabar* except two Lascar seamen.

During the night a severe storm blew up from the north. The next morning the wreck was still being lashed relentlessly, groaning and creaking loudly. Finally it split in two and sank, leaving only the top of one mast visible. Never before had we seen the force of the sea as dreadful as this; the shore was strewn with sodden esparto grass and debris as far as the eye could see. We found the bodies of the two drowned crewmen and a monkey, though what distressed us most was a dead canary still in its cage. To us, it seemed that the men and the monkey would have had some chance to swim ashore; the canary, on the other hand, had been trapped.

The crewmen's bodies were taken away by the police and various people came to make enquiries. Father went to question the ship's captain at a hotel and took Kitty with him. He had to find out if anything was wrong with the light then record all the details of the incident in his shipwreck return book. Kitty said that Father asked the captain if he saw the light and why the ship had run aground so near the lighthouse. He had seen the light, but his vessel had hit an unmarked rock or some floating object. He beached her to try to prevent her sinking.

Soon the esparto grass on the beach was gathered into big stacks and lorries arrived to take it to paper mills near Edinburgh. We had never seen lorries before; they were enormous! Then a converted tug, the *Earl of Powis*, was anchored by the wreck to salvage the silver lead from the cargo. Divers in clumsy suits and big helmets went over the side of the ship, and metal baskets were winched to her deck with dripping loads.

The Gibsons moved from St Abbs to a big house in Edinburgh, and the boys came each summer to spend holidays with us at Barns Ness. One night Father and Kitty were staying at their house when Mrs Gibson received terrible news – Captain Gibson's ship, the *Hopelin*, had been wrecked on the Scroby Sands. The local lifeboat could not get alongside because of rough seas, and there were no signs of life aboard. In great distress, Mrs Gibson prepared to leave for Norfolk the next day. But that night her youngest son, Peter, had a very strange dream. Suddenly, with his eyes still shut, he sat up in bed and shouted: 'Dinna worry, Mither. Dad and the men are a' safe an' weel in the wheelhouse.' Sure enough, when Mrs Gibson reached Great Yarmouth, she found that the whole crew, including the ship's cat, had been rescued uninjured. Later, Captain Gibson told us that the day before they were wrecked their black cat had fallen into the flour bin and crawled out all white; a white cat is supposed to bring bad luck to a ship. Peter must have been eight or nine when he had this dream. In due course he too became a master mariner and would have more than one lucky escape at sea.

We had been at Barns Ness for a few months when I contracted double pneumonia. When I was beginning to recover, I was asked what I would like to eat. 'A flounder' was what I fancied more than anything. Before long Father appeared with a delicious plateful of little flat fish – how good they tasted! He was advised that a break from the raw east coast air would do me good, so I was sent to recuperate in Perthshire for several weeks, away from the sea for the first time in my life.

2

Butterstone, Barns Ness and Chanonry

1920–1926

I stayed for several months at Butterstone with Uncle Peter (Father's brother) and Aunt Kate. Peter was a gamekeeper and Kate was the village postmistress. Originally, Uncle Peter had been at sea with Lyle Shipping Company but in time he had been offered work ashore by Colonel Lyle as a gamekeeper on his estate at Butterstone. Uncle Peter always referred to Colonel Lyle as the 'laird' and gave his game the best of care. Butterstone, near Dunkeld, was a quiet, wooded corner of Perthshire and very different from any of the places that I knew. Aunt Kate spoke of the 'forest' to describe

Butterstone Post Office, Uncle Peter and Aunt Kate's cottage.

a wide area surrounding us and I thought the woods must have extended much further when she was young. Their cottage had a rustic wooden porch and the post office, with its telephone switchboard, occupied one of the rooms.

Inside the house were many treasures from Africa. Aunt Kate was a Livingston and related to the explorer David Livingston, who had brought them home to the family. I loved the stories she told of his adventures and the fascinating objects to be seen. The walls of the staircase were lined with assegais, spears, bows, and arrows. In the two upstairs rooms were strange witchdoctor charms, furry hide shields, and much more. My feet touched a lion skin rug when I stepped out of bed. Down in the parlour, the rich colours of Aunt Kate's best china shone like jewels from her dresser. They kept a wooden box full of gold sovereigns hidden in their bedroom which they showed me one day with pride. However, someone else must have known of this secret hoard too. After they died, their precious box was found containing only one coin.

The garden overflowed with flowers and vegetables, and best of all, there was an immaculate shed. It seemed that everything for gamekeeping and fishing could be found in here, as well as all the usual necessities for garden and house. Guns and rods on racks and hooks lined one wall, and against the opposite wall stood a long work bench. Above this hung a row of shiny tools kept oiled and polished. As I grew stronger I joined Uncle Peter while he worked out of doors.

Mornings were busy around the shed. When he rose from the breakfast table he cut sticks for the day from a big woodpile. He was so clever with the razor-sharp axe; he could have split a matchstick. I was never allowed to touch the axe, though he taught me how to use a saw and I made little wooden boats. 'Now, be sure to clean that and put it back when you've finished,' I was often told. All the wood shavings were swept up immediately and burnt on the weekly bonfire. Once the supply of firewood was cut, Uncle Peter turned his attention to the garden. There was a henhouse with a wire netting run to enclose the hens. I thought these should be free to roam like lighthouse hens, so I let them out and they soon rooted up the plants that my uncle had spent hours sowing, hoeing, and weeding. He quickly put me right on that score. However after the vegetables had been harvested, the hens were let out of their run to scratch over the empty beds. But this meant trouble again – more than once they escaped when I slammed the garden gate too hard and it flew open!

After dinner he set off to check the estate game with a gun on his shoulder and pipe in his mouth; its bowl had a metal cover to protect the lighted tobacco from wind and rain. He wore a suit of plus fours and a knitted waistcoat that had a special pocket for his silver watch and chain. I was delighted when I was able to go with him.

Aunt Kate was a great baker and a flowery pinafore always covered her clothes in the kitchen and the post office. Often a telephone call came when she was busy making scones and she would run through, rubbing her floury hands together. I became very interested in the switchboard and one day I went through on the quiet. While I was having a good look at wires and switches a bell rang. I pulled out a plug that looked promising and the line went dead. However, Aunt Kate had followed me to answer the call. 'Don't ever do that again!' she scolded. 'Somebody might be calling for help!' That was the only time I saw her really cross, though she had to tick me off sometimes.

Aunt Kate rose at five every morning and her days ran ahead of mine. The housework was finished before the post office opened or the switchboard needed attention. Breakfast was at seven o'clock; we had dinner at eleven and tea was at four. We all had a cup of tea with a scone at eight o'clock every night and she went to bed at nine. Kate did not like it when I wanted to stay out later to play or fish on long summer evenings. I was never hungry; their food was so good and they always gave me extra snacks. My mid-morning 'piece' was usually a slice of bread with jam or cheese. On warmer days I ran out of the back gate and sat on the Butter Stone to eat it – farmers in olden days used to sell their butter on this black stone which had become shiny from the fat. Lemonade was sold in the post office and Uncle Peter sometimes sneaked a bottle into the kitchen for the two of us. I had never tasted lemonade before – it was marvellous.

Aunt Kate sent me out and about to deliver telegrams, for which I was paid sixpence. Usually the recipients gave me a biscuit or a drink. Every day I went to the big house to collect a can of milk. There an old lady and her daughter made a great fuss of me. They sat me down in the kitchen and put a baby on my knee to play. They chatted and the baby laughed while I had a snack.

When I had recovered sufficiently from the pneumonia, I attended the village school for several weeks. The school was across the road from our house and beside it were trees where red squirrels nested. We could see the babies come out of the nest and race after their mother, jumping from branch to branch. One of the big boys climbed the tree and caught one to show us.

Uncle Peter was well known to the operators at the Dunkeld telephone exchange and never needed a number to make a call. He only had to say something like, 'Put me through to Jessie, please,' or 'Give me Donald Macvicar.' He was very wise too. He taught me about the different creatures that lived around us, such as deer, capercaillie, and blackcock, and he showed me nests of kingfishers, yellow wagtails, and tree-creepers. We watched the roding of the woodcock and heard their strange brrr…ing noise, saw the handsome jays – whose nest-robbing habits he did not like at all – and identified calls and choruses of throngs of different birds. One day I went to stroke a tiny fawn that was lying among the trees but my uncle stopped me; the mother deer would be watching and might abandon her baby if it was touched by a human.

He took me to fish on Butterstone Loch and in little hillside burns. My favourite was the Backney Burn, right behind the house. After a night of heavy rain it would become a roaring, peaty spate that subsided as quickly as it rose. It was here that I had a close view of my first kingfisher when I spotted one diving into a pool. It then disappeared into a hole in the bank with a fish in its beak. I was surprised that this brilliantly coloured bird lived in the dark, foul-smelling nest that my uncle described.

When we went up to the hills we crossed little bridges over burns, and Uncle Peter showed me where large pike lay in wait under the water. A neighbouring gamekeeper shot them from one of the bridges to protect the fish and game in his care as pike have big appetites for small trout, baby grebes, and ducklings. When Father came to visit he and Peter enjoyed catching enormous pike on the loch, which they then fed to the laird's dogs.

In summer Uncle Peter acted as a ghillie on the River Tay at Dunkeld. He could always entice a fish to take. I thought this was due to his attitude as well as great skill; a man of inner calm, he never hurried his fishing. I always knew he had hooked something when the whistling started. His leathery cheeks puffed and bulged as if he were blowing bagpipes (he had been a keen piper when he was younger) while he patiently played the fish. It was a great day when he gave me my first rod, a greenheart – so started my lifelong passion for fishing.

Now and again we were given a lift to Dunkeld by pony and trap. These outings were very exciting. Uncle Peter would wear a distinctive tweed hat with the curved tail feathers of a blackcock stuck into the side. He would leave me in the High Street with instructions when to meet. Then I would look in all the shop windows and buy a bag of striped sweeties. I gazed longingly at the fishing flies displayed in the tackle shop; they were so beautiful, dressed in tempting bright feathers and coloured thread. Most of my afternoon was spent in this shop and the man behind the counter selected small flies which would be good for catching trout in a burn. They were two for sixpence, though he always gave me one extra. Many would end up snagged in the branches overhanging the Backney Burn, but some brought in little wild trout which were great fighters and made a tasty breakfast, fried with crispy bacon. Later, when it was time to look for Uncle Peter, I could spot the bobbing blackcock feathers approaching above the shoppers on the street. On one of these journeys in the trap, the driver had a bad bout of flatulence. Perhaps he thought his 'noisy expulsions of wind' could not be heard above the clatter of hooves. My uncle fixed me with a steely gaze, willing me not to laugh or comment.

Aunt Kate had an amusing outing with an old neighbour who lived alone. One morning Kate found her flustered at receiving an invitation to a family wedding. She said she did not have a good hat to wear for the occasion. As the lady seldom left the village, Kate offered to go with her on the bus. Off they went to the Co-op in Perth, and how she laughed when she came home. The neighbour had worried that there might not be enough for a hat in her Co-op account. 'Madam, you have enough in that account to buy the entire shop!' the assistant assured her.

One day I came in from school to find Kate very upset. She had an old collie that she was very fond of. I was fond of him too – he was a good pal when I went exploring or fishing on my own and he would wait patiently on the bank. We knew the dog was ailing, but that morning she had called the vet who put him to sleep. Uncle Peter and I had to console her for a long time and she was particularly unhappy about the vet's methods when she found bloodstains in the garden. Now there were only the estate gun dogs, the laird's spaniels.

By the time Father came to take me back to Barns Ness, I had grown very fond of Peter and Kate. They had shown me great kindness and in years to come I would go back to see them often.

Back at Barns Ness, Bobbie and I were keener than ever to catch rabbits. Our stoning method was not proving very successful, but then a man told us of a trick that was 'sure to work'. First, we had to catch a crab, put a lighted candle on its back and send it down a rabbit hole; on seeing this, the frightened rabbit would dash out and we could grab it. With great enthusiasm we caught our crab and placed it in the mouth of the burrow with a candle burning brightly on top of the shell. However, the crab promptly dug itself into the sandy soil; nothing would shift it and the flame went out. That plan was abandoned. We were then given six snares and some instruction on setting them. Once we got over our initial difficulties with killing the rabbits, we caught plenty for the pot. The local gamekeeper was not as delighted by this as we were, so we had to scale down our operation.

At that time we had a wirehaired fox terrier called Puggie. He was a great ratter and, to our knowledge, killed 200 in his day. He often joined us on our various ploys, until the day a boy, who played with us, teased him and gave him a hard kick. Puggie bit the boy who went roaring and howling to his parents. Father decided the dog would have to be put down, but how we missed our sporting little Puggie.

About two miles from the lighthouse a pair of moorhens nested on a pond. One day we found the mother bird dead; she looked freshly killed and there was still an egg in the nest. With great care, Kitty took the egg home and put it under a broody hen that was sitting on a clutch of her own. Kitty was delighted when the baby moorhen hatched. It lived with the family of chicks, feeding on oatmeal until it could launch out on its own.

We kept an eye on a pair of linnets nesting in a patch of gorse – a hoodie crow began to pick off their new brood one by one. Father bought a bird cage which he placed in the bush when only one of the young was left. He lifted the whole nest, complete with baby, into the cage. The mother still came dutifully to feed it, but the crow was afraid to go near the cage. When the little one no longer needed its parent, Father moved it into the house; Kitty took over the feeding and kept it for years as a pet. He had seen this trick in Islay when nestlings were sold as cage birds.

Climbing up the high tower and into the lantern with Father was very exciting. Some nights masses of birds flew straight for the light, attracted by the beam. We watched them run around the grating, whizzing and chattering all around us. Little faces peered through the glass and we got to know them well from such close encounters. A great rush of wings filled the air when we stood out on the balcony; the birds never collided with us in spite of their frenzied searching for a place to land. They glinted like little shining stars as the broad ray of light revolved. The greatest numbers came in spring and autumn, especially with misty weather. Lapwings, woodcock, fieldfares, redwings, blackbirds, thrushes, skylarks, and golden plovers were among the many that flew to this light.

Barns Ness was the only lighthouse where I saw owls at the lantern; they always landed softly and safely. A great many curlews circled in mist, calling all the time and usually flying higher than other birds. I never saw a curlew crash, or even land, though there were often casualties from other species.

It was easy to see when the birds were dazzled; some looked dazed or weary. Occasionally Father caught one, grasping its feet through the grating or lifting it carefully. He would examine the bird gently and hand it to us so we could let it go. A woodcock was the first that we handled. Most birds would fly in any direction when released, but a woodcock never flew back to the shaft of light. A captured blackbird pecked viciously and a starling would mess in our hands – their only methods of defence – so we were not keen to handle either of these.

Sometimes we found dead birds at the foot of the tower. One morning Kitty picked up a goldcrest from the pavement. She skinned the tiny bird carefully and managed to cure the skin. After stuffing the body with cotton wool she sewed it up with fine stitches and kept it for a long time.

When it was time to go to secondary school in Dunbar, Father gave me a bike so that I could cycle there. He also bought a heavy ex-Army tent for Bobbie and me. We slept out for a week by the beach in summer with the assistants' two boys and had a Primus stove to make our own tea – it was wonderful.

Chanonry

I was 14 when Father was transferred to Chanonry, on the inner Moray Firth. By then it was a one-man station. Bobbie and I went to Fortrose Academy, and Kitty left school to take on the role of housekeeper, though she would have liked to go to college and become a teacher. Her linnet came with her and more pets were collected before long.

The lighthouse stood on the tip of Chanonry Point at Fortrose, more or less at sea level and a few feet from the sea wall. The channel here was narrow considering

Hugh the ferryman at Chanonry, with his sister.

the many vessels that passed to and from Inverness and along the Caledonian Canal. Chanonry had a tiny tower compared to Barns Ness and birds were not drawn to its lantern. The lighthouse adjoined the golf course so the three of us learned to play. We also made special friends with Jock, the son of a neighbour.

There was a ferry from the slipway at Chanonry Point to Fort George, a crossing of about a mile. It was a dangerous stretch of water, with hectic currents where the tides met. Alex Maclean, the ferryman, lived next door at Ferry House with his sister. She was a very reserved lady and always known to us as 'Miss Maclean'. Alex was provided with a motor boat in summer for carrying visitors, but in winter he had to row his passengers across the Firth in a dinghy. Gripping the oars meant his fingers were permanently hooked like claws; but his pay was meagre. A fine old man, he was greatly respected by the soldiers at Fort George. They sometimes entertained him on a Saturday night in the sergeants' mess and gave him a food parcel to take home to his sister. Now and again Father gave him coal from the supply in our coal shed.

Alex was expert at judging the tides and crossed the Firth in all weathers. Bobbie and I spent many hours in the boat with him – it was our favourite pastime. He would often give us an oar to share the rowing, and he taught us about tides and the handling of boats. Alex was always calm, even in heavy seas. 'Big holes in the sea today, Archie,' he would say when it was very rough. Some evenings he came to our house and was

*Father spying through the
station telescope at Chanonry.*

pleased when he was asked to give us his sword dance, accompanied by Father on the spoons or harmonica.

Every night Father had to check several gas buoys in the Firth. These lighted buoys were viewed through the great brass telescope that was standard issue at lighthouses. If a buoy light failed he had to hire a boat and attend to it immediately. Several times Father asked the Inverness pilot to take him to one of those more distant. It was bitterly cold working on a buoy in winter – one day he just about froze. Kitty sat him by the fire afterwards and warmed him with blankets and hot tea. There was always a good fire burning in our kitchen, although the wee scullery beside it was a cold corner.

There was an abundant supply of sea fish on our doorstep; dolphins in particular enjoyed feasting on the salmon and sea trout in late spring and summer. Cod, halibut, plaice, skate, herring and mackerel were plentiful at other times of the year. We once saw a seal catch an enormous cod which it dropped after a long struggle. Later I went out in the dinghy to pick up the fish – it weighed 36 lbs! Father used to set a line on 'Skate Bank' and could catch up to a hundred fish at a time, mostly skate and plaice.

The dolphins came in greatest numbers when shoals of salmon or sea trout were running, usually on a flowing tide. They needed lots of the smaller fish, such as herring, to feed their large bulk. People at that time generally showed no interest in the dolphins. Some folk here called them 'louper dogs', but mostly they referred to them as porpoises, which were actually seen for a shorter season and did not swim so close to the shore.

The Firth was very rich in bird life too. In autumn, masses of seabirds gathered on the sea and the shore, and the surface of the water turned black with rafts of duck. This was a popular spot for wildfowlers who came to shoot mallard, teal, and widgeon, often from punts. In summer, terns and ringed plover nested along the margin of the beach and we helped the netsmen at the salmon station near the lighthouse. Their bosses tried to control the numbers of seals and cormorants, as they stole the wild salmon from the nets. A reward of ten shillings was offered for a seal's tail and five

Father and Bobbie feeding the animals at Chanonry.

shillings for a cormorant's beak, so Bobbie and I shot cormorants with our friend Jock. How our views on conservation have changed since the 1920s!

Father had always been keen on shooting. We shot rabbits, duck, and game in season; there were good numbers of woodcock in late autumn above Rosemarkie shore, and Jock and I snared rabbits on the hill of Fortrose. Kitty cooked whatever we bagged. Wild partridge were plentiful in the fields, and a pair nested undisturbed by the lighthouse flagpole every year – they always reared a brood successfully and none of these were ever shot. Another good sport was shooting vermin; the village dump, on the west side of the Point, was seething with rats.

Bobbie found a clutch of abandoned mallard eggs which he put under one of our broody hens. When the ducklings hatched he decided they needed water, so he set a large basin into the grass and they swam happily. But the mother hen got very agitated, fussing and clucking at this foolish behaviour. In time, all but one left to go down to the sea.

Although there were no fields attached to the lighthouse, there was enough grazing to keep a few sheep in the grounds at Chanonry. One pet lamb of Kitty's grew into a hefty, arrogant sheep that expected to be fed all the time. It butted us on sight and sneaked into the house to look for food.

Our first working gun dog was Jack, an amazingly clever collie-retriever cross. (Kitty had been given a puppy earlier, and whilst it was a great pet, it never learnt to work with a gun.) I had been beating for a local shoot when the landowner's daughter came up to me in tears, holding a lovely puppy. Her father was going to have him put down because he was not pure bred. So I took the pup, Jack, home. Father trained him, and found he was quick to learn and good with the gun. He followed Father everywhere, and did not like being left unless told expressly to stay on guard. One day Alex and Father were taking the boat from the lighthouse round to Fortrose harbour when they saw Jack racing along the beach. He swam out frantically to the boat and they picked him up.

Jack took his duties seriously. Once we went to Inverness by train and he was given instructions to 'Look after the place!' When we came home we found a tinker boy sitting on top of the large oil storage tank inside the gate. Jack was on guard, growling at the lad. 'Call your dog off, mister!' he wailed. 'I've been up here all afternoon and he won't let me down.' We all liked this boy; Father often gave him rabbit skins and he would come in for a cup of tea and a piece. Jack did not object to him when we were around.

Father with Jack the dog in Fortrose.

A well-to-do gentleman came down to the Point quite regularly in his car and Father would stroll out for a chat. One day the gentleman's trilby hat was blown into the sea and he was very annoyed.

'Do you really want it back?' asked Father.

'Of course I want it back. I only bought it a few days ago! But you can't do anything about it.'

'Jack! Fetch!' called Father as the hat headed out to sea.

Jack shot after the hat and managed to retrieve it. However, persuading him to give up the dripping trilby to its owner was another matter; he would only drop it for my father. The man was so delighted that he offered a goodly sum to buy Jack. No money could buy his dog, was Father's instant reply. That didn't stop the two men from becoming friends and my father was sometimes given a handful of cartridges on future visits.

Jack adopted a pet rabbit of Kitty's. He often carried it into the living room and laid it on the hearthrug where it would sit up, lick its fur, and hop around the floor. Unfortunately, the silly creature thought all dogs were its friends. One day it lolloped to greet the postman's dog which promptly killed it. Jack never forgot, and would attack this dog on sight until the postman stopped bringing it. He then transferred his attentions to Bobbie's tame duck and carried that into the house instead.

Sadly Jack died quite young from distemper. In time Father took me with him to look at another possible gun dog at a large house near Conon Bridge. We were shown in and a gentleman with a white beard appeared. He greeted us warmly, and a glass of whisky was brought for Father and a drink of lemonade for me. 'Please excuse us, while we speak in our mother tongue,' said the gentleman to me. A long chat in Gaelic followed, which Father seemed to enjoy; it was a rare opportunity for him to speak Gaelic. He did not buy the dog, but Jack was eventually replaced by Dash – good enough with the gun, though not as clever.

I started a weekend job with a local butcher. It was alright turning the handle of the sausage machine and even cleaning the back shop, but it was less enjoyable cutting great hunks of meat and fat into small pieces. The butcher left oddments to be thrown away and I thought some of these found their way into the mixture that his wife prepared for sausages. I liked going with him to Dingwall market to buy beasts, though I refused his invitation to the slaughterhouse, as memories of sheep killing on Scalpay were still vivid.

It was much better when an opportunity arose to do odd jobs for the minister. I hoed turnips on the glebe beside Rosemarkie manse and built a hen run. Then he bought a large roofless mill by the shore with ground that needed clearing. When the building had been re-roofed, he offered to sell it at a reasonable price to my father for his retirement. But Kitty had other plans.

A nearby farmer was often glad of help too. He had three Clydesdale horses and we took many cartloads of seaweed from the beach to manure neighbouring fields. These fields would eventually become part of the gold course.

Bobbie and I learnt gradually learnt about the varied tasks involved in lightkeeping. We helped with polishing the lens, cleaning the brass, and sweeping the tower stairs. A large area of grass had to be cut, so Bobbie trained Jack to pull the large mower for him till Father put a stop to this! We watched roofs being tarred and the tower and the house being limewashed and painted. The sea wall itself was patched by Father with a bucket of cement whenever it was damaged by storms and big tides; it was important that this wall was well maintained. The slipway outside the gate had to be kept in good order too; here the *Pharos* landed our stores and passengers boarded the ferry. Gas to fuel the light was also delivered by the ship and I was allowed to help with the hose that fed this into a manhole by the slip.

We were taught how to hoist the lighthouse flag, which was flown on Sundays, public holidays, days of national mourning and for important visitors. The flag was dipped whenever the *Pharos* arrived and departed. She always tooted when she passed the Point; we waved to the crew and Father flourished his cap.

In summer we crossed on the ferry with our bikes and cycled into Inverness. I spent hours at Inverness harbour hoping one day to find a job on a coaster. Bobbie and I had heard sailors talk of their adventures at sea, and many ships that passed our lighthouse were making for exciting places. Father wanted me to go into a bank, but that kind of life was not for me.

In the summer of 1925 the superintendent came to Chanonry for the annual inspection. He asked Father about my plans for the future, and when he heard that I wanted to go to sea, he promised to put forward my name to join the crew of the *Pharos*.

3

'What are the wild waves saying?'

1926–1932

The superintendent was as good as his word; the following April, when I was 16, a letter came to say that there was a vacancy for a boy seaman on the *Pharos*. I left home a week later wearing a brand new suit, with a new cut-throat razor in my case and £6 in my pocket. I caught the train from Inverness to Edinburgh and had lunch in a dining car for the first time. The waiter brought me a plate of delicious roast beef. 'Horseradish?' he barked, and not waiting for a reply, he deposited a spoonful of unpleasant sauce beside the meat.

The *Pharos* was a steamship of 920 tons, and was one of four tenders that serviced the Board's lighthouses and buoys around Scotland and the Isle of Man. That evening she was at her own berth in Granton harbour. Very apprehensively, I reported to the officer in charge. There were 32 in the ship's company, which was under the command of Captain Scott. The 12 of us in the focs'le included another boy seaman, Willie. He was the son of the principal keeper at Stoer Head lighthouse and we became great friends.

At five o'clock on Monday morning the ship sailed for Rockall to check the area's radio beacons. It was fine and calm for the first hour in the Firth of Forth. The wind soon rose though, and a full gale was blowing by the time we reached the Isle of May. To my horror we kept going, bucking and heaving relentlessly through heavy seas. I was very seasick and took to my bunk with a bucket. But before long a powerfully built seaman appeared beside me. 'Get out of that bunk!' he ordered. 'You're on watch for the next four hours.' That was my first introduction to Jimmy Mac. Still clutching my bucket, I was taken to the smoke room, where I was told I would be a member of the port watch and sent to the bridge as lookout. Vessels of any kind or floating objects sighted must be reported immediately to the officer of the watch. All I could see was spray and seasickness, though I stayed upright for as long as necessary. 'What are the wild waves saying?' chanted the sailors and the ship plunged on. This was their

Archie – Boy Seaman.

favourite saying, particularly in wild weather, followed sometimes by 'pump, you b…, pump!'

When my next watch was due I was left in my bunk, and I lay there for the rest of the trip. Jimmy Mac took my other watches, as well as his own, and I did not see Rockall. The crew assured me the seasickness would wear off in time; I did not believe them, and I vowed I would never set foot on a ship again. However, waiting for me at Granton harbour was a parcel containing a split new uniform with brass buttons and a cap with a brass lighthouse badge. I decided to stay on for another week, and in time I discovered that the crew were right – the seasickness did wear off.

For routine duties we wore uniform trousers and a navy jersey with PHAROS embroidered in red across the chest, and overalls protected our clothing during very dirty jobs. Our uniform jacket was usually only worn to go ashore or for smart occasions. New uniforms were issued every year and the old jacket gave us an extra layer for cold weather. I learnt that the ship's funnel gave out some warmth on winter days and leant against it when there was nothing in particular to be done. Someone always noticed before long though, and moved me on.

It was hard work aboard the *Pharos*, especially on the storing voyages to lighthouses in summer. These trips lasted about seven weeks, and we made it as far as the Isle of Man in the summer. Sometimes we had to work 18 hours a day to beat the weather and tides. Keepers' wives often brought baking and big kettles of tea to the lighthouse slipways for us when we unloaded stores. Their mouth-watering pancakes were a special treat.

Every spring we serviced all the buoys in the Firth of Forth and Moray Firth; a dirty, uncomfortable job. Some were taken on board for repair while we landed on others to repair and paint them, bobbing up and down unceasingly. The

KIRKGATE

Shirts and shoes could be bought cheaply enough in the Kirkgate in Leith – shirts at half a crown each (2 shillings and 6 pence – 12½ pence). However, the Kirkgate was not always safe. A man wielding a stick demanded money from Willie and me one night; he ran away when we chased him, but we guessed by the haircut and white face that he was just out of prison. I bought my first watch from an old salesman, Jackie, who sold trinkets around the harbour.

buoys were always thickly coated with bird droppings. At times gas escaping from the burner wafted into my face and made me sick. I was delighted when I was told to take the ship's wheel during buoy work. After this work was finished, and we had returned to harbour, the whole ship above the water line was painted.

Junior crew members took month about as 'peggy'. The peggy had to serve meals in the seamen's mess, wash dishes, clean the table and scrub the foc'sle floor. He was excused from all other duties apart from night watches. One lad who joined after me was so annoyed with these chores that he chucked the dirty crockery out of the porthole; he was sacked on the spot.

Each watch lasted four hours. The exceptions were the two-hour dog watches, from 4pm to 6pm and 6pm to 8pm. Once we were trained we took an hour at the wheel and, in bad weather, an hour on lookout (in good conditions the officer of the watch and the helmsman kept a lookout from the bridge). At the change of watch, someone would ring the appropriate number of 'bells' using the plaited rope on the ship's bell.

Buoy maintenance in progress aboard the Pharos.

While on watch, a call 'to the lead!' could come any time if a sounding was needed. Occasionally the call was for 'two hands to the lead!' to check the depth on both sides of the ship in narrow waters. The *Pharos* often went to anchor in sea lochs, where two soundings might be needed because the scouring from heavy seas and strong tides meant the seabed shifted frequently.

Jimmy Mac taught us how to swing the lead and Willie and I were delighted when we were considered proficient and could take our turn. The ship would reduce speed and the deck was cleared of men – someone could be killed if the lead fell short. One day a man let it fall too soon resulting in a dent to the deck and a dirty look from the bo'sun. The lead was attached to a length of thin rope which was marked at fathom intervals with different coloured threads. When the lead was spun overhead it flew in front of the ship then plummeted to the seabed. As we drew level, the reading was given to the officer of the watch. According to the colour of marker showing on the line, we called out numbers like 'by the mark five!' or 'by the deep ten!' As the ship still had no radar, a larger deep-sea lead was invaluable in fog. It had a cavity underneath that was filled with sticky tallow, to which sand, mud, and gravel adhered easily. Samples taken from this could be compared with the nature of seabed shown on a chart to pinpoint the ship's exact position.

Our training in seamanship and navigation included a weekly stint of rowing practice off Inchkeith. The Commissioners' gig was manned by eight men, with four oars on each side. Everything was performed in the best Royal Navy style under the direction of the ship's mate. At the end of the session he would call 'way enough!' as we approached the ship; this was the signal to raise oars smartly to the perpendicular. Then came the order, 'ship oars!' to lower them in precise succession. Boat training made a welcome change from everyday work.

The mate was an old windjammer (merchant sailing ship) man who enforced discipline rigidly. He walked around the deck with a belaying pin in one hand and a rope's end in the other. The company jumped to attention immediately he gave an order. On a bad day his likely response to a 'good morning, sir,' from us was 'good morning my arse, look for a ship!'

At this time a well-known evangelist had been converting many people in dockland. One evening our mate was persuaded to go to one of his meetings. He came back from this a changed man; gone were the belaying pin, rope, and the lurid language. At the next rowing practice he addressed us brightly: 'Right, lads! Let's have a good show today and we'll get back early for tea.' He spoke to us like a father and we felt uneasy. Everything at the session went well until we were told to ship oars. Then, by accident I hasten to add, I clipped him on the ear as I lowered my oar. He cursed and swore; his new-found piety was quickly forgotten and things soon returned to normal.

The *Pharos* was a happy ship. Most of her company were young. Some of the highly qualified seamen had come from major shipping lines; Jimmy Mac was a former quartermaster from the Blue Funnel Line. Others had been on Arctic whaling ships, one had fished off the Grand Banks of Newfoundland, and some had even served under sail. There was much practical joking in the foc's'le and yarning in the smoke room passed time in the evenings. Jimmy Mac became a great adviser and friend; he got Willie and me out of many scrapes. Our food in the seamen's mess was generally good. On one occasion it deteriorated until there was just a hunk of cheese for each man's meal, but a new caterer was found and normal service quickly resumed. For breakfast there was usually bacon and eggs, replaced by a tasty curry every Thursday. Plum duff once a week was a special favourite, and a huge Johnnycake packed with sultanas was popular with everybody. There was one day when a temporary crew member went to have an early dinner before going on lookout duty. The cook put the whole pudding on the table and left the man to take his portion. When the rest of us arrived there was only an empty serving dish left. 'Where's ours?' we demanded. 'Oh, I thought it was a duff a man,' said the sailor, having polished off the lot!

I was about 19 when the cook and his staff were struck down with flu; the chief officer told me to take over in the galley. I had little experience of cooking and on the first morning there was a heavy swell. The fiddles were up while I fried bacon and eggs for 32 on a stove that was never still.

An enormous stockpot was kept simmering on this cooking range. It was heated by three coal fires and a rack above the hotplate was used for drying pots and lids. I was in for a shock that forenoon when I lifted the lid of the pot to add some vegetables – a cloud of steam enveloped the rack and a shower of cockroaches dropped into the stock! I banged the lid back on and left the contents alone to continue cooking. I sieved the soup before it was served; there were no complaints and the next day no bodies appeared. In any case the ship was soon fumigated; apart from these cockroaches I saw no vermin.

We had a little band on the ship to amuse ourselves; this included two accordions, two fiddles, a clarinet and a drum. While we were at anchor we played in the foc'sle, or on deck if it was fine. I progressed from a mouth organ to an accordion after lessons from a St Abbs sailor. I then saved up and bought a lovely little white melodeon of my own. One or two of us liked to fish when we came to anchor. After I caught a 30-pound halibut in Loch Eriboll we sold it for 30 shillings (£1.50) at Stromness and shared the proceeds. The *Pharos* also had a football team and we played teams from other ships or local teams at ports of call. We usually socialised with the crews afterwards.

Storytelling was a memorable pastime in the smoke room and deep sea men had many tales. Not only were there black bugs in their bunks to contend with, but fishing off the rich Grand Banks was a highly dangerous occupation. The men had to leave their ship in little dories to search for fish; some were lost in fog and never returned. One of our crewmen had been missing for a day and a night before his dory was found. Whalers told of their small craft being damaged by flailing whales that had been harpooned. A dead whale would be pumped full of air to be towed back to the ship, and then the sea ran red with blood from the grisly butchering. They spoke of Eskimos as fine, friendly people who would share everything if they counted you as a friend.

Our coxswain was Andrew, a fine old St Abbs fisherman. Known as 'the auld yin', he was respected by all the crew. Andrew always wanted me to help him in the boat and seemed to value my childhood connection with St Abbs. His hobby was breeding canaries and he gave me two to take home for Kitty.

It was while we were landing stores at Cape Wrath lighthouse that Andrew saved me from nearly drowning for the second time. I was carrying a load up the slipway when a rogue wave knocked me into the sea. In a flash my heavy leather thigh-boots filled with water and I was dragged under. Andrew pushed the boat out quickly and reached me with the boathook. 'What the hell are you doing in there, Mac?' I heard as I surfaced. The crew soon pulled me aboard and I was taken back to the ship. The only damage was a sore knee, so it was straight back to work after a change of clothing.

I was not the only one who nearly drowned. One day 'Old Chippie', the carpenter, was busy on deck with a buoy anchor when he slipped overboard. We could see him on

*The ship's carpenter
with his oil can.*

the way down through clear calm water. He soon rose to the surface again though, still clutching his favourite hammer and with his cap still stuck firmly on his head. We threw him a line and helped him up the rope ladder that always hung over the bulwarks during buoy work.

The carpenter who succeeded 'Old Chippie' was seldom seen on deck without his oil can. He used it all the time 'to keep things moving', even the anchor chain received his attention. He was a cheerful member of the company. He bought the first three-wheeled car in Stromness and it was known as 'Skinner's Fart'. A story went around that he appeared once on a charge of speeding. He was asked how fast he had been driving. More used to the ship than the car, he hesitated: 'Er… six knots, Your Honour!'

The bo'sun, Dugald, was an exceptionally fine man who had spent his early days on sailing ships. Although his discipline was strict, it was fair and he was expert in all aspects of ship maintenance. He acted as our foreman and was especially proud of his deck – it had to be kept immaculate at all times. One of the first jobs we learnt was to keep the deck and its rail clean and clear of bird droppings, a hateful task. However, the carpenter was always leaving drops of oil on the deck and not in the least bothered when the bo'sun shouted at him.

The bo'sun checked my misdemeanours swiftly and nothing escaped his eye. One day, while I was polishing all the brass on deck, I decided I would save myself work in the future. I painted the casing of the stern light white so that it would need no further polishing. Some days later, when the paint was thoroughly hardened, he called me: 'You've a job to do today. Clean every trace of paint off that light and polish it!' That was a lesson I never forgot.

Every three weeks or so, less often in winter, we took on coal. We were not happy when the officers said 'we'll be going to bunker soon', as it always meant there would be a very dirty ship to be cleaned. Beforehand the decks had to be cleared and the hatches closed, and everything given a good hosing afterwards. Twice this coincided with dockers' strikes. Then we had to load the tons of fuel ourselves, taking it from the hold of the coal ship to skips on a cargo boat and on to the *Pharos*.

Looking down through grilles in the deck we could see the ship's furnaces glowing red whenever their doors were opened. The firemen were always stoking; an endless task in that dreadful place that looked like an inferno. At one point the stokers were shorthanded and two of us were called to assist. Initially, we shot coal all over the place each time the ship rolled. It was heavy work shovelling all day in the heat; it was so hot we were stripped to the waist. A steady heat had to be maintained so that the head of steam in the boilers remained constant. This was difficult to judge without experience, but large pressure gauges gave us readings. Clearing clinker from the back of the fire with long rakes was the hottest part of the job. We were glad when the regular stokers took over again, and we were rewarded with large packs of cigarettes.

In port the bo'sun taught us to sew canvas for the ship's various awnings, how to splice and whip manila or wire ropes, and many other shipboard skills. The boats needed constant attention and ropes such as the 'falls' often had to be replaced.

*Polishing brass
on the 'Pharos'.*

These were very important as they controlled the boats being lowered to the sea from the davits on deck.

There was an old able seaman called Ned, who appreciated our help with some of the heavy work for which he was no longer fit. A wonderful hand with a canvas needle, he had repaired ships' sails when he was young. When we were mending flags in the after hold we realised he was colour-blind because he sewed a yellow patch on a blue flag. A fiery character, he preached socialist doctrines at us, thumping the table at meals to emphasise a point. There was always practical joking on the ship and Ned could usually take a joke. One day however, while a lively discussion was in progress, Willie pushed Ned's plate slightly to one side. Quite carried away, Ned banged his fist down into his soup. Sputtering with rage at this cheekiness, he could take no reprisals with 11 of us grinning at his soupy face.

A large crowd gathered one Sunday afternoon to watch the *Pharos* come alongside at Granton; there had been a delay in completing the reliefs on time. She was a bonny sight and a magnet for sightseers at weekends. We were carrying a handsome goat from a keeper on the Isle of May to be delivered to the mainland but nobody would volunteer to lead the goat up the gangway in front of so many people. Finally, Ned was given the job and – to Ned's fury and the amusement of the bystanders – a cheeky lad on the quay shouted: 'Which end of the rope is the goat at!'

I nearly drowned a third time when I fell overboard somewhere near the Isle of May. My head hit the gunwale and ex-Navy man John, a marvellous swimmer, jumped in and grabbed the back of my jersey. I was floating, semi-conscious, when I heard his distant voice: 'Over on your back, Mac! On your back! Norway's a long way off!' He towed me to the side and someone lowered a rope. Back on board, hot sweet tea had never tasted so good.

During the depression our wages were cut, leading to much anger and frustration. None of us had been union members before, but now everyone except the officers joined the Transport and General Workers' Union. John, a dedicated socialist, became our Union man. Strikes became common, although we had to promise the Northern Lighthouse Board never to withdraw our labour; lives could be at risk if lights were not tended.

Several of us went to a political meeting in Leith addressed by Robert Boothby, then a prospective Conservative candidate. I asked him why our wages had been cut drastically. 'My friend, I am not interested in the past, only the future,' was his only reply. This left me disillusioned about politicians. John eventually left our ship for a career in politics and became Secretary of State for Scotland.

The second mate, Dougie, was in charge of the ship's boat at reliefs, and we soon learnt how to cope with sudden changes in wind and sea conditions. With safety always the priority, the crew worked as a team in every respect. Leaving the Bell Rock one day, the boat was caught in a gully by a big wave. Washed onto the rock, we were stranded at a crazy angle. I thought we should jump out and run to the lighthouse before we were swamped by the next rush of sea, but Dougie shouted, 'Sit still, where you are!' We sat while the next white crest curled towards us. This carried us out to deep water and we rowed away furiously so we could not be tossed back. Always in perfect control of the most difficult and dangerous situations, Dougie could calm any man that panicked. Father had known him as a boy because he was friendly with his parents. Now I had to remember to address him as 'Sir'! He took me aside occasionally to give me good advice, including reminders on maintaining the high standards of the Lighthouse Service.

A year later we were back once more at the Bell Rock in a rough sea, this time delivering a heavy load of water barrels. Again a big roller caught us and it swamped the boat. We were in immediate danger of sinking and the water was up to our knees. 'Out with the barrels!' yelled Dougie and the whole lot went overboard. As we baled furiously, the boat rose in the water and we were safe. After I left the *Pharos*, her boat was lost there in similar conditions, though the crew escaped by jumping on to the rock.

On one wet and windy night a cat joined the ship's company. It was getting dark when Andrew spotted her under the pier in the harbour clinging to one of the piles and on the point of drowning. Although he was not young, he shinned down to rescue her. He climbed back with the cat clinging for dear life to his shoulder. She became a favourite with all and visited every port with us in the course of her many years aboard, always returning to the ship before we sailed. Then one day there was no sign of her. We came back to Granton pier ten days later, and as soon as the carpenter opened his shed, a rather thin and bedraggled cat ran out. From then on the captain always asked if the cat was aboard before we sailed.

The captain gave me lessons in steering the ship in the Firth of Forth. To begin with I over-steered, so he sat with his feet on the wheel to demonstrate how little adjustment was needed for plain sailing. Soon I was often at the wheel in sheltered waters, helped by the experience gained from many hours with Alex on the Chanonry ferry. Once I was fully trained I had to 'take my trick' on the open sea. I enjoyed this greatly, and was now seldom seasick.

The best of times were those spent on lookout in good weather. What a great feeling of freedom there was, standing in the open bow! A stiff breeze blew salt spray on my face and no one could hear when I sang at the top of my voice. Dolphins often swam with the ship, leaping through the bow wave as if for joy, and fish glittered in the dark sea on calm nights. There were special moments when whales and basking sharks appeared from the waters of the Minch. On one summer's day an eerie silence fell though we maintained our speed; we were sailing through thousands of jellyfish which turned the sea to a thick soup and muffled all sound.

When the ship was in port, there always had to be one man on watch; an officer stayed on board, and two firemen kept the fires alight in case we were called to an emergency. Most of the crew lived in or around Edinburgh and they would ask Willie and me to take their night watches so they could go home. Willie and I stayed overnight on the ship while in port anyway. We sometimes went ashore together in our free time, but we were not allowed into pubs till we were 20. The others often invited us for tea with their families. Once I was asked to a house by a fellow whose brother, Jimmy, was a hand on a fishing boat. Jimmy arrived home after a long trip with no sleep; he just managed to cut the top off his boiled egg before he fell asleep. No one could wake the exhausted lad and I thought he had died at the table. We carried him to his bed, where he slept for many hours.

In spare time ashore I always found a warm welcome at the Gibson's. Mrs Gibson was kind and motherly; if she saw that my shirt was frayed she would buy me a new one. After a hard storing trip she would say that I looked worn out and give me some of her special tonic. This pink liquid from a lemonade bottle seemed to help. The four Gibson boys still lived at home and we had good times together. There were musical evenings and parties at their house and Captain Gibson entertained us in the billiard room with stories of his voyages to the Far East or America.

One wild spring night Andrew, the coxswain, stayed on board to help us; the sea was so rough that he thought we might need extra moorings. Around midnight I saw a girl, probably in her twenties, gazing into deep water from the edge of the pier. I called Andrew who walked over to her.

'What are you doing here at this time of night?' he asked. 'It's dangerous.'

'Just looking at the sea,' she said and walked away. We sailed the next day; when we returned to the same berth weeks later, our propellers turned up her body. She had been reported missing but a search had been unsuccessful.

There were others who tried to board the *Pharos* at night, either drunk or intent on robbery. When we were on a night watch we walked around with a heavy stick – once I had to get rid of two men that I found on deck; I surprised two others climbing down the ladder from the pier. On another occasion I woke to find a man beside my bunk and shouted to Willie. A fireman acted fast and grabbed the thief; all our loose change was in his pockets and the police were called.

Before each payday the captain sent me to collect the wages for the ship's complement from a bank in Edinburgh. For three or four years I carried the special yellow bag safely along the city streets. It seems amazing now that a lad could walk the same route regularly with cash to pay 32 men for a month without any fear or danger.

The Commissioners – the governing body of the Northern Lighthouse Board – comprised the sheriffs principal of the seaboard counties plus the Lord Provosts of Edinburgh, Glasgow, and Aberdeen. The *Pharos* took a group on the Commissioners' trip every summer. Various lighthouses in the Western Isles, Orkney and Shetland, and the Isle of Man (a particular highlight) were included, as well as some on the mainland. This was an easy fortnight for us on the ship, with routine work only, and sometimes we were able to go ashore as well. Our morning work would be finished by nine o'clock and then we changed into full uniform, but always wearing sandshoes so that we walked around the ship quietly. When the trip included Sule Skerry lighthouse, I glimpsed the island of Foula in passing. We sailed near enough to see the vast bird-nesting colonies on high cliffs, capped with green. When the ship sounded her siren, a blanket of seabirds rose and flew over our heads.

A special chef from an Edinburgh hotel was brought in to cater for the Commissioners. Delectable smells filled the air as grand dishes were prepared. Occasionally an extra morsel came our way, although not always legitimately. The visiting chef would grumble when we went to the galley in the evenings to make ourselves a cup of tea, not happy at the invasion of his space.

In 1928 I was part of the boat crew that took the Commissioners to St Kilda from the ship. The islanders were eager to sell us their knitting and barter for tobacco

The Pharos' boat on a storing trip to St Abbs Head
(note the barrels lined up on the slipway).

or cigarettes, but outsiders were not always keen to buy the garments, which smelt strongly of fulmar oil. It was sad to find how poor the folk seemed. We saw no young people; most had probably left for the mainland by this time. Only two years later St Kilda was evacuated by the Fishery Cruiser.

For storing trips, the hold was carefully stowed at Granton so that consignments were unloaded in the right order. The *Pharos* carried enormous quantities of stores, including water, coal, oil, machinery and spares, furniture, paint, fodder and building materials. Fresh water was delivered in little wooden barrels known as breakers. At the lighthouses everything was craned or carried by hand. Rolling the 40-gallon casks of paraffin up the landings was hard going; we had no gloves and our hands were often raw by the end of a trip. Goats to provide milk were transported to some stations, and sometimes we also had to look after donkeys and occasionally a pony in transit; we rode the more co-operative ones around the deck.

Some of the remote stations were supplied with two donkeys and little carts which were painted smartly in red and green. The donkeys at Ushenish, South Uist, were well behaved, carrying stores regularly from the landing to the lighthouse. But at Pentland Skerries I had dealings with 'Green Teeth', who always tried to bite. Leaning over a dyke there once, I watched their two donkeys grazing near a flock of starlings. I could not believe my eyes when Green Teeth inched nearer, snapped up a starling, chewed, and swallowed it! (A favourite habit of his, apparently.) At Auskerry, Orkney, one of the donkeys was an exceptionally good worker while the other ran away whenever he saw the relief boat approaching. He was easily rounded up, though he grew more and more stubborn until he refused to pull the cart at all. Finally one of the keepers had a brainwave: he tied the donkey to ropes at the back of the cart and took the shafts himself. Harnessed back to front, the donkey worked quite happily and took the weight as long as the man held the shafts.

Normally, our main duties in winter consisted of making reliefs at the Bell Rock, island lighthouses in the Firth of Forth, and the North Carr Lightship. Supplies and a replacement keeper would be delivered at each. However, one breezy winter afternoon we headed further north to replace the *Pole Star*, our sister ship, because she was in dry dock. The north-east wind soon freshened to a gale and reached storm force off the Aberdeenshire coast. I was at the wheel from two to three in the morning with the ship pitching heavily in mountainous seas that shot over her bow. Spray smothered the bridge; I had seen nothing like it before. As we were passing the entrance to the Moray Firth, there was a sudden crack – one of our lifeboats' booms had snapped in two and the boat swung loose on its davits. 'All hands' were called to secure the four lifeboats and lower their booms while the ship's head was turned away. We resumed our northerly course, but the storm was so severe off Duncansby Head that there was real danger of damage to the ship. 'All hands' were called again, this time to put on our lifejackets. These hung in clips from the rail but on the port side they had already been washed away. Captain Scott decided to run for Widewall Bay in Orkney rather than attempt the Pentland Firth.

We lay at anchor there for two days until the storm blew itself out, and then continued west. While the ship was in the bay we were invited to spend an evening at the local manse, and when conditions eased sufficiently, four or five of us crossed in the liberty boat. Meanwhile, two of our lifebelts had been found washed ashore at John o' Groats. As soon as possible, the captain sent a telegram from Longhope to the Lighthouse Board saying that the ship was safe. Despite this, the alarm had already been raised, and newspapers reported that the *Pharos* was thought to have foundered. We were unaware of these stories in the press; we were enjoying games of cards and tea and cakes with the minister's daughters.

For the whole of another winter, the *Pharos* had to take over the northern area. While a new *Pole Star* was being built, we were based at Stromness and serviced the Orkney Isles, Shetland Islands, Sule Skerry, and Flannan Isle lights. It was a long haul to the Flannans in bad weather.

On passage north from Granton to Stromness we ran into a gale again. I was hurrying across the deck and dodging the spray when something fell at my feet. An exhausted pigeon lay with its wings outstretched and its beak wide open. I picked it up and put it in our washroom for the night. The next morning the bird seemed hungry, so I started feeding it. A few days later I tried to release it several times from the deck; each time, it circled the ship and landed beside me! The pigeon stayed with us for weeks, though it looked very seasick on rough days. Most of the others grew heartily tired of 'Mac's b… pigeon', in spite of its chatty cooing while they washed their faces. Finally, I gave it to my girlfriend, Peggy, in Stromness and suggested it would be better kept indoors for a while. But the bird landed on deck again and by that time we had sailed a hundred miles. On our return to port I clipped its right wing and it stayed on dry land.

On an even stormier passage, to Lerwick this time, we received a message that a fishing boat had run aground on Ve Skerries and was in danger of sinking. Altering our course straightaway, we soon found the *Ben Doran* lying on her side being pounded by the sea. She was breaking up rapidly on the reef and the lifeboat was unable to get alongside. One of the masts was still intact and two men clung to the rigging as huge waves broke over them. Helplessly – we could not even lower a boat – we watched as one man, then the other, dropped into the foaming water. Soon the trawler was a complete wreck, and all hands were lost. On berthing at Lerwick, we were invited by the superintendent of the Seamen's Mission to attend prayers for the crew of the *Ben Doran*. We sat with the lifeboat crew and a large crowd for a very emotional service. In his address the chaplain stressed that life must go on, in spite of such terrible tragedies.

The first time we carried out a relief at the Flannan Isles, I was warned to be very careful. We came in to the exposed west landing; a dangerous place at the best of times. It was reckoned that every seventh wave could be exceptional, even if local conditions were good. I saw this the second time we were there. That day we could only watch powerlessly as a huge wave washed a heavy box of artificers' tools off the landing platform, never to be seen again. In my experience, at no other lighthouse landing was the force of the waves so extreme.

My wristwatch stopped while we were off Orkney and I had it repaired in Kirkwall. The watchmaker spoke with a heavy foreign accent and my friends thought he was Swiss. I heard afterwards that his little shop closed suddenly in the Second World War – he left just after the *Royal Oak* was torpedoed and was never seen in Orkney again. His hobby had been sailing in Scapa Flow at weekends; some locals thought he had been a German spy and had helped to sink the battleship (800 lives were lost).

At weekends we went to local functions in Stromness and this was where I met Peggy, my future wife. While Peggy's father was a lightkeeper at Sule Skerry his family lived at the Stromness shore station.

Back in our own area, the *Pharos* would sometimes be moored at Leith instead of Granton. Willie and I were fascinated by the big ocean-going ships that brought their cargoes here. Ben, Blue Funnel, and Salvesen lines travelled frequently between exotic places and Leith. We gazed at beautiful Cairn Line ships with their feather insignia on the funnel, and cherished dreams of sailing further afield. A sniff of the air often told what was being unloaded, whether it was the cloying smell of brown locust beans or a pungent whiff of oranges. A crate of fruit occasionally slipped out of a sling and shattered on the quay. The dockers were very good and gave us handfuls of spilt apples, oranges, and bananas which we would otherwise never have tasted. We also liked the sweet taste of locust beans that were imported for sheep fodder, so when they dropped we always picked up a few to chew. By late spring there was regular sea trade with the Baltic – ships such as the *Weimar* and the *Breslau* sailed through waters that left their bows impressively scarred and polished by ice. We made friends with the *Weimar* sailors and sometimes had coffee on board. They brought over jewellery and trinkets, which they sold to us cheaply as presents for girlfriends and sisters.

Bobbie followed Archie, as a boy seaman, but went on to take his tickets.

One night I found Willie very ill in the foc'sle and he was immediately taken to hospital. He was diagnosed with tuberculosis and had to resign. This was a sad end to my friend's time at sea. He died soon after; he was only in his mid-twenties.

For my last three or four years on the *Pharos* I was given a great deal of boat work. I enjoyed every minute of this. The boat's awning was only used in really bad weather so I was often soaked to the skin going to and from the ship. The others just laughed and chanted 'what are the wild waves saying?'

Captain Scott wanted me to study for my tickets and I attended several classes at Leith Nautical College. But after six years on the ship I knew that I wanted to be a lightkeeper, so I joined the long waiting list for keeper training. There were regrets at parting from my shipmates, and I gave my beautiful melodeon to Jimmy Mac who had guided me from the start.

4

Supernumerary Keeper – Isle of May, Bass Rock, Monach and Kinnaird Head

1932–1934

Isle of May

LIGHT ESTABLISHED 1816
SQUARE GOTHIC TOWER 24 METRES HIGH ON STONE DWELLING
ENGINEER – ROBERT STEVENSON

In June Bobbie arrived on the ship to replace me; he would later go on to take his tickets. I packed all my gear into kitbags and the *Pharos* took me to the Isle of May. My shipmates wished me good luck and waved as the ship steamed away, tooting twice on her whistle. With mixed feelings, I watched the familiar outline disappear over the horizon; my training as a supernumerary keeper had begun.

This was a busy station where men were based with their families for several years at a time, only leaving the island for three weeks' holiday a year. From outside, the lighthouse looked rather like a small castle, with a square tower and gothic windows; not at all like the lighthouses of my childhood. The keepers' quarters were on the ground floor; I had a spacious room. Above this was the Commissioners' Room which was very grand, with a long polished table, elegant chairs, and a bright red carpet. The room was rarely used – the Commissioners now held most of their meetings in Edinburgh – and it was only unlocked for routine cleaning by a keeper's wife.

The present lighthouse was built in 1816 by the Northern Lighthouse Board. A second lighthouse, the Low Light, stood near the shore to warn ships of the North

THE FIRST LIGHTHOUSE

The disused tower of the first lighthouse on the Isle of May was still standing. It had been built by neighbouring landowners in 1636 and lit with a large coal brazier. The keeper lived underneath this with his family – he gathered coal for fuel from the beach and carried it up on his back. His pay was seven pounds a year with some oatmeal; he often needed to fish by day to feed everyone. No light would be displayed if he had not returned by darkness. The brightness of the fire varied wildly depending on the strength of the wind and billowing smoke, and fog or rain could obscure the light completely. One night in 1790, fumes from the fire above suffocated a sleeping keeper and all members of his family, except one little girl.

Carr rocks. In time the North Carr Lightship replaced the Low Light, which was then used as a store. Limewashing this store was one of my first jobs and like all the Board's property, it was well maintained. Another job was to paint the foghorn. One day an assistant and I were busy painting the horn when it started to blast! We were sitting on top and nearly fell off with fright and the task was abandoned till all was quiet.

Four keepers made up a standard lighthouse crew, with three men always on duty and one ashore. But at the Isle of May, two crews were required because there were two fog signals, one at each end of the island, therefore six men at a time were on duty here to man these and the light. The engine room for the Isle ofMay fog signals and houses for the three extra keepers were in Fluke Street, some distance from the lighthouse. Three keepers were deemed necessary at a lighthouse in case of an emergency. A tragedy in 1960 would show how important this staffing arrangement was. At Little Ross lighthouse a furious argument got out of hand and one keeper killed another, then fled.

Every lighthouse had its own unique character to indicate an exact location. For example, the beams on revolving lights were set for different intervals of time, and some displayed a red sector to show vessels when they were heading for danger. Other stations had a fixed light that would flash, or occult, for set periods.

The light was a revolving paraffin gas burner. The clockwork mechanism for turning the light stood in the lightroom; known as 'the machine', it was enclosed in an enormous glass case and had a handle that we turned to wind its weighted chain. The frequency for winding varied from one lighthouse to another according to the height of the tower, but allowing a revolving light to become stationary was always a serious offence. The timing was checked against the lightroom clock; we had a gadget for adjusting this, though it was rarely needed.

Up in the lantern the many prisms of the lens concentrated the light. Here the lens floated on a bath of three or four inches of mercury; although it weighed well over a ton, it could be pushed around with one finger. To top up the bath, we had to carry a metal container upstairs and this was exceedingly heavy when it was full. Not all revolving lenses floated on a bath; some were set on small wheels that ran on a track. These had to be polished and oiled regularly, whereas we only had to clean the mercury bath once a year. To do this, we ran a tool that looked like a metal saw blade through it to pick up all the dust and then wiped the dirty blade with a cloth, sometimes touching stray beads of mercury with our bare hands. Not realising we were handling a dangerous substance, we didn't wear gloves. Occasionally we dipped a finger in and rubbed it on the little brass wall ventilators to see them turn briefly to silver.

The morning routine to prepare the light for the evening started at nine o'clock. A green can containing four gallons of paraffin was carried up to the light room. At high towers the spring went out of an older man's stride after a hundred steps. The lens was cleaned – its thick glass always had to be immaculate – and the prisms were dusted with a white cloth and polished with a chamois. Stubborn marks were rubbed with methylated spirit, but no other cleaning agent could be used. A bull's eye needed special attention to keep its brilliance. At night we had to avoid looking at the centre of a bull's eye as it was dazzling when lit. After dinner the watches began, with one keeper always on standby. The others might be free for the afternoon and often used this time to catch up on sleep.

At all lighthouses the first night watch started half an hour before sunset and these were kept in the lightroom. The light was lit with a long wax taper; the lens was set in motion and the clockwork mechanism wound regularly to keep it revolving.

For the first two weeks the principal keeper took me with him to keep a three hour watch at night. I had to check continually that the lens was revolving at the right speed. Every 15 minutes I went onto the balcony to scan the sea for ships and fog. When fog was sighted someone had to be called immediately to start the fog signal.

The principal keeper was in charge of training; he was an excellent, patient tutor with high standards of discipline. He instilled the ideal of the Northern Lighthouse Board – 'For the Safety of All'. He was surprised that I already knew how to clean the lantern and brass, chores I had learnt as a boy.

I was taught the golden rules: never leave the lightroom unattended; never allow the light to stand or be extinguished; never fall asleep on watch. A lightkeeper could be dismissed instantly for breaking any of these rules. While on watch we were not allowed to read or write anything except entries in the log. I soon learnt that it was a bad idea to sit down towards the end of a watch as it was easy to fall asleep; better to keep moving for the last hour. At the end of a watch I rang a bell to call the next keeper.

One night I went on to the balcony just before three o'clock, towards the end of my watch. A light mist was hanging around the tower and a flock of curlews were calling in the darkness. Winging in and out of the rays, they circled the light in a fascinating display. However, when I stepped back into the lightroom I was horrified to see that it was already seven minutes past the hour. I called the principal keeper immediately and was afraid I would be sacked. When I explained, he said: 'I believe you. But don't let it happen again.' Good timekeeping was essential; the rules were strict.

In Father's day a superintendent sometimes appeared in the middle of night to check on watch keeping, arriving unexpectedly in the lightroom. Keepers devised a warning method by hanging a towel on the rail at the top of the stairs, which fluttered as soon as the tower door was opened. I was glad that these surprise checks no longer happened.

Following my introduction to the light, the mysteries of the engine room were revealed with its pleasing oily atmosphere. I was then trained in the use of foghorns, with engines like those I had admired in Scalpay. Their oil had to be checked and filled and its smell clung to our clothing. One morning I was looking after an engine which would not run smoothly. I left the oil bucket to fill under the tap of a barrel while I went to settle the engine; when I returned half an hour later, the floor of the oil store was completely flooded! The principal helped me to sweep and scrub all afternoon, with no reprimand. I thought it would never be clear, but quantities of sand and sawdust worked wonders.

There had been several recent strandings on the May rocks. Two of the keepers had swum out to save four men from a trawler, the remains of which were still visible. 'Just part of a day's work,' one keeper said, describing the incident. We practised lifesaving drills every month in case of another shipwreck – I was taught how to fire a rocket with a rope attached for helping people to safety.

Boatloads of visitors came to the Isle of May on day trips and flocked to the lighthouse, which livened up our day. I was given the job of showing groups up the tower, with explicit warnings as to safety. I had to ensure that nobody fell down the 'traps', the steep metal stairs that lead up to the lantern, and on the balcony, children were not to be allowed to lean over the rail or climb the ladder to the dome. There was another rule too: the keeper must always go first when climbing the stairs, to save ladies in skirts from embarrassment! Another hazard was our Clydesdale horse who was an expert at stealing picnics – if visitors left their bags unattended the contents would be eaten or trampled underfoot. We needed him to carry stores from the ship; it was my job to catch and harness him.

I cooked for myself here, but my supplies soon ran out. I had brought more tins of condensed milk than anything else. This was the one item I did not need because Jock, the senior assistant, kept six goats, which provided us with fresh milk. Luckily, his kind wife gave me enough provisions to last until the ship's next visit and used my unwanted tins for her baking. I learnt very soon about the treachery of the billy goat; his long curling horns packed a wicked punch, and he never missed a chance to butt an unsuspecting person when their back was turned. I had no success when I tried milking the nannies, though they let down their milk and chewed the cud contentedly while I watched Jock fill the frothing bucket.

Seabirds nested in greater numbers here than I had ever seen. Puffins, guillemots, razorbills, kittiwakes, shags, and gulls crowded the faces and tops of cliffs, and a great many eiders nested on flat ground. One duck had hatched her brood in a hollow on the cliff. I watched the ducklings drift down the rock face like tiny puffs of down to reach the sea. This island was overrun with rabbits, probably introduced originally by monks as a source of food. The keepers snared a great many which were collected by the *Pharos* and sold on their behalf in Edinburgh.

No one other than the lightkeepers and their families now lived on the Isle of May, although a chilling rumour survived that the ghost of the engineer who installed the lights was seen sometimes at the Low Light. Artificers said they heard his footsteps, but I found no sign of him.

Bass Rock

ESTABLISHED 1902

WHITE TOWER 20 METRES HIGH

ENGINEER – D. ALAN STEVENSON

In the spring I went to the Bass Rock for three months, arriving at the same time as thousands of gannets. Their main nest site was very close to the lighthouse which was smothered with their droppings. Since this could obscure the light, much of my working day consisted of washing the lantern and scrubbing the balcony, in addition to my normal lightroom duties. Despite the mess, I never heard a keeper complain about the gannets, known as the 'Bird of the Bass'. There were two huge noisy breeding colonies that covered the rock with nesting birds and guano, making one side of it look white. Tightly packed together, they squabbled constantly and stole nest material from each other. Now and again one was killed during many fierce mid-air fights, though the quarrelling eased when the young hatched and feeding their chicks became non-stop for parents. Watching them was wonderful. But I was warned never to walk on ledges below the nests. The birds could knock a man into the sea as they took off in search of fish and it would be easy to slip over the cliff on the patches of slippery grass.

Fried gannet eggs had a fishy taste that was not noticeable in baking. Their yolks never set, no matter how hard they were boiled. Gannet eggs had also been used in the mortar for building an early chapel which was now in ruins. The lighthouse itself was above a ruined fortress that had a grim past as a state prison; Presbyterian ministers had been confined here and prisoners died in its dungeons.

Although the Bass Rock was an outcrop that covered about 19 acres, its lighthouse was classed as a rock station. The space outside gave us a chance to exercise and provided a gradual introduction to life as a rock keeper. The three men on duty had been in the Service for a long time and seemed to get on well with each other. They were very good to me in this next stage of my training. At first I was on watch with the principal and his word was law. Their spells of duty consisted of eight weeks on the rock at a time, but I stayed for three months. As usual at rocks, the two assistants took turns as cook and I washed the dishes; principal keepers were not expected to carry out these chores.

This principal said a grace before every meal. One of the others told me never to ask for a second helping of pudding at dinnertime, and I soon saw why. Every day some was left in the serving dish and the boss would say, 'well, if nobody wants any more, I'll finish this off, boys.' None of us would speak up as he spooned the rest into his bowl. 'That was very good!' he would say as he left the table. It bothered nobody, though little habits like this could aggravate at rock lights. Lovely milk puddings with crisp brown skin were baked in a large enamel pie dish. Afterwards, the empty dish was left outside in the courtyard to soak overnight. By the next morning it was always spotless, the crusty edges stripped clean by rats. The Bass Rock had plenty of rats and they obviously knew where to find a good pudding.

There was still much for me to learn after my three months here; further training followed at the Monach Isles, beyond the Outer Hebrides.

Monach

ESTABLISHED 1864

RED BRICK TOWER, 41 METRES HIGH

ENGINEERS – DAVID AND THOMAS STEVENSON

Monach lighthouse was on Shillay, one of the Monach Isles, west of North Uist. To get there, I took MacBrayne's ferry to Lochmaddy, a car journey across North Uist and a trip in an open boat.

The tricky surrounding waters bristled with rocks, and it was said that 'if you can see Monach you're too near!' Two black stone pillars marked a narrow rock-bound channel by which a boat might approach. Passing ships gave the reef a wide berth and I do not remember seeing any from the lantern. There was no foghorn, probably because vessels could not come near enough to hear a signal.

Work followed much the same routine as before but with no gannet droppings, for which I was thankful. I helped with the painting programme, though outside work was limited because the tall red brick tower was left bare to show against the flat background and there were frequent gales and rain, even in the summer.

Archie with two farmer friends on Heisker, Monach Isles.

The keepers and their wives were the only inhabitants of Shillay. Two farmers, who were brothers, lived with their families on Heisker, the neighbouring island. Weather permitting, the farmers delivered our provisions by boat every fortnight. I crossed regularly in the lighthouse boat to fetch our mail from their island.

Afternoons at the lighthouse were quiet, with one keeper having a sleep before a night watch. I was always asked in to one of the houses for a cup of tea and there seemed to be children everywhere. Between them, the two brothers had six sons and six daughters and I was glad of the company.

Neither the principal nor the assistant liked the boat and only used it when essential. Once the boss saw I could handle it, I was allowed to go fishing or explore the little islands when I was off duty. This suited me fine, and I soon found enough bits of wood and net on the beaches to make a lobster creel.

One afternoon I came across a well-built fishermen's bothy on Heisker. The door was snibbed but unlocked, and the bothy was empty apart from a lovely dry straw bed. I felt like having a snooze so I lay down. Suddenly, there was a rustling and two little ferret eyes popped up near my face! After a good stare, the head disappeared back into the straw. I often sheltered here, though I did not try the bed with its unexpected company again.

Not far from the lighthouse was a little thatched hut that stirred my curiousity. Apparently, it was used by four men from North Uist who fished lobsters off the Monach Isles every summer; in due course a fishing boat arrived. A peat fire was soon burning inside and a large stack of creels appeared outside. The men brought a few sheep from their crofts on Uist for some fresh grazing on Shillay, to the annoyance of the principal's goats – the visiting ram would chase the billy round the island. I went along to see the fishermen most afternoons and we yarned about catches as they mended their creels. They were generous with information and told me the best place to set my own; by now I had made two.

For the next few weeks I caught at least one lobster a day. Three of the fishermen went home every weekend, leaving the fourth to look after their gear in case of bad weather. They brought out a fishing line for me, which took 200 hooks, and I set this for dabs and big plaice. The keepers' wives cooked the catches for our meals. As the Uist men had difficulty getting hazel twigs to make their creel bows, I wrote to my school friend, Jock, at Chanonry. They were delighted when two big bundles, carefully tied and labelled, arrived from the Black Isle with the mail.

These were not our only visitors. Two strangers landed from a dory one day and walked up to the lighthouse. I wondered why the assistant was shouting to make them understand until I realised that these were Breton fisherman and spoke no English. Their group had arrived from Brittany in three big boats with white sails. They anchored in a little Shillay creek and set hundreds of creels far out in deep water. I admired their seamanship in the little dories, from which they worked their crayfish pots. Large strings of onions hung in rows under the deckheads, and holding tanks below held a great many live crayfish and lobsters. I visited the crews on their boats in my free time; most of them were young and were good company. Drinking mugs of strong coffee, we communicated in signs and an occasional word of schoolboy French.

I was amazed how frugally the men lived – their food came almost entirely from the sea. They ate cockles, mussels, 'spoot fish' (razors), and now and again a crab from their pots. Their dinner was in the afternoon and sometimes I was asked to share a bowl of limpet soup. The principal's wife gave me jars of her homemade jam to pass on and they loved these. In due course, the fishery cruiser moved the Bretons on. Their creels were apparently inside our territorial waters, though in fact they worked further out than our own fishermen. Years later I saw other Bretons, this time under the high cliffs of the Flannan Isles, skilfully using the backwash to prevent their tiny craft being smashed on the rocks.

I was delighted to see my friends from the *Pharos* when they unloaded the year's stores on a calm summer's day. From time to time a naturalist or writer would also visit the island. On one occasion I was asked to meet Alasdair Alpin Macgregor with the lighthouse boat, as he was coming to research a book.

We were also visited by many birds. Puffins nested all over the short grass, and in autumn bunches of weary little birds alighted to rest for a day or two, especially during gales. Hundreds of barnacle geese grazed all winter on Heisker; on calm days I watched them from the bothy. There was also a large population of seals which hauled out on the rocks and beach at Shillay; some came further to lie on grass. Their long journey back to the sea looked like hard work, with much loud grunting as their heavy bulks were dragged on short flippers.

After two years without a holiday, I was told to take two weeks' leave. The principal's wife was preparing to look after a sick relation in Glasgow, so I was asked to return with a temporary housekeeper to cover the time she was away. However, I had not a clue about hiring domestic help.

On the ferry crossing from Lochmaddy I was surprised by a slap on the back that nearly flattened me. 'Well, well, it's Archie! What the hell are you doing here?' shouted a large flame-haired man. It was Robbie, the young tinker from Kirkwall who once poured beer over one of our ship's firemen in a Kirkwall bar. Robbie was now travelling around the islands selling crockery from an old van.

I had another surprising encounter on the way back from my holiday. I was greeted in North Uist by a young man who said, 'You'll be Archie MacEachern and you'll be needing a lift over to Bayhead?' My cousin, Finlay, had told him I would be heading for Monach lighthouse! That evening he took me to watch the waulking of the tweed in a little hall. Five or six women welcomed me warmly, saying they were related to Finlay's mother so I was family. Soon a large roll of tweed was unwound over a long table. Gaelic singing set the rhythm for energetic pulling and kneading by several women on each side. Quite a crowd came to watch and sing, adding to the fun. Racy jokes in Gaelic were greeted with gales of laughter. Tea, home baking and dancing rounded off a lively evening.

The next morning the boat was due to take me back to Shillay, but I still had not solved the problem of hiring a housekeeper. I asked my helpful companion for advice. As he drove me out to Bayhead, we stopped at a thatched cottage beside the road where a woman was washing blankets in a big wooden tub outside the door. I was amazed to hear she had given birth to her fourteenth child just the day before. My acquaintance explained that I was looking for a housekeeper at Monach. One of her daughters would be just fine for the job, she said, and a girl aged 16 or 17 appeared from the house. I was delighted to have found someone, and a few hours later we crossed to the lighthouse.

The new housekeeper smiled cheerfully as she worked about the house, although problems arose when she emptied hot ashes into a sizzling bucket of water. The principal was not at all pleased with the eruption of foul steam in the scullery. 'Why didn't you pick someone older, with training?' he asked. She returned to Uist a fortnight later.

TROUBLE AT MONACH

Some years after I left Monach lighthouse, there was a tragic accident. During a winter gale two of the keepers were rowing back from Heisker with the mail. They were caught in a blinding snow squall and their boat was driven onto rocks. The third keeper was watching from Shillay but had no way of reaching them. He saw the two clamber onto a round rock, trying to drag the boat behind them, before heavy snow blotted out his view. The rock was polished by tides, with no crevices to which they could cling. By the time the blizzard cleared, the principal and his young assistant had disappeared. Neither of these keepers were at Monach when I was there, though I knew the assistant, a fine young man from Orkney.

It took some time for help to arrive because of the remoteness of the station – the surviving man kept the lighthouse running singlehandedly for ten days. Even the farmers had gone by this point. A keeper who eventually went to assist served with me later. He spoke of finding the bodies which were taken home by the *Pole Star* in lead-lined coffins, and described a poignant entry in the log, with details of the accident witnessed by the third keeper. To this had been added: 'Alone for ten nights on the island of Monach. "Watchman, what of the night? Behold the morning cometh."'

Its remoteness led to the closure of Monach lighthouse in 1942. After the war, however, the North Uist crofters returned for their summer fishing. They still went home at weekends, leaving one person to look after things. One particular Saturday the man who had stayed behind was walking round the beach when he picked up a mine. It exploded and almost blew his hand off. He was in danger of bleeding to death when he got back to the hut, so he bound a pillowcase round the wound. With no one nearby to help, he managed to start the boat's engine and make the crossing to Bayhead. It must have been a long and lonely boat trip.

I loved wild Monach where I had little responsibility and was lucky to have the use of a boat. As my supernumerary training drew to an end, I was appointed assistant keeper at Fair Isle North. It seemed a long time since Peggy and I had first met while I was still on the ship. Now, most all, I looked forward to our marriage and making a home together.

In the meantime, there was a transfer to Kinnaird Head for a month. Kinnaird Head lighthouse was the Northern Lighthouse Board's first light. Dating from 1787, it was a unique light because the lantern sat on the tower of a 16th century castle. Adjoining a canning factory beside the fishing port of Fraserburgh, it was known as 'The lighthouse at the end of a street'. However, its foghorn did not seem to disturb the people of Fraserburgh when it sounded from the headland.

Here there was all the bustle of a busy station, but life was easy for me as there were already three keepers in place and we only had to take one watch each night. We could play tennis in our spare time as there was an old court in the grounds.

After one month I left Kinnaird Head and Peggy and I were married at Kirkoswald in Ayrshire. Ever since her father died at Turnberry lighthouse, her mother had run a guest house in Girvan. A week after our wedding we went to stay with the Gibsons in Edinburgh before preparing for our new life on Fair Isle.

5

'Welcome to wur isle'

1934–1939

Fair Isle

LIGHT ESTABLISHED IN 1892
WHITE TOWER, 14 METRES HIGH
ENGINEER – DAVID STEVENSON

My letter of appointment to Fair Isle North in 1934 said that we would be provided with housing and all essential furniture. Five tons of coal would be supplied each year, and there was a reminder to buy provisions for three months before leaving Edinburgh. Our first shopping list included large quantities of flour, oatmeal, tea, salt, sugar, and tins of milk, as well as a tub of New Zealand butter and two hams. We tried to remember little items as well, like baking soda and Oxo cubes.

This station was new territory for both of us, though Peggy had spent much of her childhood in Orkney and I had seen the island when we came north delivering stores. As a youngster, I had been told by Father that there was a lot to be learnt from the people of remote communities; we should respect them and try to adapt to new surroundings. Peggy and I were worried that we might not understand the local dialect, which seemed more Scandinavian than English. Even the Fair Isle names for their two lighthouses seemed strange: Fair Isle North lighthouse was known as 'The Skroo', Fair Isle South as 'The Skadden'.

However, we were made to feel welcome from the moment we arrived. After a stormy passage on the *Pole Star* we were greeted warmly by Tom Wilson, a leading figure in the community. He shook hands with us both on the pier and presented Peggy with a gold sovereign, saying, 'welcome, welcome to wur isle'. The people of Fair Isle had known my aunt Mary and her husband when he was a keeper at the south light. Kitty stayed with

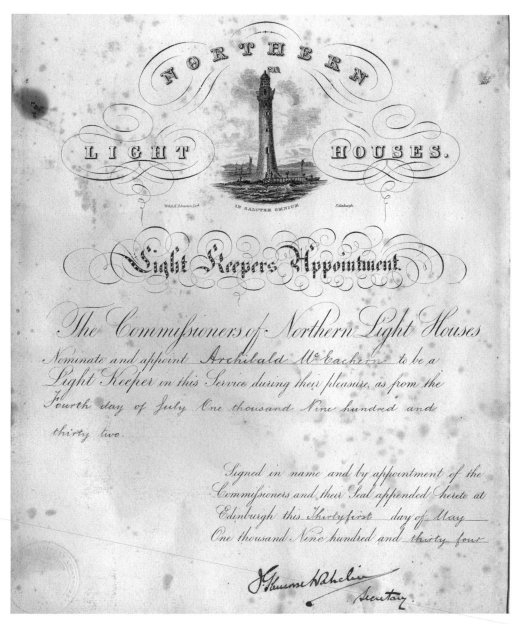

Lightkeeper Appointment Certificate.

them after Mother died, and a few folk could recall when she broke her leg sledging with school friends. At first everyone spoke to us slowly and there were no real language difficulties. We sometimes saw a young Fair Isle girl called Annie, and our paths would cross again in the future.

There was a small shop, and some goods could also be ordered by post to be delivered by Fair Isle's mail boat, the *Good Shepherd*, weather permitting. A nearby croft supplied us with fresh milk and we made our own cans for carrying it from sheets of tin supplied to the lighthouse. We bought eggs from the crofters too. Much of our meat was tinned, apart from the hams we had brought from the mainland. The islanders were generous and gave us fish from their catches or occasional pieces of mutton.

About 130 people made up this industrious community. They worked the crofts, where men and women shared the work, and major jobs were carried out on a communal basis. Each crofter kept sheep, and most had a cow for milk and a working ox for ploughing and pulling carts – there were no horses or tractors on Fair Isle at that time. Once I saw a crofter's wife pulling a harrow because their ox had died suddenly so they finished cultivating a field themselves. The men fished in small boats that were very good for their waters. These 'yoles' were built on Norwegian lines to their own design; the wood, mostly larch, was sent from Shetland.

The locals were very creative – driftwood was used extensively to make furniture and other items. The beaches yielded rich pickings after storms, especially when Scandinavian timber vessels lost their deck cargoes. The women always seemed to be knitting and I imagined that their fingers moved automatically; it was wonderful to watch. They could read, talk or listen while producing a garment effortlessly, in intricate Fair Isle pattern. Their knitting, using wool from local sheep, was very important to the local economy.

Life was certainly different on this windswept little island – it was only 3 miles long by 1.5 miles wide. No trees grew and the washing blew away on wild days. On our first washday we found we had forgotten to bring clothes pins. There were none to be had at the shop, so I made a batch of extra strong ones from the staves of a butter barrel and bound them with strips from empty tins. Although there were two churches, a Church of Scotland and a Methodist chapel, which people attended alternately, there was no doctor. All the medical care was provided by a resident district nurse.

Ox carts carried all our heavy loads to the lighthouse, including the year's coal, which was unloaded from the *Pole Star* at the North Haven. This was a novelty for us, as we had never seen working oxen before. Ox transport was very slow; the benevolent, shambling beasts were allowed to plod at their own pace. The owners seemed fond of the oxen and I never saw one being harassed. One day we had to take heavy new foghorn engines to the lighthouse and they were loaded onto three carts. We walked beside them and had to wait for each animal to put one foot in front of the other. It was a tedious business. Finally Alex, the other junior assistant, smacked the leading ox lightly on the rump with his hand. 'Dinna ever hit my ox again!' he was told and we had to curb our impatience.

Fair Isle ox transport.

Although we had three weeks' leave each year, the cost of fares meant we only went to the mainland once in our five years on Fair Isle. We started that journey by crossing to Shetland on the *Good Shepherd*, which carried passengers as well as the mail. On the return trip the sea was so rough that I had to look after a small baby whose mother was laid low with seasickness. That was the only time we saw any of our relations as it was too difficult for them to visit us. Fair Isle was not on a regular ferry route, and there was no harbour that could accommodate a ship. The *Good Shepherd* was small enough to put into the North Haven and she was the lifeline of the island. However, it had long been the custom for Fair Isle people to trade offshore with passing ships. Goods were bartered or sold and news exchanged. In earlier days when crews were at sea for months at a time, news travelled slowly.

Many ships had been stranded or spiked to pieces on the coast of Fair Isle, mostly before the lights came into operation in 1892. Ferocious seas and thick fog were common. Cliffs, stacks, and high rocky headlands bound the northern coastline, and to the southeast, the formidable Sheep Rock towered from the sea. The land at the north end was bare, hilly, and covered with heather. In the flatter south, there were crofts with grazing for sheep and a few cattle, and soil that was good enough for crops and vegetable gardens. Even the sparsest stretches burst into summer carpets of wild flowers.

The white tower of Fair Isle North was relatively small at only 14 metres high but its position on a high cliff was very conspicuous. Our fog signal played an important role and the horn itself was poised on the edge of the promontory. To reach it, we had to follow a path that crossed a narrow neck of rock and had no handrail. It was especially dangerous in high winds and we never ventured there after dark. Fortunately, the signal was operated from the engine room beside the tower.

We lived in a block of houses around a central courtyard, though there was no suitable ground for gardens. The senior assistant occupied the ground floor, and Alex

Fair Isle North lighthouse.

and I, the two junior assistants, lived on the first floor with our families. There was no electricity, but Tilley lamps gave out a good warming light. We did have running water and our own bathrooms with flush toilets. It was cold on the cliff top and the kitchen range was kept alight continuously. On bitter windy nights it was lovely to come off watch, open the roaring fire in the kitchen and bask in its warmth. Our coal allowance was very adequate and the houses were comfortably furnished.

Peggy and I soon discovered that lighthouses were a focal point on islands. They always had a telephone, even when these were not commonplace, and they were equipped with a well-stocked medicine chest, all kinds of tools, and plenty of paint and building materials. It was a standing joke in outlying communities that houses near a lighthouse were often smartly painted in matching colours – surplus tins of paint could always find a good home among the neighbours. Keepers needed to be practical men with various skills. At Fair Isle, one had been a blacksmith and was very handy at repairing implements on the crofts; another had been a trained ambulance man on the mainland. Alex and I did not accept payment for odd jobs that we did, but we were amply rewarded with gifts of fish.

Mr Ingram was the chief for both lighthouses and principal keeper at Fair Isle South. He always wore big golden earrings and indoors, a green parrot perched on his shoulder. These were legacies of his days as a windjammer captain. Every month Alex or I took the returns to the south light for him to check and sign, and receive the inevitable lecture on the traditions of the Lighthouse Service. Sometimes there was a telling-off about our handwriting while the parrot dropped large messes on his jacket and was cursed loudly. We had great respect for Mr Ingram; he ruled with a rod of iron but was always fair, and the island people held him in high regard. There was a Commissioners' visit one July and Mr Ingram escorted the party around both stations on their tour of inspection. He looked very smart in his best uniform and brass earrings, but the parrot was left in its cage.

However, the senior assistant at the north light was our immediate boss, and he was very demanding. Luckily, Alex and his wife Phyllis became our good friends, and the senior assistant's wife was very kind. She was a great baker, and when Peggy knocked at her door one day she appeared with her hands covered in flour. Her brass door handle was always highly polished, though that morning she spotted a white mark. 'Och, I've put flour on that handle!' she said as she wiped it off with her finger. She licked the finger absentmindedly while she spoke to Peggy, but suddenly she spluttered, 'ugh! Bird dirt!' and rushed indoors.

In the lightroom was an autoform paraffin light – familiar from my training – though this lens turned on rollers rather than mercury and the three massive Walsh and Clark engines that operated this foghorn were new to me. They were difficult to start and maintain but Alex helped greatly while I was inexperienced. Each keeper was responsible for maintaining one of the engines. We cleaned the huge flywheels every week and rubbed cloths dipped in Brasso over the rims as they rotated, never thinking about being crushed even though there were no protective guards. If there was a breakdown Mr Ingram was ferried from the south light in the sidecar of a motorbike – the only one on the island – to supervise the repairs. He chewed tobacco all the way and spat it onto the doormat before he entered the tower; a habit we detested as we had to clean up after him.

To start the engines for the foghorn we used a special blowlamp. On one occasion Alex lit the methylated spirits in its little cup and then turned to oil the machinery. In no time at all a bucket of oily cotton waste that was used for cleaning burst into flames. Alex snatched the blazing pail immediately and ran outside. His prompt action saved the building, but his arm was badly burned and he was rebuked severely by our boss. The superintendent was visiting at the time and intervened to praise Alex's courage. The *Good Shepherd* took him to Lerwick hospital where he was kept for several weeks.

We worked seven days a week; Alex and I had to work all afternoon, though the senior assistant disappeared after dinner each day to 'attend to his bookwork'. This was a very foggy area and there always had to be a man on watch; with the visibility often poor on long winter nights, the foghorn was used extensively. In bad conditions, three hours on watch had to be followed by three hours in the engine room, meaning we frequently had only three hours of rest each night.

Things did not get any easier during the second winter as we still had no free afternoons. By early spring there were many entries of 'fog' or 'snow' in the log, and the extra hours with the fog signal meant little sleep, though the boss's rest remained undisturbed. At three o'clock one morning I came down to the engine room and found Alex swaying on his feet, holding on to one of the engines with his head slumped forward. He was fast asleep and very close to the revolving six-foot flywheel. The situation had become intolerable and we needed to take action.

When the senior assistant greeted us at nine o'clock in the morning with 'get your paintbrushes!' we barred the doors at either end of the engine room.

'We have been so hard pressed that we can take no more,' we said. 'We're afraid of falling asleep on watch. We never have time off and if things don't improve, we shall write to Mr Ingram and the office. We'll leave you to think about it.' With that, we went to our houses to wait for repercussions and possibly sacking.

About half an hour later he came to see us both in turn. He brought a present of a carpet runner each from lighthouse supplies for our bare linoleum floors. He invited us to a meal at six o'clock. I told Peggy I wouldn't eat at his table, but she said we must go. Phyllis persuaded Alex to see reason too. We all had a glass of sherry with good food and our boss was the life and soul of the party. Poor Phyllis blushed with embarrassment while we smoked a cigarette with our cup of tea. She dropped ash on the immaculate white tablecloth and when she tried to blow it discreetly on to the floor, the contents of the ashtray flew everywhere.

The situation did improve, though we were still very pleased when this man was transferred the following year. (We heard he was beaten up by a junior colleague who was sacked as a result but said it was worth it.) After I had left Fair Isle, a keeper at Sumburgh Head fell under an unguarded flywheel and was killed. I thought of Alex's lucky escape.

The new senior assistant who came to Fair Isle North was a kind and cheerful Orcadian and the atmosphere at work was much happier. He understood the Fair Isle people well and, like them, was very clever at making furniture.

I tried my hand at carpentry and before our son, Angus, was born, I made a cradle from driftwood and Peggy trimmed it beautifully. Usually we could use the workshop and lighthouse tools when we were free, but the boss at that time would not allow it, so I worked in a bedroom with my tools and Peggy put up with the mounds of sawdust. Soon I had also made a drop-side cot from wood that I collected from the shore. This was a bigger undertaking, with no instructions and only a picture to copy. Some of the slats would not fit together and I found that these had shrunk as they dried out. Fortunately, Annie's father was a clever carpenter and came to help; another Fair Isle friend gave Peggy some sheep's wool to stuff the little mattress that she made. We used this cot for two babies and took it to our next station.

Peggy went to her mother's in Girvan before the birth. It was arranged beforehand that the passenger ferry between Shetland and Aberdeen would anchor off Fair Isle to collect her. The ship could never stop in a strong wind, though the sea was calm that day and a local boat took us out from the South Haven. I saw Peggy on board for the voyage and we kept in touch by phone. The weeks dragged while she was away, though Alex and Phyllis were gems, providing meals and company. It was a joyful day when I met the ship again, but a marathon trip for Peggy and our new son.

The challenges of living on a remote island hit home again when Angus was two and he developed croup. A fierce storm was in progress and he needed urgent medical attention. A doctor told us over the telephone that we should get him to hospital in Shetland immediately – which of course was impossible. As Angus got worse, any romantic illusions we still had about life on an island evaporated rapidly. With no doctor on Fair Isle, we relied entirely on the district nurse, Nurse Munro. She was instructed, from Lerwick, to give Angus an injection. 'How does he expect me to have these drugs in such a remote place!' she snorted as she put down the receiver. But she sat with him all night by a hot fire, working her own magic. Gradually he recovered, and we were in no doubt that she saved Angus's life. Eventually she was awarded an MBE in appreciation of her outstanding work on Fair Isle.

Ships' radio was still not in common use at that time and a red flare was frequently the only indication that a ship was in distress. On watch one evening I saw a trawler running before a gale; it was just before lighting time and there was no sign of a flare. I could see only one man on board – the wheelhouse had been destroyed and her lifeboat washed away. I tried to signal with a Morse lamp from the balcony but there was no response. We later heard that she made it to Orkney, though at least one crew member had been lost.

The weekly crossings of the *Good Shepherd* to Shetland were seldom cancelled, even in rough conditions. Her crew, all expert Fair Isle seamen, would gather at the skipper's house when she was due to sail. He would step out and look at the sky on all sides; unless he saw signs of dire weather, he would pick up his gear and walk silently to the boat. The crew would follow and no discussion was necessary. The 'Old Man's' judgement was infallible.

Alex and I had bicycles sent out from Shetland. These were our only means of transport for a year or two. One pay day I lost my wage packet and thought I must have dropped it when I cycled to the shop. The loss of a month's money was critical, so I phoned the shopkeeper in a panic. 'Dinna worry,' said Tom Wilson calmly, confident in his people's honesty. 'If your wallet is found, it will be here for you tomorrow.' Sure enough, it was handed in and I guessed Tom rewarded the finder.

When one of the keepers at Sumburgh Head was being transferred he asked if I wanted his Matchless motorbike for £12. It was in good condition, so Alex and I bought it between us. Now we could make the most of our hours off and get to the south end in no time. The artificers borrowed the Matchless to get around when they visited in

*Archie on the Matchless
motor bike, Fair Isle.*
(Stewart B. Thomson's
family album)

the summer. One always said, 'this needs a bit of work,' and serviced it in his spare time. Cans of fuel were bought from the village shop as there was no petrol pump.

Alex and I took turns to fetch our milk from a croft. On the way there I often saw 'Field George', a noted birdwatcher. He was always cheerful and full of stories and he taught me a great deal. Many visiting bird enthusiasts called on him to glean valuable information. Two or three collies were constantly at his side; he loved his dogs. Field George's father was a grand old man with a long white beard who used to transport our coal with his ox cart. Peggy always asked him to join us for tea. Very reserved at first, he became a good friend and told us a lot about the island.

I explored the cliffs near the lighthouse – they held great fascination for me. The local men were expert climbers, and ropes which had been used over the years hung from the rock face. However, they warned me never to use these in case they were rotten.

By the second Sunday in May it was reckoned that most of the gulls would have laid their eggs, so when it was calm I scrambled down to the nests to collect them for baking. I yearned to try the cliff below the foghorn, which was even more dangerous, but as this was forbidden by the boss I ventured elsewhere. One afternoon I took a dozen or so eggs from a rocky shelf and pulled up the front of my jersey to carry them, leaving my other hand free for climbing. Suddenly, I realised that I was stuck on a sheer face of rock; no one knew where I was and I had not taken a rope. Blind panic took over and I froze completely. Convinced that I would fall hundreds of feet into the sea if I moved an inch, I shut my eyes and had a think. What a fool I was! Slowly, I put the eggs back one by one into nests within my reach. This had a calming effect and in time I found a safe way back. That was my last egg collecting expedition.

A group of young crofters once took me to Sheep Rock when they went to clip their sheep. This fearsomely steep outcrop reared sharply from the sea to a sloping grassy plateau where a few sheep grazed. The rock was joined to the island by a narrow crumbling section of rock and so was only accessible by boat. We made our way up the great wall from the sea and scrambled along a narrow ledge. From there we climbed up on a chain which was attached to the rock face, with rocks and swirling waters below us. The shepherds had a saying: 'First man up tests the chain'. I marvelled at the skill

SOCIAL GATHERINGS

All ages attended the wonderful dances at the village hall in summer and winter. Their fiddle and accordion music was lively, much of it Scandinavian in flavour. After our new boss took over, Alex and I could join in – there was hardly any darkness in the brief Fair Isle summer and it was late at night before we had to put the light in. Often in the evenings, either Alex or I would arrive at the hall for dances with a reluctant pillion passenger. Neither Peggy nor Phyllis was too happy on the motorbike!

Every winter there were parties called 'lifts' in different houses and we were always invited. Peggy and Phyllis often went; Alex or I went when we could. We enjoyed the music, dancing, and spread of home baking. Guising was traditional at Hogmanay as well as Hallowe'en, with both the adults and children dressing up. Although New Year was great for parties and first footing, all keepers had to be on duty over the festive season so we could not take part; the north light was too far away for guisers to visit us anyway.

We made a golf course beside the lighthouse. It was very rough but we kept the grass well cut. Peggy and Phyllis sewed flags and we lined the holes with empty food tins – steamed pudding tins were the best. The course at the south end was bigger and had a bunker but ours didn't. Competitions were held which were fun for all; we always won on home ground, but never at the south. The opposition was used to smooth turf, whereas we knew the ball would not roll on our tough grass so we hit it hard. The prize was a packet of cigarettes or a dram, and sometimes Mr Ingram produced a bottle of port for the winner.

and strength of these men as they took six new sheep to the summit. Carrying the animals on their backs as they climbed and hoisting them with ropes looked like an impossible feat. It took me all my time and energy just to haul myself up, but this was an exciting trip on a summer's day.

One fine sunny day, a spectacular square-rigged sailing ship – the four-masted *Herzogen Cecilie* – was becalmed to the east of Fair Isle. I joined a group of men who went out in their yole to sell boxes of eggs. It was a thrill to board this ship. The vast girth of her main mast was astonishing; great numbers of ropes – thousands, it seemed – hung from hooks, all in neat coils. Her sails were furled and tied round the spars, ready for the wind. We did not stay long – the ship was drifting with the tide and the captain's sharp eyes watched the rocks. That evening the wind rose and from the lighthouse headland, we saw her sail south under full sail, bound probably for New Zealand. More sailing ships came into view that summer, yet none were as grand as the *Herzogen Cecilie*.

In the winter of 1937 there was one of the fiercest storms we had ever seen. At the end of January, the *Good Shepherd* was pounded mercilessly on her trolley above the

North Haven. She became a total wreck when the engine fell through her hull. People did not receive any mail for the six weeks that followed, which meant the lightkeepers had no wages. We had to rely on tinned food and I shot some duck and rabbits. Normally we preferred not to eat the rabbits here; many had different coloured fur which seemed strange to us and might indicate something wrong with them.

Provisions were getting low when the fishery cruiser finally reached us and the meat we had ordered was putrid. A group of Fair Isle men decided to replace the wreck with a much bigger boat and plans were drawn up in Buckie. About three months later they brought the new *Good Shepherd* north from the Moray Firth yard and normal service was resumed.

Another incident was a sharp reminder to all of us to take care out-of-doors in stormy weather, especially of our children. Our senior assistant, a big heavy man, was blown off his feet by extra strong gusts and thrown across the courtyard. We found him shocked but otherwise unhurt, and someone commented that he was 'farting like a brewery horse!' when they helped him to his feet. That though, might have had more to do with the mysterious contents of a medicine bottle that his wife administered every morning.

The first aeroplane lands on Fair Isle. Captain Fresson,
centre. Archie, holding Angus, 3rd left, behind Peggy.

Captain Fresson, Mr Ingram &
Jerome Stout. (Fair Isle Museum)

One of the islanders built a windmill. He lent me the plans and Alex and I constructed one near the lighthouse. It gave us enough electricity for a single light in each of our houses as well as power to charge wireless batteries. This was in operation until it blew away in a hurricane shortly before I left.

On the day of King George VI's coronation in 1937, the first aeroplane landed on Fair Isle. Everyone had a holiday and there was great excitement when Captain Fresson came to the village hall to meet the islanders. After a meal we posed for a group photograph and went back to the plane with him. That day the schoolteacher and his family were going on holiday, so we gathered to see them board and take off from the south end. As the plane gained height over the cliff, it dipped suddenly; onlookers gasped and, for a few awful seconds, we thought he would crash into the sea. But he levelled out quickly and roared away safely. We knew that Captain Fresson was a pioneer, though we did not imagine how invaluable flight would become for island life and medical cover in particular.

When Mr Ingram retired, a principal keeper for the north light was appointed for the first time. Roddie, our new principal, was a very good boss and an expert with the engines. He was a widower and his daughter kept house for him. We still had a senior assistant, so life became easier. However, we were sorry to lose Alex and Phyllis when they were shifted to another station

One day when Angus was three, he went missing. Roddie's panic-stricken daughter cycled down to fetch us from the landing, and my heart sank when we spotted him on a narrow ledge of the cliff. An overhang blocked any approach from above; waves crashed on the rocks below. How on earth could I reach him without scaring him? Remembering how Father had rescued Kitty, I climbed down to one side and crept across to a foothold.

'What are you doing there, Angus?' I asked quietly.

'Watching the pretty birdies,' he said, quite unconcerned.

On leave from Fair Isle. Archie & Peggy with Angus.

Puffins and fulmars whizzed past to their nests, so close he could almost touch them. I stretched up and took hold of the little figure gently, passing him to the helping hands that waited anxiously above. Poor Peggy fainted with shock. Afterwards we wondered how we could prevent him wandering again; he and his pal, Ian, were great explorers. There was no garden here, and the boys quickly sussed out the various catches that we fitted to the courtyard gate. Nowhere beyond it was safe.

Soon after that we went to the mainland for our holiday and I bought a black Labrador, another Jack. I trained him successfully to keep the boys away from the cliffs. As soon as Angus strayed, the dog would push him over gently and stand there till someone heard the cries of frustration.

Fair Isle was a birdwatcher's paradise –an ideal stopping place for migrant birds en route to the Arctic – and many rarities strayed to Fair Isle, some blown off course. Hordes arrived in spring and autumn and the absence of trees meant they could be seen easily. One spring, there was a greater influx than usual – birds seemed to be lurking by every stone and grassy tuft. Among these, I saw a bluethroat, just a name in my bird book till then. Although geese came in big flocks, few stayed for the winter; most only rested for a day or two and did not cause much damage to grazing. I came across a dead golden eagle on the moor. It was thought to have taken lambs, though these might have fallen over the cliffs. Once I watched a great spotted woodpecker working its way up an old pit prop that supported a haystack, and another time, Field George put me on the trail of a very special visitor. I nearly fell over backwards when a snowy owl rose silently from under my feet and flapped away slowly on large white wings.

Great colonies of seabirds nested on the cliffs; terns laid their eggs in scrapes on the ground, and dive-bombing 'bonxies' (great skuas) bred on the moors and terrorised anyone who walked on their territory. During wild winter weather lots of storm petrels came to the light and crept round the balcony and courtyard like little black mice. Petrels seemed to flutter and land rather than hit the lantern. They could not take off again in a confined space and were easy to catch. We carried them to the cliff edge and they flew straight out to sea, leaving a musty smell on our hands.

For about a month every autumn large numbers of migrating woodcock settled to feed. Shooting them in season was a traditional part of the Fair Isle economy and I was invited to join in. Woodcock made very good eating, but I sent some of mine south to be sold with the islanders' birds. Ducks were shot too, and occasionally an overwintering goose; the duck tasted fine, though the geese were rather tough.

The lighthouse tower was a good place from which to spot whales. Killer whales headed for the cliffs then veered away beyond the biggest stack which we called 'The Rock'. They were probably after the seals that congregated there, yet I never saw a kill. Larger whales cruised further out, in deep water.

It was springtime when I first met George Waterston on one of his early visits to Fair Isle. I was working outside when this tall smiling man walked up to the lighthouse gate. 'Ah! There they are! I heard them before I saw them,' he said, pointing to two small birds on the boundary wall. After the war he bought the island and set up the Fair Isle Bird Observatory.

In early spring 1939 a young German called at Fair Isle North and Roddie asked me to show him round. The man claimed to be a reporter for a German newspaper; however, while we were up in the lantern, I realised he had no interest in the lighthouse. He was very keen to know if the surrounding seabed was sandy and I told him it was scattered with large rocks. I was convinced that he was a spy looking for places for U-boats to shelter.

Our second baby, Kathleen, was born in March 1939. Peggy, quite understandably, did not want to repeat her long journey to Girvan for the birth, so she stayed on Fair Isle. She went into labour during the night. The new district nurse lived at the other end of the island and a local girl came to help while I sped off at four o'clock in the morning to the nurse's house. I rang the doorbell and waited anxiously until she appeared. She climbed onto the pillion seat with her black bag, but no matter how hard I tried, the Matchless' engine would not start. Finally I gave it a kick in utter despair, which must have reconnected the drive. We shot away and my passenger nearly flew off backwards, uttering something I could not quite catch. The bike's headlight was poor and the road was narrow; the nurse shone a torch over my shoulder so we could go faster while gripping my waist with her free hand. By the time we reached the lighthouse the young girl with Peggy was extremely worried. The nurse was very efficient though and Kathleen was delivered safely. She was the last baby to be born on Fair Isle before expectant mothers went to Shetland or Aberdeen to give birth.

Two months after Kathleen arrived I was transferred to Dhuheartach – a pillar rock off the west coast of Scotland – and a very different life from the one we had grown used to. Working and living amongst this friendly community for five years had been a wonderful experience. We departed as we had arrived, aboard the *Pole Star.* I left the Matchless on Fair Isle and it was last heard of in a roadside ditch after many more years of use.

Postscript

That September war broke out. The north light was bombed in 1941, though no lives were lost. Several panes were smashed in the lantern, windows were broken in the houses, and the outhouses were demolished. The hens survived but the henhouse did not. They returned the same evening to roost in its wreckage as if nothing had happened.

The south light was not so lucky; it suffered two direct hits, with loss of life. A German plane machine-gunned the lighthouse in 1941, killing the wife of an assistant as she stood at her pantry window. Miraculously, her two year old daughter by her side survived. In 1942 a plane dropped a bomb on the block of houses. At the time of this raid the principal keeper was walking back from the post office and arrived to find his wife and daughter had been killed. The only survivor was an assistant who was eventually rescued from the rubble of the houses. Roddie was still principal at the north light and went to their aid, making sure that the light was lit the same night. He managed to walk to the south light and back through atrocious blizzards, and returned in time to take his own watch. He was awarded the BEM for this.

6

The Lonely Years

First Years at Dhuheartach

1939–1944

THE SPELLING OF DHUHEARTACH WAS CHANGED TO DUBH ARTACH IN 1964.
LIGHT ESTABLISHED 1872
GREY GRANITE TOWER 38 METRES HIGH WITH A BROAD RED BAND
ENGINEERS – THOMAS AND DAVID STEVENSON

We arrived at the shore station on Erraid in May 1939. It had been a long journey by ship and train from Fair Isle with six-week-old Kathleen and Angus who was four. Before we left I sent Father a telegram telling him of our transfer. From the immediate reply, 'CONGRATULATIONS STOP FATHER', I knew he was pleased that I was going to the isolated rock where he had spent about ten years. Its name was translated from the Gaelic as 'black one of death' though others nicknamed it 'Heartache Rock'. But we knew that the houses on nearby Erraid – a little tidal island off the Ross of Mull – were fine homes for young families.

Dhuheartach lighthouse marked the Torran rocks, 14 miles west of Erraid. Many ships bound for America and the Baltic had come to grief in the area. In December 1865, 24 vessels were wrecked in two days between Tiree, Iona, Colonsay, and Islay during a freak storm. This light was established in 1872 to prevent more losses. To quote from *Scottish Lighthouses* by R. W. Munro:

It is an isolated mass of basaltic rock with a rounded black top rising 35 feet above high water with deep water on all sides… A great submarine valley stretching out to the Atlantic ensures that landing will usually be difficult and in stormy weather impossible.

Dhuheartach.

After a couple of weeks settling in to shore station routine it was time for me to leave the family for the challenges of rock life. As I approached aboard the *Hesperus*, the red band on the forbidding granite tower was the only spot of colour I could see in the grey of sea and sky. Landings here were notoriously difficult and the waters seldom quiet due to strong tides and the exposed situation. At one time Dhuheartach men were supplied with an extra 'rock suit' every year because of the extreme conditions. Now, dungarees and oilskins were standard wear and we never used the cork lifejackets that were issued because they were too cumbersome. A towel worn like a scarf around the neck helped prevent saltwater boils.

I was winched from the ship's boat to the rock on the 'button', a small wooden disc fixed to a rope. Most of us did not bother using this after a few landings, instead grasping the rope with our hands and feet. Waves often caught us as the derrick (the crane used to move cargo and passengers between the lighthouse and the ship) swung us across the water, meaning we generally arrived soaking wet. Sometimes the men on the grating were not quite quick enough, especially when hoisting a heavy person. Once Father was washed off this grating and nearly drowned when a giant wave carried away the three keepers as they prepared for the relief. The other two landed semi-conscious on the rock while Father was still in the water. He was a very strong swimmer and managed, at last, to grab hold, but he lost all his fingernails scrabbling at the rock. All the keepers were badly bruised; Father's fingernails grew back, though they always looked slightly crooked.

To reach the entrance door we climbed 40 feet up the bronze ladder on the outside of the tower. The prospect of being confined in this small space for six and possibly eight weeks was daunting; I had serious doubts. Would I be able to get on with the other two men? Could I live up to Father's example? How would my family manage? We would only be able to venture down as far as the rock when the weather was calm at a low tide. If it was a wild day, keepers often could not leave when a relief was due.

After visiting Dhuheartach while his father's work was in progress, Robert Louis Stevenson wrote this description: '... *one oval nodule of black trap... no other life was there, but that of sea birds, and of the sea itself, that ran here like a mill race and growled about the outer reef for ever, and ever and again, in the calmest weather, roared and spouted on the rock itself.*'

I soon found that the whole tower shook in heavy weather and I could not sleep when the bunks shuddered. In bad gales, waves charged up the tower and broke over the dome in sheets of white spray. When the sea fell away suddenly, the lack of tremors was very noticeable and I waited for more to come.

Weather permitting, one keeper was replaced at each fortnightly relief. The duties of the fourth member of the crew, during his time ashore, would include manning the

Nearly ashore at Dhuheartach. (NLB)

radio which linked several outlying lighthouses to Erraid. We made contact by radio three times daily from Dhuheartach and spoke to our families once a day.

I found the principal, John, to be an awkward boss, especially since I was inexperienced in rock work. The way of life and separation from the family was difficult, though Jock, the first assistant, gave me invaluable guidance. He was a good and experienced rock keeper with a practical approach to life. Full of humour and yarns, Jock gradually made me see that we had to accept being cooped up; a turn ashore would come in time. All the men had been alarmed by the shaking of the tower, he said, but they got used to it, as I did too. The fourth member of our crew was in poor health and before long he was sent to an easier station, and was replaced by Andrew.

Dependable in difficult times and emergencies, my colleagues were particularly fine men and our comradeship was very strong. Johnny, the occasional, was a cheerful and helpful young chap, well-liked by the regular crew. He was always a willing hand for heavy work at reliefs and we valued this greatly when we were unfit through lack of exercise.

Keepers for rock service were picked by the superintendent, who knew us all; some struggled with the isolation more than others and their stays were short. We tended to run out of conversation after about a week and arguments could break out over trivialities, so tempers had to be kept in check. The most provocative thing was to say that you did not believe something one of the others said; such doubts were better left unsaid.

'Sure as the cat's a hairy beast!' from Jock always amused us, yet other little habits and thoughtlessness caused annoyance out of all proportion. One man used to get upset when he was given the wrong cup at teatime. 'But they're all the same,' said the cook. 'No! I want my own,' he insisted, taking another that looked identical, and a great argument started. After stirring my tea I liked to tap 'tum, tiddly um tum' with the spoon on the side of the cup – a habit that irritated greatly, I was told. Another man never rinsed his shaving brush which stood beside ours on the dresser; the dried-on lather would 'do next time,' said the owner.

Andrew told us all that if we ran short of cigarettes we could help ourselves from his reserve supply, so long as we told him and replaced them the next time we came out. One day he was shocked to find that his supply had almost disappeared. Jock was ashore, and I had not taken any. The third keeper denied taking them and pointed at me:

'It must have been him!'

'No! Archie would have told me,' said Andrew.

When the man walked into the kitchen at teatime, Andrew was sharpening a large knife on a strop. He stared menacingly at his adversary. The man was very scared; he swallowed a cup of tea with a slice of bread and disappeared upstairs. I was uneasy too as Andrew was a tough chap who did not like to be cheated.

'You wouldn't hurt him, Andrew?' I asked.

'No! No! I'm just trying to frighten the b..!' he said and put the knife away. But the two did not speak again and the cigarettes were never replaced.

A nasty situation arose late one night when out of the blue a man ran at me with his fists up.

'Come on! Fight like a man!' he shouted. I picked up the poker from the fireplace.

'Go on and I'll flatten you with this!' I said. He calmed down and went off to bed. There was no apparent reason for the outburst and it was never mentioned again. Perhaps the isolation had become too much and he suddenly flipped. We noticed that he seemed to be afraid of waves and would never work on the grating. He left a week or two later and did not come back.

Someone was always on watch throughout the 24 hours. The two with the heaviest night duty went to their bunks for the afternoon and the third made the tea and called the others at five. When someone came off watch it was his responsibility to see that the next man was awake and dressed. He would then pour a cup of coffee for them both. One keeper was always difficult to waken which was annoying as it wasted other folk's sleeping time.

The two assistants took week about as cook and worked our watches as normal. We became fairly good cooks and there was always help with the dishes, so this was quite a pleasant way of passing the days. My first attempt at baking bread produced two rock hard loaves that were not fit to eat, so I threw them straight out of the kitchen window. A patrolling black-backed gull usually ate any jettisoned food, but he pecked at these, shook his head, and flew away. The gull was very interested in the balcony during storms – we wondered why until we found live sand eels and fresh seaweed dumped there during north westerlies. One eel, still wriggling, measured 12 inches. 'My, that looks good! Sure as the cat's a hairy beast!' said Jock, and he had fried eel for his tea.

Johnny was expert at making plum duffs. One afternoon when Johnny was cook, Jock came to waken me. 'Come on, the duff's ready,' he whispered. 'Let's eat some while it's hot!' We ate half the deliciously fragrant pudding and put back the lid. At tea-time Johnny uncovered the pot with a flourish. He was so cross to find a chunk had disappeared that he never made us another.

The principal had all the station paperwork to do, the so-called 'returns', and it was usually a job for Sundays. There were no church services at a rock light, though there may have been when my grandfather was in the Service.

Each summer the superintendent and artificers came for the annual inspection and maintenance. They were with us for two weeks and the extra company was welcome.

The base of the granite tower was solid for the first 40 feet. Inside the door was a large storage area with coils of rope, some of which were kept ready for reliefs. The safety rope was near at hand for climbing up and down the outside ladder; it was used by new keepers and visiting staff, not generally by the regular crew. A set of coffin boards lay on a ledge in case of a sudden death, but during my service I never saw these used. A curved flight of metal steps inside the tower led to all the other floors. There was a workshop that housed a complete set of engineering and woodworking tools, with materials of many kinds.

The kitchen provided our main living quarters and was very cramped, with a diameter of 11' 6". Like all the compartments, it was round; its walls were lined with pine and fitted with curved furniture. The dresser held the radio which was our only link with the outside world. Crockery and items like shaving kits sat on the dresser too. Four stools with no backs provided the only seating, and these had an annoying habit of tipping over when you stood up. They offered little comfort after a heavy day's work, so one of us generally sat on the coal bunker and leant against the wall. It was luxury to sit in an armchair when we went home.

There was no kitchen sink, but an enamel basin was used on the table for washing dishes; there was another basin for washing and shaving. Dirty water was emptied out of the window and clean water came from a tank in a cupboard. We topped this up once a week by pumping from the supply in the main water tank at the door below. There were two windows of thick glass in the kitchen, one facing east and one facing west. Heavy wooden shutters on the outside protected them from the worst of the weather. The granite floors were left bare to reduce the risk of fire and you could see how the central block had been dovetailed into the surrounding sections to hold the structure firm. Each had been shaped perfectly by men using only hammers and chisels.

Cooking was done on a small Portdownie range which also gave us a fire to sit by. It was never allowed to go out and warmed the kitchen efficiently. However, there was no other heating in the bare stone tower and it was cold in winter. A copper chimney pipe passed through the floors above the kitchen and out through the top of the dome, but any heat was lost before it reached the bedrooms. Every week we hauled three hundredweight bags of coal up and through the kitchen window on the quieter east side. We tipped this straight into the bunker and dust flew everywhere. It was soon scrubbed up by the cook whose tasks included keeping the kitchen spotless.

Our food store was over the kitchen and up the next ladder was the assistants' sleeping accommodation. Fixed to the walls were three sets of rounded bunks with blankets and a cover. Curtains around the bunks helped to keep out draughts and give some privacy. The extra bunks were for visiting artificers.

Above this level was the principal's bedroom. It was referred to as the library because of its two bookcases, though the stock of books was never changed. Here was a large leather-bound Bible with the Northern Lighthouse Board crest on the front. This was standard at rock stations and recorded inside were the names of all the keepers who had served there, my father included.

In the lightroom a big brass clock kept us right and the keeper on night watch wound up the machine here. A desk held the logbooks. Details to be logged included the barometer and thermometer readings – taken every three hours – and sightings of any of the Board's other lights visible from the station.

Two doors from the lightroom opened on to the balcony; which door we used depended on the direction of the wind. At Dhuheartach the fog signal was carbide operated and a shot was fired through the top of the dome every five minutes. The blast reverberated through the tower, especially the sleeping quarters; another background noise that we got used to in time. A safety rope was stored in the lightroom, of sufficient length to reach the rock in an emergency such as fire.

The lantern held the huge circular dioptric lens, with three bullseyes of thick mirror glass. The lens was designed so that one side could be opened without disturbing the operation of the light. We stepped inside each night with a long white taper; we did not linger because it got quite hot.

To prevent fire, we had to clean the chimney every month. From the balcony we climbed a metal ladder that was fixed to the outside of the dome. It was quite tricky working from the cramped perch on top; we had to drop a brush on a rope down the pipe and retrieve it. I never heard anyone complain about this, despite the lack of helmets and harnesses. A job for a calm day, it had to be abandoned immediately if the wind freshened. There was a wonderful sense of freedom up there.

Heavy deposits of salt would reduce the power of the light, so we had to make sure the glass was kept clear. Sometimes we could use a stepladder on the balcony, but to reach the top we stood on the iron grating that surrounded the lantern and held on to the iron rings between the astragals while we worked. Luckily it rained a lot, which washed off the worst. Snow blotted out the light very quickly if the flakes were allowed to accumulate, so in blizzards it was a non-stop job for one man to both keep the lantern glass swept and wind up the machine. He had to hang on like grim death while waves sprayed the tower and the narrow grating became slippery. It had no guard rail and no one could see if the man on watch fell to the rock.

While I was fairly new, the *Hesperus* delivered the year's coal. To beat the tide, we only had about three hours to lift and store five tons. I was appalled at how difficult it was to heave the bags up 40 feet on a rope; I suggested rigging a downhaul with double blocks, which was a method often used on the *Pharos* to tackle heavy lifts. The principal did not like this idea, though he was going ashore at the time and in his absence we found it to be successful. He agreed to the new method when he returned.

Our water supply also came by ship and a keeper's daily allowance was three gallons – for all purposes, including drinking. The main delivery of water was made in June in breakers and we hoisted these to the door on the downhaul that was used for the coal. The storage tank held 2,000 gallons. There were tanks for 3,000 gallons of paraffin in the oil cellar above and a small amount of petrol was kept here for a generator to charge the radio batteries. Handling hundreds of gallons in barrels was hard going when we were unfit after weeks on the rock.

We were very fussy about keeping ourselves clean. Very occasionally in summer, we had a quick dip in a deep pool in the rock. Its water was renewed with every tide and was always clean. One day though, Andrew jumped out in a hurry. 'A big crab tried to catch me,' he muttered, and we speculated as to how many more skulked in its dark corners. Another day we found a lot of old cutlery caught in a deep crevice nearby, possibly from a wrecked ship. As far as we knew the last to founder there was in 1871, a year before the light was established.

Sanitation consisted of a bucket inside the main door. For emergency needs, there was another bucket on the balcony. Each man kept a two-pound jam jar beside his bunk at night. There were no drains; all waste, dirty water, rubbish was emptied straight into the sea. Lack of sanitation was one of the worst aspects of rock life, especially when the artificers stayed with us.

During my first spring we repainted the red band round the outside of the tower and I had a major row with the principal about safety. A heavy wooden stage was suspended from the balcony on a strong block and tackle, with a tiny inadequate shackle bearing all the weight. The principal said it was alright, but I was not prepared to risk my life and refused to use the stage until the shackle was replaced. An argument followed. By the next morning, however, we found that a much bigger one had been fitted and Jock and I completed the job in a couple of days.

Another morning we were repairing the landing steps which were beginning to crumble. The boss was starting the day in a bad mood and criticised Jock's work.

'... and that's not the right way to mix cement!' John added.

'Well, this is how I mix cement. And I've done a lot of it.'

'It's time you learnt to do it properly then.'

'You can mix it with a fork and spoon if you like! This is the way I do it!'

When we finished, we were surprised to find that John had cooked dinner for us. It was not usual for a principal to cook for his assistants and it defused this situation.

At this time we were still not very happy with the small wages the principal was handing out. A new assistant joined the crew and when he asked questions, he was told that some of our money had been burnt by mistake at the shore station. We were given no explanation but the payments were correct from then on.

One night the boss went up to the balcony to start the charging motor for the radio. We wondered why he did not reappear and then we heard a faint tapping. He was on the balcony, unable to move – his back had given out and he was in intense pain. The problem was how to bring him down the ladder. After two hours we had manoeuvred him as far as the library where, with one swift move, Jock lifted him onto his bed. This was beyond the scope of our medicine chest, so we radioed Oban for advice. A doctor issued instructions and we checked his pulse, but we did not have the equipment to test his blood pressure. We took it in turns to sit with him all night and the next day the *Hesperus* came. Still in agony, the poor man faced his biggest challenge: how on earth would he get to the rock from his bed near the top of the tower? We lashed him to a stretcher, but since it was impossible to negotiate bends in the stairs, the only solution was to let him down the outside of the tower. Luckily, it was a calm day and we pushed the flimsy contraption gingerly through the library window. 'Good luck!' we said. His face was as white as chalk and we could not imagine his feelings as he was lowered a hundred feet or so. Three or four of the ship's crew stood below and he reached the ground safely on the block and tackle we used for coal. He was transferred to another station after he recovered.

No alcohol was allowed at rock stations, but in Father's day each man was given a glass of beer at 11am every day. We were paid a 'rock victualling' allowance and the keeper in charge radioed our provisions order before the *Hesperus* was due. Tinned food made up a large part of our diet and dried fruit was essential. Green vegetables were a luxury.

A three-month supply of emergency rations was always kept on hand and included tins of salmon, corned beef, and tinned milk, ships' biscuits and dried figs. These supplies were eaten when a new consignment came – it was the only chance I got to eat ships' biscuits, which I thought were delicious.

When our stores arrived, the cook divided the meat into suitable cuts for a month. There was fresh meat for the first week and the remainder was salted because there was no fridge. The cook prepared the preserving brine by adding salt to fresh water; when the solution was strong enough, a potato would float on top. Then the meat went in and was stored in the 'harness cask'. This was a broad-based oak container bound with bands of polished brass. Even preserved like this, the meat was barely edible by the end of a month in summer.

Salt fish was always good and a great standby. On calm summer afternoons we fished with a line for big lythe and saithe. We weighted the line with lead and cast as far as possible. Some we salted and hung to dry on lines in the storeroom so they would keep until winter, and blackjacks from Oban were added to our supply.

Long loaves of bread – fired extra hard to make them last longer – were made specially for us by an Oban baker. We stacked the loaves on open shelves, separating them with wooden slats to stop them going mouldy. Even so, before a month was up they were always too stale and we had to bake fresh. It was easy to build up the heat of the oven for making bread, with plenty of draught from the long chimney. A bowl of dough was left to prove in the warmth by the side of the stove. A pot of coffee always stood on the hotplate and we added a piece of salted fish skin to a fresh brew as we thought it improved the flavour.

Reliefs were set for the lowest ebb on a spring tide. Usually the keeper in charge decided if conditions were suitable, but after our first principal left I was often asked to make the decision because I had been a seaman.

One of the ship's officers would radio early on the morning of a scheduled relief to ask if a landing would be feasible that day. If conditions with us were fair enough, the ship would set out on the 40-mile trip from Oban and call again about halfway to see if our weather had changed. Then a keeper would go out on the balcony to look at the sea and check the strength and direction of the wind. From the west side of the balcony we would watch the waves break on the reef beyond, then count the number of seconds until they reached our rock. If the intervals grew shorter it meant there was a heavy sea further out and wild weather in the offing. Gaps that grew longer indicated improvement for us and a good chance of a landing.

Relief at Dhuheartach around 1923-1927. (NLB)

As soon as we reckoned the ship was approaching, we went down to make preparations; it took roughly an hour and a half to erect the derrick and safety lines. From inside the door we threw the coils of rope onto the rock. After that, we set the stanchions into their holes in the grating and threaded the safety rope through the eyes. Once this line was in place we set up the derrick on its three metal stanchions and rigged it. Fixed permanently to the rock, these three were the most important and nearest to the sea.

We watched the water like hawks while we set up the equipment. At any time, and without warning, an extra-large wave could sweep round the south end of the rock. This meant we had to react fast or be washed away – immediately we must run out along the grating, going against our natural instinct to head for the tower. The only way to survive was to cling to the derrick before the wave struck; the secret was to hold tight, keep your head down, and wait for it to wash over. It was difficult to breathe under a wall of water; fortunately, gigantic waves only came from time to time. More often than not, we just wore dungarees over our clothes for reliefs, as oilskins filled with water and hampered movement, and sou'westers could make it impossible to hear a warning shout.

At difficult places like Dhuheartach, tensions ran high among the boat's crew and the keepers who were coming or going. Everyone was 'up to ninety' and worked as a team. The boat would be moored outside the grating, rolling around on even the calmest of days. The ship was anchored too far off to act quickly in an emergency and everyone knew conditions could change by the minute.

A man due to leave at the relief was often on edge, worrying if he would get away. It was a grand moment when we caught the first glimpse of the ship heading our way from Skerryvore. Sometimes, however, she slowed and turned at the last minute with two toots on her whistle. It was especially demoralising if you had to decide against a landing when it was your own turn to go ashore. The captain would try again the following day. If conditions were unsuitable after five consecutive days, the attempt was abandoned for that fortnight. The ship's schedule had to be kept for other reliefs and for emergencies over a wide area. The ship could be called in an urgent situation, but never for toothache. Having toothache on the rock was what we feared most and any suspect tooth had to be extracted on a routine spell ashore.

The relieving keeper arrived by derrick and was hauled across as quickly as possible, though it was not unheard of for someone unpopular to get soaked because of a slight delay! As soon as the new arrival landed, the man departing caught the rope. He in turn gripped it with hands and crossed legs. 'Right! Heave away!' came the call as the others played out the rope. Safely in the boat, he made his way aft with pats on the back. Once the stores were landed, the crew headed for the ship – some waved, especially the man leaving his colleagues. (We were comforted by the knowledge that this would be us soon.) Meanwhile, we had to work fast on the rock before the tide could carry things away. Stores were taken to the foot of the tower; landing equipment was dismantled and secured; supplies and gear went up the ladder to be stowed. Then came greetings and chat with the incoming keeper over a cup of coffee.

As well as receiving stores, mail, and general news from home, we had a great treat for tea that day. A feast of bacon, sausage, and egg was served, along with fresh bread and butter, cake, and large mugs of coffee. Wives always sent out a freshly baked cake packed among clean clothes. Slices were handed round and I only met one man who would not share his cake. That evening, as we listened to the waves, the kitchen seemed safe and cosy. There was plenty to talk about with a different keeper, and the lighthouse families exchanged news at the pier when the *Hesperus* put in to Erraid.

Once I was asked to decide on landing conditions when a new assistant was to go ashore for the first time. On the early morning radio call I told the second mate the signs looked promising. But the

Dhuheartach – another relief.

Hesperus was late that day and by the time she approached us the tide had already turned. As I watched, a large wave suddenly broke six feet above the grating. More followed, and anyone standing there would have been washed away.

'That's it; there'll be no landing today!' I called to the others. The ship tooted and turned for the Sound of Iona. The man due to leave was furious.

'You're yellow! That's your trouble!' he shouted. I restrained myself with great difficulty and went upstairs. The radio was tinkling as I reached the kitchen.

'Sorry we couldn't stop,' said the second mate. 'We were delayed at Skerryvore and missed the tide. There was no chance of lowering the boat when we reached you. We'll come tomorrow.' All went well the next day; the assistant apologised and got away with no problems.

When a relief was late we were given no compensation in time or money for days lost. I was ashore only once for Christmas and New Year in my five years at Dhuheartach; either due to duty schedules or the weather. I was often on the rock for eight weeks at a time.

A cabin on the ship was kept for the use of keepers. It was wonderful to change into uniform there, have a delicious meal in the dining room and mix with the sailors. Best of all was knowing that I was on my way home. No clothes were washed on the rock – there was too little water and nowhere for drying. We were issued with big red kit bags which went home full of dirty washing.

One late September, after a heavy storm from the northwest, we discovered serious damage to the landing equipment. The three fixed stanchions on the grating had been snapped off. We called the office and asked for three new ones, with two three-inch jumpers for fitting them. The girl in the general office said she would pass on the message. 'But what's a jumper?' she asked. 'I only know the kind you knit!'

It was essential to complete this repair before winter, but we could not start at the first of the ebb while waves still splashed the rock. The tide only allowed us a few hours at a time, and it took several days just to cut new holes with the jumper. Then we melted lead in a long-handled ladle over a small brazier; we had to make sure the rock was dry before we poured this in, as the smallest drop of water would make it explode. We had to smear lubricating oil around the hollow first; however, Andrew was always in a hurry and the first time he did not notice a little water floating on the oil. He tipped in some molten lead and there was a great bang – holes appeared in the lobes of his ears and blood trickled down his face! A few plasters from the medicine chest were slapped on and he got on with the job. We did cover the holes with a piece of sacking before pouring in any more lead. It was still impossible to avoid occasional drops of water and small spots of lead shot through the hessian, but not so fiercely. Quick-drying cement was piled around each base for added protection. We called the new stanchions Faith, Hope, and Charity.

When some of the nuts and bolts holding the grating together were rusting badly, we realised they would soon be unsafe. Jock stood on a ladder to remove the bolts and replace them. Loosening these long thick bolts was quite a feat; again we had to work fast through the ebb tide. While we stood back afterwards to review the completed job, Jock took off with a yell: 'Oh my God! We've bolted the ladder in!' Hastily, we lashed the ladder to a leg of the grating and the next day we loosened the new bolts and retrieved it.

Hobbies were very important in any lighthouse especially at rock lights. There was a good deal of carpentry and metalwork carried out in the workshop here. Sheets of tin were supplied by the Lighthouse Board, handy for making our baking tins among other things. Wood washed up on Erraid beaches gave us ideal material for small items of furniture. Ships in bottles were popular and interesting to make; we also read, played cards including cribbage, dominoes, draughts, and chess. Music from a mouth organ or spoons cheered everyone in the kitchen after tea. Father had made boots and shoes for the family while stationed here.

Each keeper had a 'rock box' – a heavy wooden chest for transporting personal belongings – which we made ourselves, often out of wood from the sea. A rock box had to be very substantial to stand rough handling on the boat and derrick. The corners were mitred, and tough metal handles were fitted at either end. Straps to hold the lid open were handy and could be made from the wick fabric supplied for domestic lamps. A narrow compartment with a sliding lid was used for small items.

In winter, when the fierce and leaden sea swept the rock continually, our only exercise was climbing the inside stairs or pacing to and fro on the balcony. We were quite unfit by the time we went ashore and swinging on the derrick took all our strength. Colds were rare while we were on duty, though we usually caught one when we went home. On a good day in summer the sea looked beautiful from the balcony; deep blue, though always fickle. Even a clear sky could not be trusted, as one or two tiny clouds might build rapidly, bringing wind and spray. When it was fine enough we made the most of the limited area by walking round and round the base of the tower, or sometimes fishing from the gratings. I set a creel once, but the sea smashed it and I realised that even the quietest conditions would be too rough.

An important task was to cut, splice and bind new lengths of rope. All ropes had to be kept in good condition and were inspected every time they were used. If any were lost or showed signs of fraying they were replaced immediately – lives depended on them. Fresh coils of manila in different thicknesses were supplied each year.

One winter we had spent two days replacing every rope only to find that there was not enough room to store the individual coils properly. It was against the law to dump rope in the sea in case it fouled propellers. We secured the old bundles neatly to the rock, ready for the *Hesperus* to collect them in a day or two. Unfortunately, there was a terrific gale that night and the sea carried the whole lot away; we watched helplessly as lines were strewn everywhere. After reporting the incident, we were relieved when the superintendent said to Jock that 'these things happen in storms and last night was so wild the crane at Skerryvore was badly damaged.'

Whenever there was a gale, outsize slaters (woodlice) invaded the kitchen and storeroom and ran around the stone floors. Down on the rock they infested crevices and lurked under stones. 'Something's biting me!' exclaimed Andrew one afternoon as he sat at the kitchen table and he brushed one of these giants off his arm. Occasionally a housefly would emerge from a box of provisions, but it never lived for long.

There were seabirds of many kinds here throughout the year. Looking down from the balcony in summer, we watched huge numbers of gannets feed off mackerel around the rock. The birds plummeted at great speed to the outside of a shoal and then turned deep underwater. They caught the fish on the way back up and swallowed them head first. We never tired of watching their beautiful displays of dive-bombing. On a very fine day we could make out the mackerel in clear water, over 130 feet below us.

One night when Father had been at Dhuheartach, a keeper on watch had a tremendous shock when a gannet crashed through the glass of the lantern and landed dead at his feet. There were another nine or ten out on the grating, quite dazed. He called the other men and they caught them all. They carried them downstairs, their hands getting thoroughly pecked on the way. The gannets were locked in the oil cellar for the night so they could not crash again and the shattered glass was replaced immediately with an emergency storm pane. In the morning the birds were pretty lively, dodging between the oil tanks before they could be grabbed and released.

Great numbers of seasonal migrants were drawn to the lantern at Dhuheartach. Some alighted safely, but many collided and died. On a single autumn day I picked up 200 casualties from the rock alone, mostly fieldfares, redwings, and blackbirds; many more had fallen into the sea. Bird traffic was always heaviest in easterly wind and haze – we thought the birds lost their way in these conditions and gravitated to the light before being dazzled in full flight or seeing the beam too late. Some would take avoiding action at the last minute. Storm petrels always landed successfully; we tossed these, and stray swifts, into the air to help them on their way. We collected lots of goldcrests, willow warblers, and other little birds as quickly as we could, put them in boxes, and took them indoors overnight. These birds would soon be trampled by bigger birds on the lantern grating or balcony if left to fend for themselves. They flew off happily when released in daylight.

For us, the birds were a welcome link with land and home. Seeing the little figures through the lantern helped to pass the hours on watch. Their calls could be heard from inside, especially the strident babble of starlings and the urgent notes of blackbirds.

They seemed quite unafraid as they ran to and fro, trying to get in, perhaps not noticing me behind the glass.

Hawks were not far away at migrating time and although they never crashed into the light, they did take their toll on life at the lighthouse. The window ledges outside the kitchen and bedroom made great roosts for swallows and martens on their autumn

Dhuheartach from the air in the late 1940s.

journeys south; sometimes 20 or 30 lined up at a time. One particular night we watched from the kitchen as a kestrel took one tired bird after another. The pickings were too easy and we wanted to slow the bird down. I am ashamed to say that we caught the kestrel while it slept on the ledge and attached a tiny piece of paper to its tail. We thought this would stop it killing so easily, but to our horror it fell straight into the sea. Needless to say, we did not repeat the experiment.

Rumours became reality in September when war was declared. All lighthouses came under control of the Royal Navy and an element of secrecy crept into every communication with ship and shore.

7

'Sure as the cat's a hairy beast'

War comes to Dhuheartach and Erraid

1939–1944

In order to comply with the wartime instructions for west coast lighthouses, the power of our light was reduced to a dull red glow and the red band on the tower was painted grey, to avoid recognition by the enemy. Use of the radio link was restricted and messages such as 'all well' or 'everything normal' had to cover a lot. We were warned to be careful what we said on the air and the names of the Board's ships must never be mentioned. Arrangements for reliefs were very non-committal: an anonymous 'probably be out in an hour,' was the most we could expect from the *Hesperus*. Time for speaking to families each evening was also reduced.

During the first few months little was noticeably different around the lighthouse. There was not much to see, apart from an occasional convoy passing a few miles away. Initially our food rations at the lighthouse were not adequate and there were no opportunities to supplement the diet by fishing or shooting. We did gather carrageen from the rock at low tide, and made puddings with it that bore a passing resemblance to custard. In time, three Lee Enfield rifles were issued which we used to sink floating mines. Then we shot a seal, intending to use the liver. When we cut the carcass open we found the liver was emerald green and we could not bring ourselves to eat it.

At one point the ship was overdue because of a persistent gale and food was running out. For breakfast on the last morning Jock handed us bowls of orange porridge full of lumps. 'Well lads, I've got a treat for you this morning. Sure as the cat's a hairy beast!' he said proudly. 'I added a tin of baked beans to fill you up.' One mouthful was enough! Luckily the ship could make a relief that day and we had managed not to break into the reserve supplies, which were only for a real emergency. Not long after this we were issued with seamen's rations which were more generous.

We had a fine surprise one summer's morning when a friend in a trawler landed a basket of fish for us. Another day his brother, serving on a minesweeper, managed to nose his ship in to the rock; then, to our great delight, a container of Navy rum arrived on a line.

When German U-boats began attacking the convoys, our tenders sailed in dangerous waters. Submarine periscopes would pop up on all sides, often near the lighthouse; once while we sat at our dinner with the kitchen window open we could even see the sunlight glinting off a periscope. They moved through the water and disappeared again; an eerie reminder of how powerless we were. They were probably only using us to take a bearing, but we had no way of telling if they were German or British.

British-based trawlers and some Antarctic whalers were requisitioned as minesweepers and escorts for our tenders. The fishing crews were hardy and courageous men, many of whom died clearing the channels of mines. Lighthouse reliefs never failed, though submarine activity, as well as weather, would cause delays.

Captain Mac was master of the *Hesperus*, a tough, god-fearing man of the old school who brooked no interference from anyone. I had known him since he was second mate on the *Pharos*, and he would call me up to the bridge for a chat when going to and from Dhuheartach. One day I asked him whether he would be the last man into the boat if we were torpedoed. 'Not so-and-so likely! I'd be first off!' he chortled. But I knew he was joking; this was a man who did not know fear.

The escort for the *Hesperus* was usually the *Silver Spray*, an Antarctic whaler. Her plump and jolly Fleetwood skipper was a brave sailor who did not give a damn for the Germans. They probably considered his boat too small to bother with; little did they know that she carried guns and depth charges. A large gun was mounted on her stern and a smaller one on the bow. Normally the escort sailed ahead of the *Hesperus* to pick up any submarine presence on the echo sounder and warn her to alter course. The Fleetwood man, however, took delight in annoying the captain and knew his quick temper. Now and again he dropped back and then nipped sharply across the ship's bows at the last minute. After one of these exploits, I heard a volley over the loud hailer: 'Cut it out, you so-and-so!' At that, the *Silver Spray's* skipper appeared on deck in his shirtsleeves, his thumbs through his braces. 'Get away to your wheelhouse, Captain, and have your breakfast!' came the cheery retort. 'You'll feel a lot better after that!'

On another trip Captain Mac showed me two newly installed machine guns, one on each side of the bridge. After examining them in detail, he thought he would try one out. He aimed out over the bow, but the recoil was much more powerful than he expected and the gun kept firing in rapid succession. It swung him round in a semicircle and before he could stop, he had shot a hole through his own funnel! For once he was lost for words and I tried hard not to laugh. In time a naval gunner joined the *Hesperus* to man the guns, though no shot was ever fired in anger.

One day the *Hesperus* crew rescued a tiny monkey, Jacko, from a torpedoed vessel. None of the crew could be recovered, but Jacko was found adrift on a plank, crying and alone. He stayed on board with Captain Mac's consent, and was very well treated by the crew. Spotlessly clean, he was also extremely mischievous; his special friend was the bo'sun. Jacko slept in his bunk with his arms around the man's neck, and whenever he was in trouble, he ran to hide inside the bo'sun's jacket, his little face peering out between the lapels. The bo'sun fed him in the mess room – he was especially fond of lettuce.

He loved to creep under the long mats on the floors, dashing along at great speed and reappearing at the other end. As if he was playing in the treetops, he would dart up and down the rigging and onto a knee or shoulder or on top of the door. Jacko became a great pal of mine and would jump onto my knee in the lightkeepers' room, searching my pocket for the raisins I always brought from home. He stuffed them into his mouth and watched us intently, as if he was listening to our conversations.

Jacko used to drive Jimmy, the chief steward, mad. He would hide in a ventilator above the mess room and dive at any open jar on the table. In went the fingers and away he shot with a fistful of jam or pickles. Although Jimmy was a kindly man, he soon grew exasperated with having to dump jars that had been spoiled by this wee hand. One breakfast we were ploughing through a heavy sea. Jimmy put up the fiddles (restraining rails) on the captain's table and set down a plate of bacon and egg at his place. While he went to the galley for the coffee pot, Jacko slipped in, carrying a tube of toothpaste. He squeezed it quickly over the tasty breakfast and crammed the mixture into his mouth with both hands.

Jacko loved wild seas. When it was very rough and the ship rolled steeply, he raced precariously along the deck rail and we feared he would fall in. I was on board one gusty day when he sneaked into the captain's cabin and stole his very special Rolls razor. He careered along the foredeck with a furious captain in pursuit. He climbed the shrouds and leant against the mast, examining the shiny chrome case thoroughly. He lurched over the sea with the tossing of the ship and we all gathered on deck to watch. The captain was tearing his hair out and ordered us to disperse. When the monkey realised he had no audience, he climbed down carefully, carrying his prize. He sat on deck trying to open the case again; then someone threw a piece of wood, causing him to drop the razor, undamaged.

Captain Mac was a great man for his Bible and Jacko must have seen him reading in his day room. One day Jimmy called me, and, through the porthole, we watched Jacko sitting on the captain's chair with the open Bible in his hands. Looking up and down each page as if he was reading, he would turn it carefully before tearing it out and moving onto the next. Then the enraged captain walked in, seized Jacko by the tail, and carried him to the deck rail. 'You've gone too far this time!' he yelled, dangling him over the sea. At the last minute he turned and let Jacko race to the bo'sun for refuge.

Unfortunately, Jacko's love of lettuce proved fatal. On one of the ship's visits to the pier at Oban he stole some leaves from a garden that had been treated with derris dust, a deadly insecticide.

After about a year, signs of war were becoming increasingly evident at the lighthouse. Depth charges, fired by our destroyers and frigates to protect convoys from the patrolling enemy, thudded loudly making the tower shudder. Mines drifted close by, so we shot at them with a rifle to prevent them exploding against the rock and shattering the lantern. Wreckage from torpedoed ships floated by and many upturned boats and empty ships' lifeboats were seen.

Then came the dead animals, horses and sheep among them – ships carrying livestock to Canada had been sunk. A usual greeting when we came to the kitchen for our tea was: 'Well, what went past today?' One afternoon I came down after a sleep.

'What's doing?' I asked.

'Just the usual,' replied Jimmy. 'Oh, and a hen went by!'

'How do you know it was a hen?' asked Johnny.

'Well, I know a hen when I see one!'

'And which way were its wings going?' Johnny persisted.

'Don't be silly! It was floating, not flying,' said Jimmy with his wry smile.

We looked out of the window very quickly the time Jock shouted, 'There's an elephant! Sure as the cat's a hairy beast! Come and see.' A huge bloated elephant drifted towards us, followed by two mules and various other bodies, though strong tides prevented the corpses from stranding on the rock. These must have come from a consignment of circus animals being shipped to America.

On one occasion a crate of whisky caused great excitement. Andrew was used to salvaging things of value around his Orkney home and we had to restrain him forcibly from jumping in. When the crate was ten yards off the grating he was set to dive in with a rope around his waist. He could not swim, but he reckoned on us hauling him to safety with his loot. These waters were not to be trifled with though, and sadly we had to watch the case float away.

We did catch the occasional bit of driftwood before it was washed back off the rock. Once, Andrew pulled out two huge pit props, and for a laugh we set them up to look like a machine gun. When two Spitfires flew over, he swivelled round, pretending to take aim. One peeled off, swooping low, as if to return the mock fire. It flew away with a cheery waggle of wings.

For a while, a heavy Canadian plane flew over Dhuheartach regularly, seeming at times to be only about 20 feet above the tower. These visits were a treat, as they gave us something to wave to. We could not see how many men were aboard, or whether they waved back, but we hoped they did. These Canadians were doing valuable work to counteract the threat to our shipping from the German Focke-Wulf aircraft.

One day though, an enormous four-engined Focke-Wulf circled us for at least a quarter of an hour. Sheltering inside the door, we waited for a blast, but nothing happened. It then flew on to Skerryvore and dropped six bombs – the plane's bombing mechanism must have jammed while it was flying over Dhuheartach – but luckily none made a direct hit on the lighthouse or the rock and nobody was hurt. They exploded in the sea and the blast broke the lantern, disabling the light. The men fitted emergency storm panes and repaired their light for that night. A few months later we were supplied with an inflatable life raft, which wouldn't have been much use in those waters.

As the war at sea intensified we became pretty depressed by the destruction we witnessed. Towards daylight during one night watch, I heard repeated explosions to the north. When it was light enough, we could see that one of our frigates was sinking an enemy submarine on the horizon. The U-boat reared up to the surface and the frigate went in at speed. We watched through binoculars as the U-boat was blasted in the middle; it rolled over and sank.

I can never forget the day that seven lifeboats full of people drifted past us. Of these huddled figures, we could not tell how many were alive; none were strong enough to row. Some waved feebly in a mute appeal for help. Confined to our tower, we were powerless to assist. Finally, we decided to break radio silence and call for aid, but it was two days before a frigate came. By then the boats were out of sight and probably all the occupants were dead. It was surprising that a ship came at all while the Navy was so hard pressed by the submarine menace. We were reprimanded mildly for calling.

Our morale was not improved by Lord Haw-Haw's radio broadcasts. The sinister, confiding voice of 'Germany calling' relayed false reports of Allied defeats. For instance, we heard that the people of Mull were starving, though we saw this was untrue when

Lifeboats full of people drifted past…

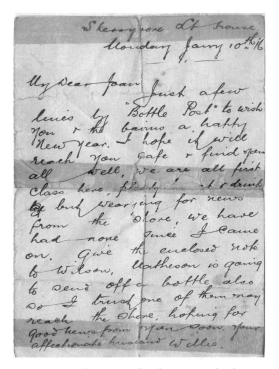

Bottle post. This letter reached
Erraid in 1916, from Skerryvore.

we went ashore. However, specific mention of Mull left a lingering unease that the island might be invaded, particularly given that Hitler's friend, Unity Mitford, was still living on Inchkenneth, a small island off the west coast of Mull. Surprisingly, Jock, who was usually so positive, could not accept that Haw-Haw was an enemy agent, and he came to believe implicitly in the negative propaganda. We persuaded him not to switch on the radio while we were in the kitchen, but he still managed to listen every day and recount the fictitious tales of disasters hitting our forces. Nothing would convince him that the point of these broadcasts was to spread fear, and we were already worried enough about our families.

Our feeling of isolation was increasing, so we thought to try bottle post to make contact with home. Though very chancy, a letter from Dhuheartach just might reach Erraid. I never heard anything from the six I despatched, but one of Jock's bottles was found on the coast of Norway and the letter was forwarded by conventional mail. The sea is full of tricks.

We were asked to be even more sparing with water. I was given a stern talking to by Captain Mac on one journey home. Too much water was being used, he said.

'But we're only using it to make food and wash our faces and hands.'

'Well, it's too much! Be very careful. With this war, I cannot come out as often as I should.'

Generally we were only shaving once in ten days by now, and the water for washing hands would be thick and black before the basin was emptied.

While I was making a small table in the workshop I nearly severed my forefinger with a sharp chisel. The others radioed immediately for help but the *Hesperus* could not come; she was in the Firth of Forth. So a motor boat belonging to my mother's cousin arrived from Fionnphort. Submarine activity was at its height and we faced a hazardous 14 miles to Mull in such a small vessel. Periscopes appeared around us, and before long a killer whale, seemingly as big as our boat, came alongside. Again and again it dived under us and reappeared on the other side. After several miles it came closer and one of the crew took aim with a rifle. 'Don't fire!' shouted the coxswain. 'If it is injured, it'll turn on us.' Instead, he took a can of petrol from the locker and poured some on the sea. The whale surfaced through the oily film, blew once, and swam away.

During one of my spells ashore a carrier pigeon came to the lighthouse. Pigeons had visited a window ledge before and usually moved on after resting, but this one stayed. When I returned, Jock, Andrew, and Jimmy had been feeding it and calling it Archie. Time passed and our little friend stayed, living on a diet of barley and lentils. There was no green food to give him, so when the *Hesperus* came we asked the crew to release him in Oban. The ship left us at noon, but that evening Archie was back, tapping on our window after a 40-mile flight.

The pigeon was a comforting companion when times were grim and Andrew built him a wooden cage. At night Archie would hop in and, after a coo or two, put his head under his wing. By December we were in the grip of gales and he had grown frail. We decided to send him to the shore station; however, the next relief was delayed because of a storm. One evening he walked feebly to a corner of the cage, closed his eyes, and died. We made a small canvas satchel for the body and added lead cuttings for weight. The storm raged for four more days. As soon as it calmed down, we went onto the rock and committed the remains to the deep. This faithful friend was not forgotten by three lonely men.

Something that did remain constant throughout those troubling times was the nature of the sea. Once Johnny was helping to erect the derrick during routine preparations for a relief, and while he was bending to tie a rope, an extra-large wave threw him against a rock. He had not heard our warning shout and he was cut about the face and hands. He was badly shaken and was especially careful on the grating after that.

Another time Jock and I were rigging the equipment when Andrew shouted – there was a roller heading straight for us. We ran to clutch the derrick, but Jock had not moved fast enough. Water was still pouring over my head when I heard Andrew again: 'Quick, Archie! Jock's away!' Jock had been carried off the grating. As our eyes cleared, we spotted him in the water, semi-conscious and caught on a derrick stay. We hauled him in before the next wave broke; he would have drowned if Andrew had not reacted so quickly. This incident affected Jock very badly and after he recovered, he was transferred to an easier station.

Life on Erraid

Erraid was beautiful, an oasis to men coming off rock duty, with its flourishing gardens and welcoming homes. How we valued the contrast to our other, stark, existence! The Stevensons had built a street of nine houses for Dhuheartach and Skerryvore families,

Erraid - the 'street' of lightkeepers' cottages viewed from Mull.

nicknamed 'Harmony Row'. There were four for each lighthouse and the ninth was their school. A whitewashed doorstep distinguished each principal's house. The only other residents on Erraid were the schoolteacher and Hugh, the lighthouse boatman. In this close-knit community, Peggy found the same camaraderie among wives as occurred between keepers on duty.

As a toddler, Kathleen would run and hide when I arrived back from rock duty, seeing me initially as a stranger. But picnics with Peggy and the children would become highlights, as well as the white beaches, carpets of heather in high summer, and the best strawberries ever. Balfour's Bay was a favourite spot for our picnics and walks. Jimmy's wife, Anne, often came too, with their little girl. In sunshine the sea turned turquoise and the children paddled, played and caught little flounders. One day a mob of gulls screeched over a huge dead halibut lying like a hearthrug on the white sand.

My father used to say that Erraid was a paradise and the time he spent there was the happiest of his life. From old letters of my mother's, we have glimpses of their early days together. She had not moved far from her family home in Bunessan after her marriage in 1907.

For her wedding in Oban she had a hat of fancy crinoline straw with the palest pink roses and a fall of knotted ribbon down the back. Angus wanted her to wear a wreath and veil so to please him she gave in to his wishes. They hurried home to Erraid after

Left: A picnic on Erraid and time to knit. Peggy 2nd left, Kitty, who was visiting, far left.

Right: Time ashore on Erraid, with Angus and Kathleen.

three days because Father's sister was getting married in their house. They lived next door to each other and the husbands worked together on the rock. Mother wrote, 'I did not know Angus' worth until he became my husband. He is a tower of strength ...'

She corresponded regularly with this cousin, Mary, often lamenting that she was too far away. But she closes one letter saying, 'The penny postage seems to have brought us nearer'.

Soon after her marriage, my mother wrote:

> My home is very comfortable, a free house of four apartments and a scullery and outhouses, eight tons of coal a year and as much oil as we can burn, two gardens. The houses are also partly furnished, bedclothes and linen for three beds are supplied – in all our kitchens there are close ranges. Dear Mary, father presented us with a new boat he built himself, so we should do well now. P.S. I forgot to mention that the Bunessan public presented me with a purse of sovereigns as a token of good will ... Angus has been away for three weeks now and it is a new experience for me to live in a house alone. Angus's sister and I are practically living together as our houses adjoin, we have always been the closest of friends so you can understand how happy we are now.

Another cousin wrote home to New Zealand while visiting my parents on Erraid:

They have a very nice house and are very comfortable. There are five rooms and a scullery and they keep a servant. If they were only living in a town I could stay with them a couple of months or so, it would be lovely, but this is a terrible place they live in and Jessie says it is the quietest place and the most out of the way place in all Scotland. It is a little island of its own about three miles wide and only the lighthouse keepers' wives live here. There is a row of houses and they each have a house of their own. There is not a thing to be seen and not a sound to be heard except one's own voice. There is no road, only a track up to the top of the hill. They only get provisions here once a fortnight. They are so kind to us.

Robert Louis Stevenson spent time on Erraid with his father and uncle during the construction of Dhuheartach lighthouse; he portrayed it in *Kidnapped* as the isle where David Balfour landed.

As Erraid is a tidal island we could walk across the stretch of sand from Mull at low tide; otherwise it was a short boat crossing from Fidden. We often took our wives and families to Mull in the boat, which Hugh used to bring us supplies and ferry the doctor and minister. This narrow gut of water could be very rough, so in strong south-westerlies we helped Hugh with the boat. Our dances and ceilidhs in the schoolhouse became so popular that crowds joined us from crofts on Mull. Late at night we took them back by boat which was fun when the water was choppy.

Every day one of the keepers ashore walked across at low tide to fetch milk for all the families from the nearest farm. Cans for the milk were made on the rock. We usually stayed for a cup of tea with the farmer, Evander, and his wife. (Her brother, Johnny, was our occasional. Previously they had farmed on the Falkland Islands where Johnny's schooling was a bit sketchy. He was a very clever shepherd though, and could tell by a lamb's face which ewe was its mother.)

When I was ashore, I shot pheasants, ducks, geese and woodcock, and set creels and lines from the lighthouse boat to supplement our diet – we shared catches between families. Here I caught my biggest lobster ever. It was too big to fit into any pot and we had to cook it in the washhouse boiler. Andrew caught one that was so huge it could not get into the creel and was trying to grab the bait from outside! As well as lobsters and crabs, we brought in cod, haddock, lovely big plaice, mackerel, and saithe. Baby saithe – also known as 'sillocks' – were delicious fried. Fish were gutted before they were brought home, as were any birds or animals that we shot. One evening we were amazed to see a pair of antlers moving through the water. Then the head appeared and we watched a stag swim to a small isle nearby. He landed, shook himself vigorously, and headed for green grass.

Poaching salmon or sea trout for the pot was an exciting pastime on a summer's evening. Once we were all standing chest deep in the sea to haul the net – this catch needed a hearty pull. Suddenly, the person at the back of the team fell flat on her back and everyone else keeled over like dominoes – we all had a good laugh. We landed some beautiful sea trout; however, soon a metal hook was set in the sand to snag our net in such operations.

Hugh kept a few hens but his henhouse had grown dilapidated. Andrew and I decided to rebuild it after plenty of suitable boards came ashore. On our second day of rhythmical hammering, I heard a sudden soft 'clunk' from Andrew's side of the shed. 'What was that, Andrew?' I said. He held up a hugely swollen thumb. 'Oh, Archie, I hit the wrong nail,' he said mildly, and went back to the job. As usual, Andrew did not let pain bother him.

We grew a variety of vegetables, including potatoes, to store for winter; winters were generally mild on Erraid and strawberries did well in the soft climate. Seaweed from the shore was used to prepare the ground. Household rubbish went onto middens outside the gardens where I trapped rats. Each house had a toilet at the end of its garden and these were emptied into the sea; that was a job for the men.

There was a lot of hard work for the wives when we were out on the rock. The two washhouses stood on a slope behind the street, one for the Skerryvore families, and the other for Dhuheartach families. Each had a boiler and a strict rota for use, with Mondays always for the principal's wife. All the water was pumped by hand and carried up from the well, in addition to buckets of coal for the boiler – not easy on stormy winter days.

Very occasionally we were given venison from Mull, and when food got scarce, Peggy and Jimmy's wife, Anne, snared rabbits to eke out the meat rations. The worst part was the killing, but Peggy learnt to whack them effectively with a scrubbing brush. One day when I arrived home the wives were complaining about having no meat. There was a herd of wild goats on the moor, so I offered to shoot one. I picked out a young brown and white billy in his prime that would give plenty of tender meat. Alert, handsome and unafraid, he stood high on a rock and stared me straight in the eye as I took aim. But I could not pull the trigger on this beautiful creature. Instead, I shot some rabbits and felt slightly foolish returning without the promised goat.

Two or three years later I came across an old billy lying in the heather, ousted as leader by the fine son that I nearly shot. In his day the old boy used to jump into our gardens and help himself to vegetables; now he was frightened and too weak to stand. I sat stroking him until he went to sleep and when I returned later, he was dead.

All eight keepers who lived on Erraid had to join the local Home Guard. This unit was highly trained because of Mull's connection with Hitler's friend Unity Mitford. Early in the war there were not enough rifles; we used our own guns and Mother's cousin, the Iona boatman, supplied ammunition until we were issued with rifles from Canada. Our drill took place in the school. 'Get in line, MacEachern, and stop smirking!' was a typical greeting from our sergeant major. One day I was showing a new keeper how to fire a rifle. After some practice loading I aimed at the fireplace and a shot went off – the ammunition hadn't been taken out! The school fireplace was smashed to pieces and Andrew's wife, Elsie, ran round from next door, greatly alarmed, as the blast had rattled her fireplace. I was peppered with splinters of metal, which Peggy patiently fished out of my ear and chest. That evening we had shooting practice again and the sergeant major asked me:

'Why did you close your eyes when you fired that?'

'I don't know,' I said.

'And what's that hole in your ear?' he added, with a trace of a smile. 'You've been firing that rifle when you shouldn't, haven't you? Well, there's a lesson you'll never forget!'

One of us had to patrol the Erraid shoreline daily with rifle and bayonet, starting at first light. This was a lonely trek in winter, though the wildlife often made good company. A large dog otter once crossed my path without seeing me. When he heard my 'good morning, sir!' he departed in great haste.

A young keeper, new to the Home Guard, returned from one of his first patrols after finding a body on the beach. He had not wanted to approach it so two of us retraced his steps. It was actually the corpse of a cormorant partly buried in the sand, with most of its feathers missing. He had assumed the worst after hearing much talk of wrecks and lives lost. Another time Andrew did find a badly decomposed human corpse at the edge of the water, but it floated away before he could reach it.

On one patrol I spotted a mine and when it grounded I went to investigate. I scraped the top with my penknife and saw a gleam of copper through a layer of verdigris. Although we had been told to sink mines that floated near the lighthouse, we had not been given much information on identifying them. This was quite different from anything we had seen during training, so I reported the find to the Naval Authority in Tobermory. I was instructed to leave it alone and no one should approach it with a metal object of any kind! I was to surround it with red flags immediately and have it guarded until the mine disposal unit arrived. It turned out to be a magnetic mine and I had had a lucky escape that day. Angus was also lucky when another mine exploded in the sea near the pier, where he was standing.

The Erraid beaches became festooned with wreckage making us realise how much damage was being caused in the northwest channel. One day the sea was yellow with bobbing oranges and grapefruit from a torpedoed cargo vessel. Though they were not fit to eat, I took an orange home because none of the children had seen one before and Angus took it to show everyone at school.

There was tragedy behind many of the finds. I was very shocked after picking up a small tin of cigarettes from above the waterline. Inside the lid was a label that identified the owner, 'Able Seaman Tom Jones', and his ship, the *Fitzroy*. Amazingly, I had actually known Tom. He and I had become friends years earlier when our ships met in port and the crews played football – the *Pharos* versus the frigate *Fitzroy*. Both of us had been young and we enjoyed the company on these occasions, the get-togethers and singing after the games. Tom had been a Barnardo's boy from London, with great hopes and plans to marry his girlfriend. Now his ship was lost with all hands. Cigarettes were usually confiscated by Customs, but I kept Tom's tin on our mantelpiece for a long time.

Much of the flotsam reaching Erraid was worth salvaging. We had to be quick off the mark though, as boats from Iona tried to beat us to it. Huge quantities of wood appeared – more than we could ever use. There were many deck planks from wrecked ships, some massive beams of mahogany, still intact, were probably en route from Honduras. From some I made a small sideboard.

We retrieved crates of lard that we purified for cooking by boiling it in fresh water and skimming the layer of fat off the top. One day I found a big sack containing three pig carcasses floating in a gulley on the neighbouring isle of Goman. These had been cleaned and trimmed for the table but unfortunately were no longer edible. However there was nothing wrong with boxes of coffee that were packed in watertight tins. Large bales of latex covered the sea at one point and we were paid a few shillings for each of these by the Receiver of Wrecks as rubber was in great demand; bundles of wax were also welcomed. Local shepherds found a cask of cognac on the shore which kept everyone happy for a while – the nearest pub was several miles away on Mull.

In 1940 Jimmy and I were particularly touched when we came upon a sturdy ship's boat from the liner *Arandora Star*. She was empty apart from a child's shoe and jacket. Having young children of our own made us particularly sad for these little victims of war. The ex-cruise liner had been torpedoed while transporting 'aliens' to Canada – Italians and Germans who had been rounded up in Britain. We heard that the captain had been flying a swastika under the Red Duster to show the Germans she carried some of their nationals, but this was ignored. Of the 1,600 aboard, about 800 people died.

A lot of wreckage arrived from the *Arandora Star*, such as thick mahogany doors and planks, half a mast, and wash basins in wooden surrounds. I made a tea trolley and a little table from wood that was probably hers; lasting reminders of this disaster.

From the hill behind the houses, we could see Dhuheartach and Skerryvore on a clear day. At the top of the hill was a round hut, the lookout, and inside was a big swivelling mirror. Sometimes we used it for fun to signal to the rock. Before the days of radio, this was used to contact the lighthouses. When the sun was bright enough, Morse code messages could be flashed by heliograph. 'All's well' was the usual signal to Erraid, with distress flares being kept for emergencies. The messages received had not always been accurate; a keeper once asked for an extra hundredweight of potatoes but received an extra pound of butter at the next relief.

THE *OSTENDE*

In January 1943 the *Ostende*, a cargo ship, was wrecked in Bunessan Bay. Immediately the captain had ordered his crew to abandon ship. Two of the sailors ran below to get their kit while the rest took to the lifeboats and rowed to safety. Before long the ship exploded with such violence that the decks were blown apart and her funnel was squashed flat; a piece of the topmast was found lodged in the hillside a quarter of a mile away and debris littered the sea. She had carried a mixed cargo, including explosives which blew up when salt water ignited the calcium flares. The two who had gone to collect their gear were never seen again.

I was out at Dhuheartach when this happened. Jimmy's wife, however, heard about the wreck the same afternoon, but she did not tell Jimmy about it until they were in bed knowing fine he would rush to the scene. He got up straightaway and went to find Andrew. In no time at all they were crossing to Mull in the boat, in spite of the darkness. They took two bicycles with them to cover the several miles on the other side. Andrew, though, had never learned to ride a bike and kept falling off, so by the time they reached Bunessan he was in agony with two broken ribs. Then, of course, they had no way of getting from Bunessan to the wreck, so they made their way to the village hall where a dance was in progress. Although someone there agreed to ferry them out, they found the *Ostende* still burning and the metal hull red hot. They decided to leave well alone for the time being.

By the time I came ashore an official salvage crew was working to save as much of the cargo as possible, especially the torpedoes, shells, guns, and large quantities of ammunition. After sailing all the way from Erraid to the wreck in Andrew's boat, we were asked by the salvers to take away sacks of white flour and crates of egg powder; these were stowed on top and hampering their operation. In the main hold, barrels and crates were jammed against flour bags and rolls of cotton cloth, the rest of which had spilled out with the flood tide. Another hold was still full of aeroplane tyres. Crates of screwdrivers and magnetic hammers had been blown over the side and burst open. A diver told me that the seabed looked like a rose garden because all the screwdrivers had red wooden handles and were sitting upright. A salver gave me two screwdrivers and I used them for many years.

When we had loaded the boat with as much flour and egg powder as she would hold, we set off for home. Although sailing to Bunessan Bay had only taken us about an hour, a strong southwesterly was springing up as dusk fell on this cold winter's night. It was dark when we reached the Sound of Iona, and we were faced with the incoming tide as well as a headwind. Eventually, we had to lower the sail and take to the oars. Fortunately, there were four of us to take turns at rowing, but soon the boat sprang a leak and things got really difficult. We debated whether we should jettison the load and run for shelter. Instead, somebody pushed a bag of flour over the leak and sat on top of it; it plugged the crack in the hull as the bottom layer of flour solidified, allowing us to battle on.

Arriving home at two in the morning, exhausted but pleased, we found the whole street in a state of alarm, fearing we had been drowned. The flour and egg powder were divided equally between everyone. The water had only penetrated about two inches into the sacks of flour before forming a protective seal, so there was still a large amount of good flour in the middle. The white flour was a luxury as brown flour was all we could buy. Every available container was filled and wives made delicious bread. The egg powder kept fresh for a long time and was fine for baking, though rubbery when scrambled. Nothing was wasted – the women used some of the enormous rolls of cotton material for sewing. We made several more risky visits to the *Ostende* to bring home boatloads of goods. It was exciting, but I am surprised we did not drown.

A minister crossed to Erraid one Sunday every month and called at each of our houses. The schoolteacher lived alone and during one visitation she came to us in great distress, saying that the minister had chased her around her sitting room. At the end of the day he came to us. 'I am ready to go now. Get the boatman please,' he said solemnly. I took him across myself and it was a silent trip. As we parted, I said I would report him to the Lighthouse Board. He got angry, but that was the last of his visits.

Relatives often visited us here; they loved the white sandy beaches, the walks and fishing. Eating cockles – quite a delicacy during the war – straight from the beach was a particular thrill. We took our visitors by boat to little islands, especially Goman as it had a big patch of white heather. Bobbie loved Erraid and often went shooting accompanied by the principal's black spaniel, Laddie. Laddie followed him devotedly; everyone knew when Bobbie occupied the toilet at the end of the garden as the dog sat patiently outside. Once Bobbie was stung by a viper weever while taking fish off a line, and it made him so ill that he had to go to hospital in Oban. Peggy's brother, Jim, also came whenever he had time off.

In summer we used to cross to Iona, but the Sound of Iona is quite dangerous for a small boat and we treated it with care. A streak of green marble lined a rock fissure on the island. Little pieces could be broken off easily and our visitors took fragments home. After we left, the marble was exploited commercially.

After five years at Dhuheartach lighthouse, and with Jimmy having been moved already, I longed for a change. In 1944 I welcomed the news of a transfer to Buchan Ness, a big mainland station in Aberdeenshire. When the ship's boat took me off the rock for the last time, the second mate asked:

'Aren't you going to wave goodbye to your lighthouse?'

'No!' I replied. 'I never want to see the place again,' and I left without a backwards glance. Our only passing regret was at leaving Erraid, the island of happy memories for our family.

8

'The Floor of Heaven'

Buchan Ness

1944–1953

LIGHT ESTABLISHED IN 1827
WHITE TOWER 35 METRES HIGH WITH A RED BAND
ENGINEER – ROBERT STEVENSON

It was a cold April day when we arrived at Buchan Ness, where we were greeted by Alan, the principal keeper, and his wife. Our first impression was of a happy station, and this would prove to be correct. After a superb tea we met my fellow assistant, George, his wife Stella, and their family. George had been the only survivor at Fair Isle South lighthouse when a bomb demolished the housing block; three other people were killed. Luckily, Stella and the two children were in Orkney at the time. The only possessions they managed to retrieve were a few charred photographs, papers, and a gold sovereign – their wedding present from Tom Wilson.

Buchan Ness lighthouse stood on a tiny island that was linked to the busy fishing village of Boddam by a short bridge. The brilliant red and white bands on the tower had been covered with grey paint so that it was no longer conspicuous to the enemy. Alan remembered well what life was like as a rock keeper; since I had spent so much of the war at a rock light, he wanted me to

Buchan Ness lighthouse.

make the most of my time here. I was told I could go to the village any day when our morning work was finished, as long as I let him know, and he would take an occasional afternoon watch for me. (All keepers were now entitled to one day off a week anyway, unless they were at a rock.) True to his word, I was given as much free time as possible, though he insisted that we attend church on Sundays when we were not on duty. It was a novelty to walk across the bridge and post letters whenever I liked!

We watched over a busy shipping lane, though in keeping with wartime naval rules for the east coast, the Buchan Ness light was only exhibited for passing convoys. When instructed, we had to display this at full power, usually for one or two hours at a time but occasionally for three if it was a larger convoy. Fog was common here and daylight watches were very important. The foghorn, known locally as the 'Boddam Bull', boomed frequently through the village. A fisherman told me he once heard the signal 30 miles out at sea on a calm day and wondered if the blanket of fog amplified its sound. I never heard the villagers complain; perhaps it was reassuring in uncertain times.

Although we thought the east coast was very cold after the relatively soft climate of Erraid, the folk here radiated humour and friendliness. Stella introduced Peggy to everybody at the shops and broad Buchan accents greeted us on the street: 'Ay ay man! Fit like?' or 'Hoo are you the day?'

We soon found ourselves part of the local community. The lighthouse wives attended Boddam Church regularly. Kathleen sang in the choir, which faced the congregation, and was mortified when I fell asleep during sermons. She and the salmon fisherman's daughter noted whose father dropped off first. Peggy was involved in church activities and we all took part in the concerts, dances, whist drives, plays, and a panel game called 'Matter of Opinion'. I valued the consistent family life, the company and freedom.

People frequently came to the lighthouse asking for help because many of their men were away on active service. Money was often scarce in these households. One day I was asked to change a lightbulb for two elderly sisters. I laid my uniform cap down on a table while I was busy and their little cat jumped up to investigate. I thought it rather odd when he sat in it – I found a little pool when I went to put it on again. 'Eh me! He's piddled in your bunnet,' said one of the ladies calmly. Quite a new cap it was too!

Another old lady came for help to fix her leaking roof. This was a bigger undertaking and I arranged for a builder in Peterhead to carry out the necessary repairs. When he gave her the bill, she stared at it. 'Ah well, I canna pay ye, but the Lord will,' was all she could say. He knew he would not be paid; she just did not have the money, so he let it go.

Our children had new shores to explore; pieces of broken china and coloured pebbles were ideal for playing 'shoppies' among the rocks. During the hours spent beachcombing they often came upon seamen's hats washed in from wrecks, though they were too young to realise the tragic implications of these finds.

Alan was very keen on sport, especially tennis. He helped us to mark out and prepare a full-sized court on the lighthouse green. It was difficult getting a net so a fisherman brought us a piece of herring net; we got on well with the Boddam fishermen. Every fine evening the court was busy and several good players from the village joined us. We made little wooden shields as tournament prizes and after the war we bought a proper net – then we could adjust the height. An old fisherman with a long white beard came regularly to watch. 'Ye'll play much better if ye tak awa' that net,' he told us from time to time. The children called him Black Bob because of the long dark coat he always wore; the smaller ones found him rather frightening. He lived alone and Peggy or Stella often gave him a couple of eggs from our hens. With great care, he would put these into the deep pockets of the black coat before he walked home.

In due course Peggy and I bought a spaniel puppy – a tiny jet black dog with the longest ears we had ever seen. Sultan of Buchan was highly intelligent and his coat grew as shiny as silk. At night he liked to sneak into Kathleen's bedroom when he heard her singing her little song 'Sultan of Buchan'. We would find them asleep, both heads on one pillow, and remove him gently. Sultan was especially fond of Black Bob and sat by his side while he watched tennis.

George and I played in the village football team while there were gaps to be filled. When the local lads returned from the war they took these places again and we became referees – after an unpopular decision we sometimes had to run for our lives! Feelings ran particularly high after one disputed penalty, and I was chased to the bus by the women of New Pitsligo. Divots were hurled as 'wash yer bloody e'en oot, ref!' rang in my ears.

Salmon fishing was a treat on days off at Buchan Ness, and I would cycle to the River Ugie or the Water of Cruden. Some free days I spent aboard the *Fruition*, known locally as the *Ferution*, trawling for haddock and plaice inshore; my main task was to shovel undersized fish overboard. When it was sunny we had our flasks of tea and ate our pieces on deck, which was glorious.

Men dyed kippers by hand in big tubs of yellow liquid that stood in an open shed at Boddam harbour. They had red spots on their bare arms from plunging them into the vats to turn the fish. One day a meeting was called – people had complained about the dye and I was asked for my opinion. I thought it must be harmful in foodstuffs if it caused such irritation to the dyers' skin.

I reported to the Boddam Home Guard and was asked to teach a group of new recruits how to handle guns, especially Sten guns. In general, this unit's role was not as vital as in Mull, and the training was easier. Morse signalling was considered very important; both George and Stella practised hard and were highly proficient – I could never reach their standard.

One night I had to put on our light for an hour to allow a damaged Flying Fortress to get its bearings. Alan thought this American plane was looking for somewhere to land.

When a mine exploded on the beach, the blast cracked three panes in the lantern and brought down bits of ceiling in our rooms; fortunately, no one was injured.

There were suspicions that an enemy agent was active in Aberdeen. Any instructions for the light always came by telephone, with a password, without which we could never accept an order. One night I took an order as follows: 'Exhibit your light from midnight until 0200 hrs.' But no password was given. Twice I asked the caller to repeat the message and still there was no password, so I said that I could not accept their call. The naval officer at the end of the line got angry. 'I am sorry, I cannot accept this call,' I repeated, and he rang off abruptly. I watched anxiously after midnight as the convoy's shadowy shapes slipped past the rocks without our guiding light; each displayed a small stern light only. At three o'clock I called the principal to take the next watch, and reported how the order had been given.

The next day a high-ranking naval officer, all gold braid, stepped out of a car at the tower door and asked to see the principal keeper. George and I were summoned and the officer addressed me:

'You refused to act at midnight on a call from our operator. Explain this!'

'Simply because no password accompanied the order, even when I asked him to repeat it.'

'Are you quite sure?'

'Yes sir, I am.'

'Ah! That's rather different.' Alan backed me up, saying that I had reported this as soon as possible.

'Thank you very much,' said the officer, and that was the end of the conversation. Nothing came of the matter, though we heard through the grapevine that the instructing officer had been reprimanded.

Soon a new system was introduced for conveying these orders – two lightkeepers were on duty all night at NLB headquarters specifically to relay the Navy messages. My cousin Finlay was one of the men chosen for this. Before it was fully operational, however, the general manager took over for a spell. At that point the week's password had not come through, but in the early hours he instructed the keeper on watch at St Abbs Head to exhibit the light. 'I do not have a password yet, but you know who I am,' he added. The keeper refused to take his instruction, saying, 'you might be Lord Haw-Haw for all I know!' This annoyed the general manager and amused lightkeepers; the keeper was not disciplined because he had stuck to the rules.

Emergency transfers to other stations began – sometimes a man was needed at short notice and I was sent to provide cover. These temporary attachments to five other stations – Rattray Head, Rubh Reidh, Barra Head, Skerryvore, and the Flannan Isles – disrupted my time at Buchan Ness. The first call was to Rattray Head; there would be four spells there. Mostly I had to use public transport to reach the ship and comply

RATTRAY HEAD

Rattray Head lighthouse is 22 miles north of Buchan Ness on reefs called Rattray Brigs. Standing about three quarters of a mile offshore, access was mostly by boat, but at spring tides we could cross a rough causeway by tractor or on foot. Once, I heard the tractor had become stuck on the way out and could not be retrieved until the next low tide. At high water, we looked down from the door at the seals that swam around the tower.

Posts marked a minefield near the lighthouse. The station had been issued with twin Hotchkiss machine guns, and instructions that they were only to be used if the lighthouse was attacked. Prior to my arrival a ship with a cargo of foodstuffs had run onto the rocks and a young keeper watched a Heinkel bomber attack it repeatedly. Eventually he had fired at the plane which retaliated with a salvo that broke panes in the lantern and chipped the lens.

During my second stint at Rattray, we were alerted by the assistant on watch – he had seen a fishing boat heading for the rocks. I tried to divert her with hand signals, but she grounded with a sickening crash. The screech of iron on rock sent me hurrying for flags and I signalled in semaphore. The skipper launched a boat and came to the lighthouse with two of his crew. His boat had just been decommissioned after working for the Navy in Scapa Flow and they had very little food left. While they had a bite to eat with us, I asked why he had come so close to the reef. 'I was in a hurry to get hame to the family and back to the fishing,' he explained. The disabled vessel was not holed and a tug towed her off before the wind freshened. In his haste, he had forgotten a local saying: 'Keep Mormond Hill a hand-spike high and Rattray Brigs ye'll ne'er come nigh.'(That is, sailors should keep the landmark, Mormond Hill, looking no higher than a hand-spike to avoid being wrecked on Rattray Briggs rocks. This was especially useful before the lighthouse was built. All sailors would be familiar with a hand-spike, a tool like a lever, for various uses on board such as turning a capstan.)

with orders such as: 'Get to Kyle of Lochalsh as quickly as you can,' or 'Go to Oban tomorrow'. Peggy and I learnt to budget for these sudden demands; it took some time to be reimbursed for the travel expenses.

Back in Boddam there was a widowed fisherman, Davey, with two daughters, one of whom was blind. They were entirely dependent on what he could earn from lobsters and crabs; his sons were away in the war so he was alone on his boat. Occasionally Alan took my watch and sent me to help Davey; I worked the creels while he looked after the engine. At the end of the day we crossed to Peterhead to land the catch.

On the way in to the harbour we would see a fleet of small fast Norwegian naval craft that were stationed there. These went out on sorties to attack German ships around the Norwegian coast, sometimes returning badly shot up. When they came back in high spirits, with flags flying, they would sing into the early hours of the morning. If it was calm, we could hear the sound waft over the water to the lighthouse. On one crossing we passed close to a boat where the crew looked elated, as if they had been victorious, and loud music blared from below. Half their deck was shot away, and more damage showed on the hull and mast. We wondered how many men were lost on these dangerous missions.

Davey was a joker. One summer's night after the war there was a bonfire party by the harbour. A good crowd had gathered and Davey sat yarning with an old friend who had a wooden leg. While they chatted, the man took off his leg and laid it on the ground. When the fire began to die Davey picked up the leg and threw it on the embers – instantly it went up in flames! In the rumpus that followed, some were not convinced that Davey had mistaken it for a stick. The boat builder soon made a new leg for the friend.

After a brief spell at Skerryvore, I was back on watch at Buchan Ness. A lovely autumn morning was dawning and a local boat passed on the way to her lobster pots. To my surprise she returned an hour later, her deck crammed with people, making for Peterhead. A German U-boat had been laying mines in the shipping lanes when it was blown up by one of its own devices. This little boat picked up the majority of the submariners and they were imprisoned overnight at Peterhead.

The weather deteriorated throughout that morning, and a gale was blowing when George and I caught sight of a life raft with a single man on board. It was being carried swiftly towards the rocks below us where it overturned before we could call for help. We were able to retrieve the raft and on it found only a small bag with a hunk of black bread and some cheese. The man had disappeared.

In the late afternoon we were called out with the Home Guard – we were needed to rescue two of the U-boat survivors. In even wilder weather, the men had scrambled ashore and got stuck trying to climb a cliff. We lowered ropes from the top and pulled the first man up. He leapt to his feet defiantly and shouted 'Heil Hitler!' with a brisk Nazi salute. However, we had great difficulty in bringing up the second man, who was exhausted. He collapsed as soon as he reached us and lay quite still. One of us ran for the doctor, who tried hard to revive the young man and could find nothing wrong except hypothermia. We covered him with a jacket, but he died soon after. I was glad the doctor spoke gently and stroked his brow; we must have looked terrifying with our rifles and bayonets. How we wished he had known that any one of us would have taken him home and given him tea and food. He was too young to die and I have never forgotten him.

In time, George was transferred and replaced by Stewart, a young keeper and superb craftsman from Shetland. We had known his wife, Annie (a prolific knitter), as a girl in Fair Isle. Stewart was also the fastest runner we had ever seen; sometimes when playing football he could not slow down in time. When he ran straight past the

BARRA HEAD

Towards the end of the war I had an urgent call from the Lighthouse Board asking me to get to the clifftop lighthouse at Barra Head as soon as possible. Tom, the principal, had been injured in an accident, and his two assistants were young and inexperienced. I was able to lodge with Tom and his wife at the lighthouse on the isle of Berneray, near Barra. The keepers and their wives were the only inhabitants of the island.

It was wintertime and the weather was wild. On the way I spent a night in Castlebay and heard that the lifeboat had recently rescued the crew of a torpedoed ship. At the lighthouse, I was told that the Navy believed a German submarine was using a sheltered cove on the lee side of the island in bad weather. Tom had been informed in case the crew should land.

The howling wind brought snow and I was glad of my greatcoat and long felt watch boots. When I went on watch at three one morning, a heavy blizzard was blowing. I crossed the courtyard from the house, gripping the handrails on either side. Amazed to find the tower door standing open, I quickly shut it behind me. As I made my way up the unlit stairs, I began to notice a strange smell, like an object that had been dragged through the sea – damp clothing possibly. Gradually I became aware that I was not alone, and thoughts of the U-boat lurking in the bay ran through my mind. The smell grew stronger as I crept up quietly. Suddenly my hand touched something woolly and alive. It moved and I froze. Nothing happened for a few seconds. Then I struck a match, convinced I would be confronted by an armed German. Instead, the biggest, hairiest billy goat I had ever seen faced me from the steps above! He had huge horns, a long beard and was very frightened. I could have hugged him if it was not for the rotten smell. I opened the door to let him out and took over happily from the keeper on watch. Minutes earlier I had feared that I would find him shot or bayonetted, but he had nothing unusual to report. He said there were wild goats on the cliffs and we guessed that this billy had been searching for shelter when he found the tower door blown open.

The station had a Jeep for bringing water up from a well by the landing. The principal was their only driver and I had never been taught to drive. The station was very short of drinking water and as he was out of action, I had to learn quickly. After a dodgy start and reversing into the shed door, I followed a track of sorts that zig-zagged down the hill. The assistants helped to pump the water and we loaded a full tank on to the vehicle. This would last a week, for cooking and drinking. Although the well water was brackish and foul tasting, it did not seem to harm us. Rainwater collected from the flat lead roof of the house supplied our other needs.

One day Tom took me to the headland and we looked through binoculars at two round objects that looked like the end of barrels embedded in the opposite cliff. He had guessed these might be aircraft engines and reported the sighting to the RAF. Investigators had identified them as engines from a Hampden of Coastal Command; the plane had gone missing without trace in the North Atlantic. It must have crashed into the rock face, probably in poor visibility. No one at the lighthouse would have heard the impact above the perpetual noise of breaking waves. Other parts of the plane were never found, but a set of false teeth, two pairs of gloves, and a flying boot lay on a ledge.

When my time at Barra Head was up I was glad to rejoin my family, but the company at the lighthouse had been good.

ball, cries of 'fit aboot the ba', man?' or 'tak the ba' wi' yer, man!' brought him skidding to a halt. They settled in quickly at the lighthouse and we became lifelong friends.

Our occasional was Jim, a kind and likeable man, and we had another good boss at Buchan Ness when a new principal, John, was appointed. His wife always addressed him by their surname, never as John. Before long, he, Stewart, and I bought an old Norwegian dory that was lying derelict in Peterhead harbour. We rebuilt it and started cod fishing off the lighthouse. We brought in big catches with hand lines.

Bobbie in the meantime had become second mate on the *Pharos*. One day he was in the ship's boat near the entrance to the Moray Firth, checking the position of mines with three other crew. A German submarine opened fire, injuring the men and destroying the boat's engine. A British frigate came in at speed with guns blazing, and the U-boat disappeared. The four were taken to hospital in Aberdeen. Bobbie had a leg wound and refused to eat anything, but a kindly nurse persisted, tempting him with repeated offers of pudding. 'There's fruit alane, puddin' alane, fruit an' puddin' thegither,' she reeled off brightly – her 'puddin' pronounced like 'buddin'. This worked eventually, by making him smile.

On another occasion the *Pharos* was heading for Peterhead escorted by an armed fishing vessel. A German aircraft flew over, fired at the escort, circled, and repeated the attack. She was badly damaged but did not sink. Bobbie radioed immediately:

'Have you got casualties?'

The answer came: 'Yes, we have a casualty; one case of venereal disease!'

These fishermen could lighten the toughest of times with their humour.

The fishermen were religious and hardworking; many were Brethren. Their boats, like their houses, were immaculate. No local men went to sea in January, as all their time was spent on cleaning, painting, and repairing. Once the boats were ready they painted and repaired their houses, which would be kept spick and span by their wives. In February, the Boddam line boats returned to work; big drifters from Aberdeen and Peterhead set out for Rockall in search of cod, ling, and halibut.

The local waters were especially good for cod. Before the lighthouse was built generations of fishermen had spread their catches and their nets to dry on our little island, but fish were no longer dried and salted in such quantities. The fishermen's wives retained these rights, however, and laid their sheets and pillowcases out to bleach on washdays. Before our time here, a principal had disliked this practice and threw a bucket of ashes over the lighthouse wall. That evening an angry group of fishermen appeared, demanding replacements for the damaged sheets and a promise this would not happen again.

One foggy day after many hours of the Boddam Bull, I heard a whistling through the gloom. I thought it was an SOS in Morse but John reckoned I was havering. He soon agreed that somebody was in trouble though, and I was sent running to the

RUBH REIDH

When the principal keeper at Rubh Reidh lighthouse became ill, I had to get there as quickly as possible. It was a slow journey to this far peninsula in the Western Highlands, which looked across to the Cuillins of Skye. An overnight stay at Achnasheen was necessary, but it was a meagre dinner that night – two lonely slices of corned beef and one small potato sat in the middle of a large plate.

The following day our bus stopped several times at hotels en route and most of the passengers disembarked to visit a bar. An army sergeant sitting beside me was going home on leave. From our last stop at Gairloch, we walked together along the road feeling quite merry. When we reached his house I was invited to join the family for a meal. A glass of pale golden whisky came with the dinner of roast lamb. 'Pure nectar, straight from the hills!' they said. After that I walked on air, in spite of my heavy suitcase, to cover the remaining desolate miles to the lighthouse. There I found that the two assistants were shorthanded and I took the watch from three till six in the morning.

They told me about a major incident in 1944 when an American steamship, the *William H, Welch*, had been wrecked while making for Loch Ewe in a winter storm. The keepers walked miles across the rocky hillside in blizzards to help the survivors. There had been little they could do, but comfort those still alive and pull bodies above the high tide line. Local crofters, who were Gaelic speakers, helped with blankets and flasks of tea. Some of the rescued Americans thought they had reached a Russian shore when they heard the strange language. Twelve of the 74 people aboard survived.

A pony and trap provided our only transport from the end of the rocky point to the nearest shop. Jean, the lighthouse pony, was a frightened animal, so I broke the whip and threw it away. We soon made friends and before long she whinnied for attention outside my bedroom window in the morning.

A few mines drifting off the lighthouse were then the only visible debris of war and I sank some of these with the station rifle. I repaired a broken creel with twigs from bushes and scraps of old herring net. This made a very effective new lobster pot and the second time it was hauled, it held four lobsters. Because no one had fished regularly in the war, I brought in consistently good catches. From a ledge below the lighthouse we could catch large pollock on rod and line. One of the keepers had his own boat and we caught jumbo haddock from this.

Twice we went trout fishing near Loch Ewe. After a long walk we came to a row of small lochs strung together by dark, bubbling burns and teeming with fish that had been undisturbed for years. I landed 92 one day and returned 60 to the water.

I returned to Buchan Ness after three months with a suitcase containing 11 cooked lobsters. The work at Rubh Reidh had been run-of-the-mill, but the fishing was unforgettable.

garage where Peter, the owner, had a big motor launch. By the time we got underway the whistling had stopped. The fog was thick and we could not locate the vessel at all. Luckily, the *Ferution* found a small coaster drifting without a propeller. She was towed to Peterhead with no casualties, and the *Ferution*'s skipper was awarded salvage money.

When another bad fog came down a Faeroese fishing boat, making for Aberdeen, anchored off the lighthouse. We knew all the rocks where we set our lobster creels and John exclaimed:

'That boat is on top of a big rock. When the tide goes out she'll be wrecked!'

'I'll go and warn them,' I said.

I rowed out in our dinghy but had difficulty in making the crew understand, so I pointed to a safe channel. They were so pleased that they gave me a pound of tea and some oranges, which delighted our families.

Not all rescue missions had such a happy outcome. A local boy had been given a new bike for his thirteenth birthday, and was trying it out on a road from Boddam that ran to the top of the cliffs. He pedalled as fast as he could but lost control at the summit and went straight over the edge. We were asked to pick him up immediately, to beat the tide. The little body felt like crumpled eggshells as we lifted him down from a ledge. One of his shoes had been caught in a crevice and I climbed back to fetch it – it seemed wrong to leave anything of his, though he would never need it again. He was still alive when we reached the pier, but he died soon after.

Angus was great friends with John's sons, Willie and Angus. On Willie's tenth birthday Angus went to tea at their house. Afterwards, the boys set off for the harbour and found a wooden box on the shore; inside it was a little metal object wrapped in straw. Willie lifted out the treasure and carried it under his jersey. This soon became tiresome, so he threw it down on the shingle. There was a tremendous explosion, and he screamed and rolled down a bank.

Peggy and I heard the bang, saw a cloud of blue smoke, and ran outside. Angus came rushing towards us with Willie's brother, both white faced and crying. Two fishermen carried Willie indoors and laid him on the kitchen floor. They put a pillow under his head and Peggy tried to stop the bleeding from a dreadful wound above his heart. I fetched John from the village. He was in shock; all he could do was say, 'He's dead! He's dead, isn't he?' again and again. The village policeman arrived and tried to make Peggy leave, saying, 'This is no place for a woman!' But she stayed to comfort Willie and wipe away the blood. Nothing more could be done though and the little boy died before the doctor came.

Police enquiries indicated that it had been a German booby trap device that had been washed in on the tide. Willie had been a cheerful, popular boy and most of his classmates attended the funeral. They came to see their friend's open coffin first; a moving sight, as each child filed past solemnly and touched Willie's forehead. His parents were left distraught and many of us mourned with them.

One morning at sunrise, quite late in the war, I extinguished the light and went to the house to make a cup of tea. It was about five o'clock, and suddenly the bell rang. I opened the front door to find a tall, tired-looking man with a bicycle. His trousers were soaking and dripped onto the stone step.

'Good morning,' I said. 'What can I do for you?'

'Will you give me a drink of water, please?' he asked in a guttural accent.

'Where have you come from, so early in the morning?'

'I come from the north.'

'And where are you going?'

'I go to a place called Aberdeen. Do you know it?'

'Yes,' I told him. 'Wait here and I will bring you water.'

I went through to wake Peggy and asked her to tell the principal immediately – I was sure the stranger was a German spy. I kept him talking on the doorstep and held on to the glass. He repeated that he had come from the north but would not say why. Finally, I handed him the water, which he drank greedily before cycling off. John had acted promptly, for as the cyclist reached the gate, two policemen stepped from behind the pillars and grabbed him. By this stage of the war any remaining enemy agents were not highly trained and we had been briefed about their activities. Four spies had landed on the Moray coast from a U-boat and were captured within 24 hours.

Two of us stood on the lighthouse balcony one night to watch strange lights flashing in the distance. We heard later from someone with a key job in London that they were probably rockets. It was about that time that the Germans were testing their newest weapons at Peenemünde.

Shortly before the war ended I was asked to show a group of Luftwaffe officers around the lighthouse. They had all been shot down in action and were housed at a nearby prisoner of war camp. A guard accompanied the men, who were quite pleasant; they seemed to accept what had happened to them.

Soon after the war, I was involved in the rescue of several Germans. Whenever we had stormy weather, I listened to the distress frequency on the radio in the house, which was not popular with the rest of the family if there was a programme they wanted! One evening I picked up a very faint call. It came again, slightly louder and clearer: 'Mayday! Mayday! Mayday! This is the German ship ——. We are sinking off the Heligoland buoy and require immediate assistance.' Exact details of their position followed and the message was repeated in German. I phoned the Peterhead coastguard. He had not heard the call but quickly contacted a Dutch lifeboat station, and the Scheveningen lifeboat rescued 15 men. We received a letter of thanks, but not everyone was happy that I aided a German crew so soon after the war, with some saying that I should have let them drown. There was also consternation among the coastguards as to why they had not heard this SOS; they had powerful radios while I picked it up on an ordinary set. A wireless expert suggested that the signal had bounced, missing their area yet coinciding with ours.

When Stewart was transferred he was replaced by Bill, with his wife Margaret and their family. We had wonderful musical evenings at Buchan Ness – Kathleen played the piano, Angus and his pal John sang, our friend Ian played the clarinet, and Bill joined in with his fiddle. Soon Angus started to learn the bagpipes and John asked his father for fiddle lessons.

In the first spring of the new peacetime we were particularly busy painting at Buchan Ness, restoring the imposing tower to its former brilliant white with a broad red band. Covering the sombre grey was a long job. Once, John sent Jim, our occasional, to paint the outside of the lantern astragals. This was a very tricky job that involved standing on the unguarded grating 100 feet or so from the ground. Jim was not used to working like this, and after a while I went to see how he was managing. I found he had frozen and was hanging onto the grips between the panes with both hands. 'I'm getting on fine,' he said bravely. 'But I canna pent.' He had to be helped down.

Another year, our spring painting was delayed by bad weather; when a brilliant day came along John decided to lime wash the tower. Upon sorting out the gear, we found that one of the ropes for the wooden stage had been badly chafed, probably the work of rats during the winter. In our haste to replace it, we did not straighten every kink thoroughly from the coil of new manila and we wasted no time in lowering the platform with John and his bucket of lime on board. Jim went to the balcony to push it round as required while I stayed below to handle the ropes. To our dismay, the stage spun two or three times, tightening the lines. 'I'm completely stuck, Archie!' John shouted. 'I can't go up or down. I'll be here the rest of the day.' I shoved a pickaxe handle down the leg of my trousers and shinned down a rope from the balcony. John pushed the stage away from the tower with his long-handled paint brush and I spun the twisted lines till they were clear. That was pretty tiring and I only managed the climb back with difficulty. As I approached the balcony, Jim tried to help by pulling me up by the hair – extremely painful, but I did not have enough breath to shout 'let go!' When I clambered over the rail I could see Kathleen down in the courtyard. Biting her knuckles with fear, she had watched the whole episode.

On a different occasion, I was working on top of the dome with an artificer, and we were servicing the weathervane when a screwdriver slipped out of his hand. This landed in the gutter below the dome, and the man slid after it. I nearly died of fright, thinking he was away. Just in time, he dug his heels in to brake. 'I often do that!' he laughed.

About four years after the war our friend Ian came to the lighthouse with a young Austrian, Rupert, who had cycled all the way through England and Scotland to look for a grave at Peterhead. Ian remembered our talking of the submariner who died on the cliff and wondered if it might be the same person. Now Rupert produced a photograph of a young lad, his brother, proudly wearing a new uniform and I looked at the face I could never forget. He told us that his brother had been only 17 when he died before our eyes. We had tea and cycled to see where he was buried. Rupert wept as he found the grave, which was beautifully kept with a vase of fresh flowers. Eventually his family took the boy's body back to Lentz, where their father was a goldsmith.

After restrictions on the light had been lifted, birds gradually came back to the lantern. One morning I picked up a Leach's fork-tailed petrel from the balcony, the only one I saw on the east coast. In Boddam we had become friendly with the local doctor who was a keen naturalist. He took the corpse to illustrate a talk he was giving on seabirds. As he showed it to his audience, he said, 'a living bird is a beautiful creature, but just a bundle of feathers when it is dead.' One sparkling sunny morning I stood outside our door with him.

'The sea looks wonderful today,' I commented.

'Archie,' he said, 'that is the floor of heaven!'

He drove down to Perthshire periodically on his way to Blairgowrie, and several times he took me to Butterstone, where Kate welcomed us with tea and boiled eggs.

After nine years, we had to pull up our roots and leave many friends – we were bound for the Isle of Man. I said farewell to the fishermen, some of whom I would

Left: Uncle Peter & Aunt Kate in their later years, revisited at Butterstone.

Right: Revisiting Uncle Peter – from Buchan Ness.

meet again in other ports. As well as remembering these folk, we often recalled their song, 'The Boddamers hanged the monkey, oh!' It told of a ship that foundered as it came into Boddam harbour. The only survivor was a large black monkey that the villagers thought was the Devil, so they hanged it on a post by the harbour:

There was a ship came roon the coast
And a' the men in her were lost
Except the monkey, it climbed the post
And the Boddamers hanged the monkey oh!
Dirra ma doo ma daddy oh!
The Boddamers hanged the monkey oh!

The folk came doon fae Peterheed
And they were gan tae have a feed
They made it into potted heed
And scoffed the blinkin' monkey oh!
Dirra ma doo ma daddy oh!
The Boddamers hanged the monkey oh!

9

Skerryvore

1944–1953, *INTERMITTENTLY WHILE AT BUCHAN NESS*

LIGHT ESTABLISHED IN 1844
UNPAINTED GRANITE TOWER 138 FEET TALL
ENGINEER – ALAN STEVENSON

The telephone call to Buchan Ness instructed me to: 'Get to Oban tomorrow and join the *Hesperus* for Skerryvore'. Their principal keeper was ill and I was to replace him for six weeks.

My grandfather had been a keeper at Skerryvore from 1870 to 1884, and Peggy's father served there during the First World War. Her mother had received a letter from him by bottle post, dated January 1916. Cast into the sea at the lighthouse, this was washed up on an Erraid beach:

Skerryvore Lighthouse, Monday Jany 10th 16

My Dear Joan

Just a few lines by "Bottle Post" to wish you and the bairns a happy New Year. I hope it will reach you safe and find you all well. We are all first class here, plenty to eat and drink but wearying for news from the shore, we have had none since I came on. Give the enclosed note to Wilson, Matheson is going to send off a bottle also so I trust one of them may reach the shore, hoping for good news from you soon. Your affectionate husband

Willie

Unlike Dhuheartach, this grey pillar did not appear forbidding as we approached. Often called the most beautiful lighthouse in the world, Skerryvore had the elegant lines of a tall oak's trunk. Dark granite from Tiree was used to build the three lower courses of the tower, but this was so hard that the workmen kept breaking tools during the early days of construction. Softer pale granite was taken from a quarry in Erraid to complete the building.

The light marked a seven-mile reef that bristled with outcrops; a series of flanking skerries helped to break the tumble of rough waters. Great numbers of seals covered these rocks; some hauled out on ours when we were indoors. Generally the landing conditions here were not as extreme as at Dhuheartach. The main rock was usually exposed, except in gales. There were two landings at Skerryvore, the Gulley and the Grating. The Gulley was only used on calmer days, typically in the summer. Here the crane was fixed permanently into the rock for winching men and equipment ashore; water, coal, and the annual delivery of stores arrived here. With the crane always in place and ready for use, the Gulley was the quicker and easier of the two landings. Further round at the Grating, the derrick was stored at the base of the tower and had to be erected when needed. However, the ship's boat could anchor broadside on to land keepers and their gear here.

Once a keeper had lost his rock box when it dropped off the derrick; it was washed up on a Harris beach eventually.

Skerryvore – landing at the Grating. (NLB)

LANDING ON THE SKERRYVORE ROCK

In 1814 Sir Walter Scott had joined the Commissioners and Robert Stevenson on the lighthouse yacht, a forerunner of the *Pharos,* for a six week cruise around the Scottish coast. The purpose of landing here was to survey the site for a new lighthouse in dangerous waters where 31 wrecks had already been recorded. Scott wrote of their arrival at the Skerryvore rock:

> At length, by dint of exertion, come in sight of this long ridge of rocks (chiefly under water), on which the tide breaks in a most tremendous style. There appear a few low, broad rocks at one end of the reef...These are never entirely under water, though the surf dashes over them...Pull through a very heavy swell with great difficulty and approach a tremendous surf dashing over black pointed rocks. Our rowers, however, get the boat into a quiet creek between two rocks where we contrive to land well wetted...and but for their assistance with the help of ropes some of the party must have been left in the boat...We took possession of the rock in name of the Commissioners...the rock was carefully measured by Mr Stevenson. It will be a most desolate position for a lighthouse - the Bell Rock and Eddystone a joke to it, for the nearest land is the wild island of Tyree at fourteen miles distance.

Robert Stevenson had reported:

> At Skerryvore we found the landing difficult, and the nimblest of sailors found it a task to climb up the sloping face of the rock...owing to the glassy smoothness of the rock, rendered so from being the resting place of hundreds of seals.

The *Hesperus* anchored in a heavy swell. After a trouble-free landing at the Grating, we dismantled the derrick and climbed the 25 feet to the door. There were 11 floors from there to the light room. This was the roomiest and most comfortable accommodation I found at a pillar light. The kitchen had small chairs with padded backs and arms, a great improvement on the stools at Dhuheartach. The walls of the kitchen and food store were lined with wood, and the balcony was the most ornamental I had seen in the Service.

Looking down on the scattering of rocks, we could see why many ships had been lost here; at times we were surrounded by foaming white water and lots of the jagged tops were submerged. It was said that before the lighthouse was built, rents in Tiree were higher on the Hynish side because so much flotsam could be salvaged there from shipwrecks.

The tall lens was quite beautiful in design; complex, with smaller bulls' eyes. It took a long time to clean, usually with a dry chamois, but methylated spirits removed the most obstinate marks. The light itself presented no problems. It was very well maintained and the autoform lamp was familiar. Because the tower was so high, the machine did not have to be wound as often as every hour.

The ship delivered the water supply a week after I arrived. The day and the weather were chosen so that she could lie off for hours. Her boat made repeated trips to the Gulley, loaded with barrels. We worked hard all day, though it stayed fine and the *Hesperus* crew were fit and efficient.

A sling full of breakers was winched in from the boat. Each was manhandled along the grating to the tower – some were rolled and others were pushed. I found it quicker to roll as there was a knack to pushing a breaker – it was better tilted on end to make it slide. From the foot of the tower, we heaved each one to the door by block and tackle. Bringing a breaker safely through the door was the most dangerous part of the operation. If it was knocked, the clips on the end of the rope would fly off. I had seen someone badly injured at the Bell Rock when a full barrel broke loose and fell from the door, glancing off a step with full force. This time I was up at the door and guided each breaker in, took off the clips and rolled it to the man behind me. He emptied it into the tank and passed back the empty. Empties were removed the same day as there was no space to store them. The ship always carried the year's coal on the same trip in case it could be delivered too, but there was no time for coal today. (Years later Bobbie simplified the watering operation when he was master of the *Hesperus*. He designed a tank for the ship's boat; used with a hose and portable motor pump, this saved a lot of time and work. Soon paraffin was delivered by similar means.)

The two assistants were conscientious, so everything was immaculate and up to date. I could rely on either man and had no worries that the light might fail or stand; I knew that the last person on night watch would close the lantern blinds as soon as he extinguished the light. However, as acting principal I did not intend to wash dishes, and that was unpopular with one.

After breakfast two of us started the daily programme of cleaning before carrying the big paraffin can upstairs for that night. We kept an eye on the little container of methylated spirits and saw that there was always enough for lighting up.

A small polished brass container on the lightroom wall was the petrol tank for a small Stuart Turner engine which charged the batteries in the radio beacon. It was housed on the east side of the balcony and had to be topped up once a week. All the fuels were stored down in the oil cellar. Some years later a fire raced through the inflammable liquids and gutted the lighthouse.

The fog signal here had to be triggered by hand from the lightroom. When conditions required, a charge of guncotton was fired through the top of the dome

Hoisting up fresh water at Skerryvore. (NLB)

every five minutes. The guncotton was loaded into the top of a metal tube; the keeper turned a handle to wind up the tube and the trigger was pressed. The height of the tower meant that the report could be heard quite a long way out to sea.

There was not much to do here in spare time. On good days we could walk around the base of the tower or along the grating. A couple of times I went swimming with Danny, one of the assistants, when the surrounding water was exceptionally calm. One afternoon we set an iron bar into a rock for a joke – we thought people would wonder why and how it got there. Danny stuck the bar into a belt round his waist and I took a hammer. We swam out in sunshine at low water in a quiet sea. Danny held the bar while I drove it securely into a crevice. Quite pleased with ourselves, we were heading back when I heard a scream from Danny – a seal was attacking his legs under the water. Twice it came at him with its mouth open. I yelled and thrashed the surface to scare it off. It only turned at the last minute and did not bite him, but he felt it touch his skin. We had never heard of a seal attacking anyone, though we thought that the movement of white legs in the sea had attracted its attention. Danny was much shaken and we never swam there again.

At the end of my first month, Danny was due to go ashore. That day the weather was bad and a heavy sea was running. When the chief officer radioed, I said I did not think a landing would be possible. Danny was very angry and grabbed the microphone to say it would be all right at low water. The chief asked me again, but I repeated that in my opinion, no relief could be made. 'That's what we think too. We'll call you again tomorrow,' he replied. Our tempers frayed easily when we were due to be taken off and Danny probably resented my taking charge of his station. He went away to his bedroom and I did not see him for hours. But he recovered his usual good humour and left the next day with no ill feeling.

About 50 years later a Lighthouse Board engineer came to visit me. By then the Skerryvore light was automatic and he had just flown by helicopter to carry out maintenance. Did I know why there was an iron post on one of the outlying rocks? He could not understand what it was for in the middle of nowhere. I was amazed to hear it was still there!

A year or two after my first spell at Skerryvore, I was sent back as an assistant. The principal, George, was on duty, but he and his crew were new to the station and needed help with the landing gear. George and I had first met first years before when he was a young keeper at North Ronaldsay and I was unloading stores from the *Pharos*. We had family connections: his sister was married to my cousin Finlay.

As we approached the lighthouse on this occasion, a strong easterly was blowing. Because of the shallow water, the *Hesperus* had to lie off about three quarters of a mile. It was going to be too rough to land at the Gulley.

'We can't use the Grating, with no derrick set up. I don't know what we'll do,' Jim said. (Peggy's brother, Jim, was now second mate of the *Hesperus*.)

Barra Head viewed from the Sound of Berneray (watercolour by Duncan Baillie).

Barra Head (photograph by Ian Cowe).

*Above: Flannan Isles
(photograph by
Ian Cowe).*

*Far left: Tarring the
Chanonry dwelling
house roof in the 1970s
– Archie supervises a
junior helper.*

*Left: Archie tending
the Chanonry light
in the 1970s.*

Right: Covesea Skerries.

Turnberry lighthouse (watercolour by Duncan Baillie).

From inside Chanonry lantern, looking east.

The view to the west from inside Chanonry lantern.

Still fishing lobsters in retirement.

Fingal's *last visit to Chanonry, 1999.*

Preparing the creels, 1982.

Sunset at St Abbs Head (photograph by Ian Cowe).

Archie at Chanonry – a year before retiring as principal lightkeeper.

'There's no way we can land with this sea. But if you take me round, there's a ledge I can jump on to.'

'Are you sure?'

'Yes, I've done it from the *Pharos*,' I said.

The motor man was not happy at having to keep his engine running in unfamiliar water; however, it was calmer round the south-west corner. I jumped from the bow on to a flat patch of rock and was grabbed by George to stop me from slipping on the seaweed. One of the crew tied a line to my kit bag and threw it after me; the boat left rapidly with cheery waving.

The young assistant on duty with us was a nice fellow, but he had never worked at a rock before. Earlier, George's hot temper had finally got the better of him:

'The other day I found that lad boiling his dirty shirt in the soup pot. It was the last straw! And I did not know how to put up the derrick,' he added.

'We'll soon sort that, when the weather's better. It's like the one on Dhuheartach. By the way, what happened to the soup pot?'

'I threw it straight out of the window!' said George.

I thought it better not to ask if the shirt had gone with it. Our soup was made in a smaller pot for the rest of that month.

As soon as the weather improved I showed the others how to rig the equipment at the Grating. The derrick was kept bolted to the base of the tower with strong clips. We always followed a strict routine, working swiftly. Everything had to be absolutely ready when the boat arrived, but nothing was set up in advance in case of damage.

The grating would be covered from half tide. Preparations began towards low water on the ebb. Throughout the operation the man in charge watched to see that the other two would not be swept away. They threaded the safety rope for a hand rail through iron stanchions. Reminders were given that a shout of 'look out!' meant run out along the grating, clutch the derrick with hands and feet, and keep your eyes shut till the wave subsided. Once the safety rope was in place, we carried the derrick to the seaward end of the grating. We attached three rope stays and the block and tackle. The other ends of the stays would be fixed to rings on the rock, two on either side and one at the top. This made a stabilising triangle so that the derrick went into the right position and the pintel slotted into its socket in the grating. The time for dismantling and stowing was brief.

For practice, we carried out the procedure twice. At the next relief the crew set it up perfectly, but a gale blew up before everything was dismantled. We rushed to get the derrick stowed and had just screwed it down when the seas broke heavily over the rock. Abandoning the lines, we scurried like ants up the ladder to the door. The lines were washed away and we made a new set the next day.

Since I was acting assistant this time, I took a turn as cook and shared the dishwashing. Our food at Skerryvore was pretty good. New bread had to be made when the last of the loaves went mouldy; fortunately, my baking had improved and there were no complaints! I often made semolina, tapioca, or rice puddings – tasty and easy. The usual barrel of salt meat sat in the store room above the kitchen, and dried fish hung on a line. As at all rocks, we ate plenty of soup at midday, often with the piece of meat that was sliced for the main course.

After dinner one day, my fellow assistant went upstairs to sleep; George was going to take the afternoon watch.

'Before you go for a sleep, take a look. There's a mine coming in to the rock,' he said, gazing out of the kitchen window. I saw it, 50 or 60 yards off, being driven by the tide. 'I'm going down with the pole to try to fend it off,' he added. The pole was like an extra-long boat hook and kept inside the door for fishing objects out of the sea; very useful for anything that fell over the side of the boat. Although we had three rifles, we could only shoot at mines from a safe distance.

'I don't think that's wise,' I said. 'If you touch one of the horns it'll explode and kill you. If you do go, I'm coming with you.'

'You'll stay to look after things in case it does explode,' said George. 'I'm the principal and you'll do as you are told.'

'You may be principal, but I am still coming with you. If it explodes, it will demolish the tower and us with it. So I might as well be down there.'

He was not pleased, but muttered, 'Alright,' adding that I was a thrawn so-and-so. By the time we reached the rock, the mine was only ten yards away and then it became stuck at an angle. 'Look! I think the tide has turned. It might drift away with the ebb,' I said. Although the waves seemed to be getting smaller, the mine still leant to one side. We waited and watched for at least 20 minutes. At last it started floating off to the west and we heaved a sigh of relief. From the kitchen we watched till the mine disappeared, possibly caught in a large patch of seaweed that Danny and I had seen during our swim.

German visitors

Occasionally, for fun, we picked up the flashing of the heliograph from Erraid. One message from Skerryvore had proved invaluable during the First World War. While Peggy's father was there, a German submarine was wrecked in the vicinity. Some of the crew survived and swam to the lighthouse where the keepers looked after them – the duties of a lightkeeper included rescuing seamen in distress, whatever their nationality. I cannot imagine how difficult it was to live so closely confined with enemy sailors. The Germans were glad to be alive after their ordeal and grateful to be fed. When the provisions began to run out, a heliograph signal to Erraid indicated that something was wrong and a ship took the Germans off the rock.

My old friend Jimmy from Dhuheartach arrived as relieving keeper for my second month, and there was plenty of news to exchange. From Skerryvore we could actually see Dhuheartach lighthouse and the flat outline of Tiree, albeit through a telescope on a clear day. Ships were visible in the distance, but they seldom came close.

There were noticeably fewer birds at Skerryvore than at Dhuheartach, though both my spells here were in summer, so I did not see any migrants. Gannets did not dive near the tower in the shallower water but they could be seen at a distance. Guillemots and razorbills perched on points of the reef or swam in the sea. Sometimes clouds of gulls would fly around, 'circling for wind' we said; a sign of wind that generally brought rain. No unexpected visitors crashed into the lantern – stronger panes had been used since a mallard duck burst through a pane at Hyskeir lighthouse.

Both Jimmy and I left at the next relief and the regular crew took over again. As the *Hesperus* approached Oban we passed a group of Catalina flying bnoats anchored in Kerrera Bay. These occasionally flew over Dhuheartach, although we had not seen them on the water before.

George and I kept in touch and he was a much-valued friend. We both fought for better conditions in the Lighthouse Service and met from time to time at meetings in Edinburgh. George would put forward spirited and well-presented arguments on behalf of keepers, and sometimes I had to calm the situation when his forthright approach was opposed by the Commissioners.

Years later, when Bobbie was master of the *Fingal*, he spoke of making reliefs at Skerryvore. 'It was a dangerous place,' he said. 'One day the boat was approaching the landing and the three keepers were ready to meet it when a heavy sea swept the grating. Only the top of the derrick was visible. When the water subsided only one keeper could be seen; the other two had disappeared. They found one man in the water under the grating, holding on to one of its legs; the other man was hanging over the side, with one arm caught in a cleat. The men were very lucky. My boat crew did not think they would see them again.'

10

Flannan Isles

1944–1953, *INTERMITTENTLY WHILE AT BUCHAN NESS*

LIGHT ESTABLISHED 1899
WHITE TOWER 23 METRES HIGH, ELEVATION 101 METRES
ENGINEERS – D. ALAN STEVENSON

It was October when I was sent from Buchan Ness to take charge at the Flannan Isles, 16 miles west of Lewis, for a spell. Two retired men, Malcolm and Norman, were coming to assist. We were needed because the principal and one assistant were ill; the other had resigned. Few new lightkeepers had been appointed during the war and there was now a shortage of manpower. Malcolm had been the occasional here but had retired a few years previously. Norman had no experience at all as a keeper; he had been a fireman on the *Hesperus*. He and I had glimpsed this little white tower on its cliff, though neither of us had ever climbed the steps from the landing.

I had been given no information about this particular light. Although my father had been stationed here before I was born, he had mentioned no details to do with the lighting. Rather, he had spoken about the Flannan Isles disaster and his three colleagues who disappeared without trace during a storm in 1900. On the way to the lighthouse I had to spend two nights near the shore station at Breasclete until the *Pole Star* collected us. I was made welcome at Malcolm's croft where I tried to glean some information from him about operating the light. His only response was: 'I have forgotten, Archie!'

The lighthouse was in a prominent position on the 200-foot cliffs of Eilean Mhor, the largest island of the Flannans group. The top of Eilean Mhor was covered with rich-looking grass that was nibbled by rabbits, though no one could say how or when they first came there. The rest of the island was pure rock. Lightkeepers here knew that they had exceptionally wild and unpredictable waters to contend with; there was an east and a west landing used by the ship's boat according to the weather's variable moods.

Flannan Isles Disaster

The last entry in the log, on 15 December 1900, recorded a storm of exceptional violence. It left such dreadful damage at the west landing as never seen before or since. An excerpt from the Official Report to the Commissioners by the superintendent of the day described:

> The iron railway at the side of the path … was wrenched out of the concrete, and twisted in a manner difficult to believe unless actually seen. A large block of stone weighing upwards of 20cwt had been dislodged from its position higher up and carried down and left on the concrete path … A lifebuoy fastened to the railings along this path had been torn away from its fastenings by the force of the sea, pieces of canvas adhering to the ropes by which it had been fastened to the railing.

In the middle of the month a ship reported that no light could be seen when passing the Flannan Isles, nor could it be seen from the nearest point on Lewis. The *Hesperus* was sent to investigate, with Joe Moore on board as the relieving keeper. No one was at the landing to meet them, despite the ship being visible from the lighthouse while several miles away.

Two of the sailors walked up to the lighthouse with Joe; they found the door of the house shut, but not locked. Two sets of oilskins were missing, and one was still hanging on its hook. After a quick search, they ran back to the waiting boat. They reported that there was no sign of life and it looked as if the men had left in a hurry.

The *Hesperus* left, returning in a matter of days with Joe and two more keepers to man the light. Four armed sailors accompanied them and stayed for a month. Replacements for the men who had disappeared were not easy to come by – there was a psychological barrier to be overcome – in spite of keepers being a hardy and stoical bunch.

Father had been part of the team that helped to build the lighthouse, and was there for the ceremonial lighting in October 1899. He therefore knew the keepers – James Ducat, Thomas Marshall, Donald McArthur, and Joe Moore – well, and said they were sound, experienced keepers. He was sent back in February 1901 as part of a replacement crew, then stayed as an assistant for three years, but Joe Moore was transferred in March 1901.

The new principal thought the three had been swept away by a wave while working on the crane and devised a hook on a rope to stop anyone else being lost. The superintendent's opinion was 'that an extra large sea had rushed up the face of the rock, had gone above them, and coming down with immense force, had swept them completely away.' His report suggests that the men had 'gone down to secure a box in which the mooring ropes, landing ropes, etc. were kept, and which was secured in a crevice in the rock about 110 feet above sea level.' Ropes were strewn crazily across the cliff face, and although the 40-foot crane was still secure, some of its holding clips had been loosened. Some people thought that one of the keepers had gone mad and killed the others, or they had all drowned in a struggle; others supposed they had been abducted by aliens.

The missing oilskins suggested something out of the ordinary, but there were no more positive clues. Unless they faced a 'life and death' situation, all three would never have abandoned the lighthouse. It was a rule in the Service that keepers must never leave a lighthouse unattended; one man should always stay.

I dismissed immediately the fantastic theories that surfaced from time to time, and became convinced that an emergency far more urgent than saving ropes had demanded that they risk their lives. Father said that they always kept a spare hundred fathoms of rope in their store. Keepers were used to preparing lines from a new coil; it would only take a couple of hours to replace all that they needed for the boat and the crane. These men were practical and used to extreme weather conditions; some, if not all, had been at sea before becoming lightkeepers.

I visited Joe Moore around 1930; by this time he had retired and was living on the north coast. He was still a tall, strong-looking man and spoke freely about looking for his lost colleagues. 'We searched every nook and cranny on the island,' he told me. 'Three good men; they were drowned, but I don't know how.'

A steep flight of steps had been cut out of the rock face above each of these platforms. On the east side the neighbouring island, Eilean Tighe, gave a little shelter but the west landing always posed danger, open to the North Atlantic and exposed to every blast. We were very aware that its destructive rollers could take us by surprise.

From my time as bowman of the *Pharos* at reliefs I remembered the 'seventh wave' – a phenomenon here that could produce colossal, life-threatening waves. While we were landing a man or stores, the ship would signal when an exceptional wave passed under her. One toot on her whistle warned of something big; two toots for extra big and a sign to move the boat out as the water washed over the landing. Usually we did not leave anything moveable on the lower platform, but I had seen a box of artificers' tools disappear into the sea for good.

During a relief in 1911, a keeper had lost the station's mail bag and all his clothes. The ship's captain reported that the men were almost swept away themselves when 'unexpectedly overwhelmed' by the sea. The keeper was severely reprimanded however and told that the mail bag should 'invariably be kept in a place of undoubted safety'. How the safe place could be found was not explained!

The day I arrived the wind was easterly and we landed on the west side in relative calm, though even then the waves were charging into the deep gulley beside us. There the boat could take us right in to climb the fixed steps to the platform; easier than being winched ashore. The three departing crew members were waiting for us on the lower landing, shook our hands, and the principal said, 'Everything's ready for you. Good luck!' All our gear and supplies were transferred quickly to the relative safety of the upper platform. Small items were carried up the first flight of steps by sailors

A derrick landing at the Flannan Isles. (NLB)

and keepers while heavy goods were lifted by crane. We had to get a move on as it was already afternoon and lighting time would be early.

A small bogie ran up the cliff on a miniature railway line to carry fuel and provisions to the lighthouse. This truck was cleverly designed with larger wheels at the back to keep it level on the steep incline, and a steel cable connected it to the engine which was housed in a hut beside the lighthouse. Branch lines from each of the landings met at a junction known as Charing Cross. In the hut at the top there was a telephone and another, in a sturdy metal box, was fixed to the rock at the west landing.

I asked Norman to go up and start the steam engine for the bogie. I thought this would be familiar to him as a ship's fireman, but before long a frantic voice came over the phone: 'There's an enormous fire under this boiler and no water in it. It'll burst any minute and I'm getting out!' I hurried to the top, where he was waiting for an explosion at a safe distance from the hut. The boiler had been overfilled by the departing crew, which explained why the level did not register on the gauge. Having used steam winches on the *Pharos*, I had enough experience to get the engine running. Care was needed as someone once started the engine too soon and a sailor who was still loading the truck had his hand crushed under its wheels. Now it arrived safely at the top of the line with its load. It hit the buffers with a resounding smack because I did not shut off the steam in time; fortunately, no harm was done. Leaving Norman to shovel hot coals out of the firebox to calm his nerves, I walked over to the empty house, which was attached to the tower. There was an eeriness about that lonesome, grey autumn afternoon. Thinking of the men who had vanished, I wondered what I would find when I opened the door. Everything had been left in perfect order by the previous crew however, and the fire in the kitchen was set and ready to light. I looked into the bedrooms and threw my cap on the bed in the single room, leaving the bunks for Malcolm and Norman in the second.

There were urgent matters to deal with now and the three of us went to look at the light, which, I was glad to find, consisted of a familiar type of lamp and machine. Malcolm remembered how to operate everything after all and I soon found that he was a good and reliable man. We lit the light and had it revolving to character in plenty of time.

Then we discovered that the radio would not work. The batteries needed charging, but we could not find any jubilee clips – these were essential. Eventually I improvised by cutting two strips from a sheet of brass and hammering them until springy enough; a tip once learnt from an artificer. This enabled us to get on the air that evening. Since the tragedy of 1900, vigilance here was especially strict, and we were expected to speak to our shore station, Breasclete, three times a day. If no message was received by night ime, the *Pole Star* would set off immediately to see what was wrong.

As Norman had never been a keeper, we showed him quickly what to do on watch. The first time he took over on his own though, he got into difficulties, and before long the alarm bell rang in the kitchen; the light had stood very briefly when he allowed the machine to run down too far. To remedy this, he needed to turn the lens by hand, while I righted the weight on its chains. I told him to wind up every 25 minutes to prevent it happening again. Years later a warning device comprising a clicking brass tongue (because the clockwork mechanism worked silently) was fitted at lighthouses. This sounded as the weight approached the bottom of the chain.

The lens was huge, with two hinged panels forming doors. While one man was busy with a chamois leather inside, the second polished the outside, and we used a ladder to reach the top. We worked well as a team for a fortnight, until one afternoon when I found the other two locked in combat. The row was about tobacco, often a cause of trouble at rock lights. As both men were over 60 it was not difficult to separate them. I always kept a spare box of cigarettes in case of emergency, of which I gave 40 to Norman, with a warning that there must be no more trouble.

At first there was little time to dwell on the past. But I noticed that whenever the tragedy was mentioned, Malcolm walked away or changed the subject. 'Och yes, that was a bad thing,' was all he would say. I found it strange, though, to sleep in the bed of a man who had vanished and to eat at the table where the three took their meals.

One day the wind went into the northwest and battered us at storm force, straight from Nova Scotia it seemed. Everything moveable was taken indoors and we listened to the raging outside. From the lighthouse balcony we watched waves break over our cliff and drench Eilean Mhor. Two trawlers sheltered near the east landing and at daylight, with the easing of the wind, they moved on. We suffered no damage.

Some afternoons I went to watch the sea above the landing at the west side, though it was too dangerous to stand near the edge. Even in a moderate gale water would charge up the rock face. Such massive storm damage had occurred at the time the men were lost, it was no wonder our crane had been fastened securely to the rock. When it was fine enough, I saw the seals in this favourite gathering place of theirs. Dozens would jostle into the gulley with strange, haunting cries. They could not be seen when it was very rough and the sea thundered through the ravine. I wondered where they were on the day the men died; if they saw what happened from safe niches below. In more fanciful moments, I remembered myths in which human spirits assumed forms of seals.

This was a great stopping-off place for migrating birds. Although it was late in the year, I was lucky to see a few Leach's petrels scurry awkwardly to their stony hiding place at dusk. Their legs were designed for efficiency in water, not on land. Once when we opened the door on a day of strong easterly wind a very large goose walked in. One of the men wanted to kill it and give us a change of diet, but I would not let him. Instead, I mixed some oatmeal with bread and water and the bird gobbled this up. Then, to our amazement, the goose settled down in front of the kitchen fire. When the wind dropped we put it outside and it flew away. We thought this was probably a domesticated goose, driven over the sea to Eilean Mhor by bad weather.

I could see some sheep on neighbouring Eilean Tighe through binoculars. One ewe trailed a large fleece behind her and it was obvious that she had dodged the annual clipping for some years. We heard there were ruined houses which gave the island its name, but we could not see them. When we scanned the sea on moonlit nights we could make out the shapes of the other Seven Hunters (Flannan Isles).

After six weeks it was time to leave for home, with hospitality again from Malcolm and his wife. While I was with them I heard that the people of Lewis had not wanted a lighthouse to be built on the Flannan Isles – they were regarded as sacred and steeped in many superstitions. However, Eilean Mhor, the largest of the group, had offered a key position for a warning light, particularly for American ships. While low cloud lingered over the water, this higher site was often clear and visible from a distance.

I was glad to be back at Buchan Ness for a family Christmas and New Year; Malcolm and Norman could resume their retirement and I hoped I had seen the last of the Flannan Isles.

However, I was back the following November, this time to replace an assistant. A big sea was running as we sailed from Lewis and the *Pole Star* climbed doggedly over each great wave. While we watched fierce rollers on all sides, the captain promised he would take me ashore for Christmas. 'I'll see you are home in time,' he repeated, as I left in the ship's boat, but I wondered whether I would be lucky again.

On this occasion the keepers were waiting for us on the east side. Reluctantly, I climbed the steep steps from the landing. After a toot on the ship's whistle and a wave from her bridge, the three of us were alone. However, this was very different from the chill of my first arrival – there was a warm welcome from the two remaining men and a homely fire burned brightly in the kitchen. Acting as an assistant, I would have less responsibility and more spare time to explore.

The principal made our lives as agreeable as he could, with free afternoons when we were not on watch. He was extremely fond of chocolate and was frequently munching. Neither he nor his assistant left the house much apart from an occasional walk to the landings, whereas I used every opportunity to look at all the corners of the island. To pass the time I made a creel, though I could only set this on the east side as the west was always too wild. I caught a few crabs, but they were poor and watery, so we only ate the meat from their claws.

Below the lighthouse was a tiny chapel, a relic of sixth century Christianity in the Western Isles, and I crawled inside to have a look. St Flann had lived here as a hermit and people crossed from Lewis to bring him food. I was puzzled when I came across a group of grassy mounds which seemed, from my probings, like the remains of little stone houses. When I asked about these in Lewis some called them the 'last homes of the little people,' while others spoke of Druids and of bothies.

I still gravitated towards the west landing to watch the seals and wonder. I was preoccupied more than ever with trying to fathom why three keepers had vanished.

Again, it was the wrong season to see seabirds nesting on the Flannans, but I was fortunate to see a huge fall of migrants that came with a strong easterly gale. All the most common garden species were there, plus bramblings; most of these birds would have seemed more at home in a Butterstone wood and I wondered how many made it to the mainland. The wind changed after three days and they departed, except for a few that seemed too weak for the flight, and these were picked off by a peregrine falcon. He lived in the cliffs and swooped with wild cries that panicked the little birds, sending them into the open with nowhere to hide. His bloodcurdling calls suited the desolate place.

As Christmas approached I recalled the promise made to me on the ship. My hopes faded though when a gale arose a few days before I was due to leave. Then it eased a little, and to my delight we eventually sighted the *Pole Star* ploughing towards us through white water. 'I told you I would come,' said the captain, though we all knew how much these reliefs depended on weather and good seamanship.

I stayed at Malcolm's again on my way back to the east coast. He showed me the shed where they dried seaweed on the roof in summer sun, and on its other side they spread fish. His wife gave me a box of dried carrageen for Peggy who used it to make vanilla flavoured milk puddings, reminiscent of Scalpay dinners.

11

'Come and see the wild men at the Chicken Rock!'

Chicken Rock Lighthouse, Isle of Man

1953–1954

LIGHT ESTABLISHED 1875
GRANITE TOWER 44 METRES HIGH
ENGINEERS – DAVID AND THOMAS STEVENSON

Chicken Rock.

The sun shone on a patchwork of little green fields as the *Hesperus* drew near to the Isle of Man. We docked at Douglas, a cheerful holiday town with palm trees in front gardens. Horse-drawn charabancs carried sightseers along a seafront lined with hotels and guest houses.

Our new home was in Port St Mary. The block of houses was conspicuous in the street because a flagpole stood outside where the Board's flag was hoisted on Sundays and important occasions. In 1875 this shore station had replaced one at the Calf of Man, where it was said that 'nothing could grow in the garden for legions of rats'. Kathleen soon settled into school at Castleton; Angus had joined the RAF and came to the Isle of Man for every leave.

The Chicken Rock, known in the Service as 'The Chickens', earned its name from the colony of Manx shearwaters or 'Mother Carey's chickens' that nested on a nearby island.

In due course the lighthouse boat took me out from Port St Mary harbour. Reliefs here were easy; the boat could enter a gulley, making it possible to step straight on or off the rock. There was therefore no need for the dangerous business of rigging a derrick. The prospect of rock duty here was not so grim, with no more soakings on a derrick and no more wet clothes. What a novelty to come away in dry uniform, collar and tie, and walk a couple of hundred yards home from the harbour! Also we could be sure that turns on the rock would last only six weeks and we would have two weeks ashore.

The grey granite tower was 130 feet high but lacked the graceful lines of Skerryvore. As usual, we carried everything up the outside ladder to the door and pulled it on a downhaul, to the storeroom window. From there, each man collected his kit and stowed it in lockers under the bunks.

I found a very congenial team of keepers: Charlie was the principal, Alan and another Jimmy were the two assistants, and Neil was the occasional. He was quite elderly and stiff, but well able to stand in for anyone who was on leave or ill. His main duties were cooking, lighting up, and keeping a night watch. Charlie always made sure that Neil was given the opportunity to sleep in the afternoons. The islanders were very outgoing and made lighthouse staff welcome.

Although we had quite a lot of fog here, there was no foghorn, so in poor visibility we fired a guncotton charge; a signal that could be identified by its timing sequence. We also had more sunshine than was usual at Scottish lights and needed to be extra careful to pull the lantern blinds promptly in the morning. Sun could damage the installation because of the bullseyes – at one station a keeper had a hole burnt in his jacket when a blind was opened on a hot day. In summer we often wore shorts for work and could all have free afternoons if the weather was good (though one man was officially on watch and always on hand to fire the fog signal should conditions change). During the winter there was someone on watch all afternoon.

Charlie was a gem, leaving us to our own devices most of the time, and unlike any

Chicken Rock aerial view.

other principal I worked with. He did not believe in hard work and spent summer afternoons sunbathing on the balcony or on the rock. Among the signs on the pier at Port St Mary was a prominent notice saying: 'Come and See the Wild Men at the Chicken Rock!' Boatloads of sightseers circled the lighthouse rock in summer and waved to us. Charlie did cover up for modesty's sake when boat trips were in the offing.

A lot of work needed to be done when I arrived, so Jimmy and I had a major spring clean while Charlie was ashore, and at low water we lit a huge bonfire on the rock. The accumulated rubbish included boxes of surplus guncotton. It happened that HMS *Hermes* was in our area just then and her captain reported that the lighthouse appeared to be on fire! This was soon after Skerryvore had been gutted by fire so, not surprisingly, reactions were swift. As it happened, the Chickens was badly burnt seven years later.

At high tide our rock was underwater, and a coating of seaweed grew thickly on the exposed west side of the lighthouse to a height of 20 feet or so. This stubborn growth needed to be scraped off each spring using a rigged stage and ladder; it was a tough job the first time as it had not been tackled for years. We cleaned a large square at a time, giving the tower a chequer-board appearance until it was completed – a period of about four weeks.

Three times a day the keeper on watch took incoming messages on the VHF, and twice a day we contacted our radio station at Craigneish. This was manned by Bert, who was really a lightkeeper, but the radio demanded his full-time attention. He and his wife lived alone at Craigneish and Bert learnt to play the piano to relieve the tedium.

For some reason Charlie always started his radio messages by saying: 'Ring, tingaling ting, ting ting. This is the Chickens Rock.' Bert would respond: 'Hello Charlie! I hear you.' One day the *Pharos*, carrying the Commissioners, intercepted a call from Charlie to Bert. Later the general manager took me to one side at the lighthouse.

'Does the principal signal "Ring, tingaling" as a coded warning that the Commissioners are on the way?' he asked.

'Oh no,' I assured him, 'that's quite normal.'

We all knew this was just one of Charlie's little habits; the idea of his being so devious was absurd.

From the lighthouse, we kept in radio contact with the Morecambe Bay light vessel and gave them weather reports. During the Round Britain Yacht Race we reported the progress of each competing boat to the controller on the Isle of Man. The yachts came close, through the sheltered passage between us and the Calf of Man. Their crews waved, looking as pleased to see us as we were to see them.

There were other diversions too. This was the only pillar rock where we had 'droppers in' and very welcome they were too. Most weeks a local fishing boat came out with post and fresh baking from our wives, and the crew landed for a cup of tea. They often gave us a bag of scallops, which were prolific in the waters off Port Erin.

One day a group of schoolgirls with two teachers came over to see the lighthouse. It was quite tricky getting them safely up the ladder to the door – we had to put a safety rope round each child before escorting them on the long climb. They were quite nervous going up, but thrilled by the view from the balcony.

We were close to the route of the Canadian Pacific liners – huge white ships with red diced funnels going to and from Southampton. It was exciting to watch the *Empress of Canada* and her sister ships with passengers lining the decks. Jimmy and I always semaphored 'bon voyage' or 'welcome home'. Once, the *Empress of Scotland's* captain came to the Isle of Man for a holiday. He met Charlie, thanked him for these messages, and offered him a free passage to Montreal. We were so disappointed that he turned it down – we had sent the signals and would have loved a trip to Canada!

Jimmy and I joined the Port St Mary lifeboat crew and went on several training exercises. However, the Lighthouse Board informed us that this was against the rules and we had to give it up.

Charlie made huge quantities of wooden clothes pegs which he sold. He shaped them with great care from the staves of our butter barrels, puffing at his pipe as he worked. Mounds of shavings and chips accumulated until they were knee deep all round him. One day while he was on leave, I thought it was time for a big clean-up, so I removed all the debris from the workshop. But when he returned, he was angry – the only time I heard a cross word from Charlie. The artificers were flabbergasted to find a clean workshop when they came to service the lighthouse.

We played a lot of chess, though none of us had a hope of beating Charlie. If there was a classical concert on TV he would sit and conduct the orchestra with his pipe. When I commented, he said wryly, 'the trouble with you, my friend, is "The Four-legged Friend" is the only music you understand!' Jimmy made Morocco leather handbags and purses to sell and taught me how to make wallets. Alan did embroidery for his family.

Birdwatching became particularly interesting when we were asked to ring birds and record rarities for the Manx Museum. Jimmy was an expert birdwatcher and we had a great vantage point to observe the rich variety. Hundreds of Manx shearwaters flew between us and the Calf of Man. Several green woodpeckers landed at the lighthouse, probably en route from Europe. Jimmy found the body of a most unusual bird which was identified as a yellow-browed warbler, a first for the Isle of Man. Once we sighted a sooty albatross. It glided around with an occasional flap of its wings and stayed for two days; twitchers came over from England to catch a glimpse. In poor visibility, the Chickens was a haven for songbirds seeking the light. We collected boxfuls of little ones to save them from being trampled and released them the next morning: chiffchaffs, willow warblers, pipits, and goldcrests (20 goldcrests on one night alone).

We fished a lot from the rock. Saithe, wrasse and conger eels came to the lines, and plenty of crabs and occasionally lobsters to our creels. Only once did we eat a conger; it was good – with beautiful white flesh – but very rich. The saithe we gave to the visiting fishermen for bait.

Neil was fond of fishing and used a long, heavy bamboo rod. Jimmy decided to make one that would be easier for him to handle; a lovely little three-piece greenheart that he fitted up with a reel and line. Neil was delighted and tied on a lead weight so he could cast well out. He had never used this type of rod and reel before. After the first cast, he released the line too soon and the lead landed back at his feet, so he tried again and cast with an almighty heave. This time the line spiralled through the air; he let it go even sooner, and the lead landed on his bald head. Neil had a fiery temper and we could see him cursing; with gritted teeth, he broke the rod in pieces and stamped on it. He had cooled down by the time he had climbed to the kitchen, but he went back to the 16-foot bamboo rod for his next fishing session.

One day when I came out to the rock, I found Jimmy making an enormous kite in order to give us a new method of fishing. I helped him build the wooden frame, six feet by four, which we covered with discarded yellow blinds from the lantern. We sat on the rock and wove an exceedingly long line from old mooring ropes. The finished kite was cast off from the balcony with high hopes. But instead of flying over the sea, it spiralled downwards; repeated efforts also ended in crashes. Eventually, one of us climbed to the top of the dome and threw the kite into the air while the other stood on the balcony controlling the line, and this time it caught the true wind. Success at last! Now we could add a pulley half way along to carry our fishing line with its hooks and feathers attached.

Once the kite was flying steadily, we lowered the fishing line slowly to the seabed, pulled it up a foot or two and kept it moving. When the kite bobbed and we felt a tug on the line, we had to act quickly. During the long and precarious haul to the balcony fish often wriggled off the swaying line, some at the very last minute. Hungry gulls circled hopefully. After a few adjustments had been made we caught plenty; mostly saithe, but one day we had a sea bream. We never knew what was hooked till it was landed safely; it was an exciting new method of fishing.

The kite came into its own when the sea was too rough for the boat to land stores safely. Provided conditions were not extreme, Johnny, the boatman, attached a strong bag to the end of the line. In this he put mail, newspapers, and bread to be hauled to the kitchen window, though he could not send more than two loaves at a time. Once we even took up medicine for Alan. We never lost anything, despite the load dipping now and then; the kite did not break, but the screws on the frame needed tightening sometimes.

As time went by, we realised that Alan was actually a very sick man. Our fears were confirmed at a relief when he accidentally stepped into the water and had to be taken straight to hospital. He came back for one more spell despite being far from

THE *PRINCESS VICTORIA* TRAGEDY

In bad weather and emergencies we kept the radio open at the lighthouse and listened on the distress frequency. During a dreadful storm in January 1953, the passenger ferry *Princess Victoria* was passing to the north of us, en route for Larne. She ran into difficulties soon after leaving Stranraer and we caught her calls for help. We could only wait and listen for further news, while our tower shook in the worst of the weather. In despair we heard the words: 'We are preparing to abandon ship.'

Apparently, the captain was turning the ship back in worsening conditions when a wall of water hit her stern and began to flood the car deck. Fearing that the doors would burst open, he turned the disabled ship's head to face the waves. She made slowly for Larne until her engines finally failed, not far from Belfast Lough. A small coastal tanker, the *Pass of Drumochter* was among several vessels that went to help. She found the drifting wreck of the *Princess Victoria* on her beam ends. It was impossible to get alongside, though she was able to pick up a few people from one of the lifeboats. The tanker's captain watched the ship sink and announced: 'It is with great regret I have to inform you that the *Princess Victoria* has sunk with a great many people still aboard.'

We were shattered; 130 people were lost and about 40 were saved (none of them women or children), and we had been powerless in spite of being so close. Charlie began to sing 'The Old Rugged Cross' very quietly and we sat at the table, paying our own silent tribute before each spending a little time alone. A couple of hours later Charlie called us: 'Come on lads! Tea's ready. Life must go on.' Trying to console us, he said there was nothing we could have done.

well and I was asked to inform the office about his ongoing health problem. He never complained, but was retired on grounds of ill health and must have suffered greatly. He had a lot of courage to stay on rock duty for so long.

In the 1950s, thousands of holidaymakers came to the warm and lively Isle of Man. We were very impressed that the beaches were cleaned every morning. Parties of Lancashire mill girls were regulars and one day Peggy found a large wad of pound notes on the chemist's floor. She took it to the police station and a girl came to say thank you that evening, delighted because this was her spending money for the week.

Every June people flocked to watch the famous TT racing. Many of the spectators came with their own motorbikes and toured the island on days when there were no races. We found it was better to watch on TV because the bikes flashed past too quickly for us to see on the twisting roads. Before we had our own set we were invited to watch big football matches, sometimes by people we did not know. Each Christmas a tea chest full of goodies was sent to the lighthouse by a generous group of Manx people, which we appreciated greatly. I was on duty for both our Christmases there, but my family were asked to join local people in their festivities and had a wonderful time. Christmas was special in the Isle of Man, though New Year would always hold pride of place for us.

At one point Jimmy asked me to keep an eye on his mischievous younger son when I was ashore; the lad was about ten and had a habit of climbing out of the bathroom window. I managed to catch him one night when he shinned down the drainpipe and landed at my feet. One afternoon I met him coming out of the house with a bunch of flowers and a sour face. His mother told me that the flowers were her contribution to a sale of work. 'He can't eat those, can he?' she added ruefully. Another day he fell into the harbour. He had been wandering along with his jersey pulled up over his face and could not see where he was going. Luckily, a young fisherman saw him walk over the edge and jumped in to rescue him.

There were beautiful places to explore, with masses of wildflowers and the biggest brambles we had ever seen. Locals gathered these by the bucketful; they were great winemakers and bramble wine was particularly popular. Our effort was not very successful; the corks flew off as the wine fermented, leaving one full bottle out of twelve and a large red stain on the floor. The island bird life was much the same as in Scotland, though black redstarts were common – lovely little birds flitting here and there after insects.

In November 1954 I was promoted to principal keeper at the Butt of Lewis. We flew out, leaving behind the kindly people of Port St Mary and my friends at the Chickens; the rich green fields; the leafy lanes; and the consistently warm summer days when we could work in shorts.

12

Butt of Lewis

1954–1960

LIGHT ESTABLISHED 1862
RED BRICK TOWER 37 METRES HIGH
ENGINEER – DAVID STEVENSON

We reached Stornoway two days after leaving the Isle of Man following a very rough crossing on the *Loch Seaforth*; Peggy and Kathleen had both been seasick. On the pier, a stranger greeted me: 'Are you the new principal keeper at the Butt? I've got news for you! The lighthouse is in a bad way; your radio beacon has been off the air for days and the foghorn engines won't start!' With that he walked off, and we hired a taxi for the 30 cold miles to the northern tip of Lewis. It was a dreich arrival that November evening.

Butt of Lewis lighthouse.

At the lighthouse the assistants handed round cups of tea and I arranged to see them at nine the next morning. The bulk of our belongings would follow in a few days. Kathleen was 15 by this time and would continue her schooling at the Nicolson Institute in Stornoway, staying in lodgings and coming home at weekends.

Neither of the two men knew what was wrong with the radio beacon, nor did they seem interested. The previous principal had been on lengthy sick leave which explained the signs of neglect everywhere. The fellow on Stornoway pier had not exaggerated; things were in a bad way. With my promotion came the full responsibility of bringing the station up to scratch. Given the poor crew, the problems would be unrelenting and I could take no free time. It would be a year before this changed.

The Butt was a major lighthouse with a foghorn – which sounded two blasts every 30 seconds – and a beacon. Beacons were very important to navigation before radar. A beacon's range was far greater than that of a foghorn, which only warned of immediate danger and identified the lighthouse, making it especially useful in fog. A Morse code signal sent hourly by the beacon assisted ships in the Minch and North Atlantic to fix their position; 'BL' stood for 'Butt of Lewis'.

However, I had no training in operating radio beacons. Luckily, Bert at Craigneish had given me a detailed run-down before I left the Isle of Man. I was therefore able to find that the brushes were worn on the code-sender, replace them, and do a little maintenance, so we were back on the air quite soon. Each beacon was set to signal at specific times. Inside was a highly accurate Mercer clock; occasionally this lost or gained a second and we checked it regularly using BBC time pips. Whenever it was incorrect, sometimes by as little as two seconds, our radio engineer in Edinburgh would ring the lighthouse – even if it was the middle of the night. There was also an alarm with a red light in the principal's bedroom which called me if there was a beacon fault. Huge batteries provided a standby power supply and had to be charged frequently by petrol motor. (Two years later we were supplied with starting batteries and a petrol engine for charging.) Here the radio room housed the beacon as well as the radio for our busy link. Radio played an important role at the Butt of Lewis. We made contact three times a day with the lighthouses on the Flannan Isles and Rona in the Sound of Raasay, relaying family news as well as official messages from the Lighthouse Board. The men there were always glad of contact with the outside world. Unofficially, I kept in touch with Tom at Barra Head, and the principal on Muckle Flugga, in particular to swap weather news; it governed so many aspects of our life.

In addition to this, we had a very busy link with the coastguards and the lifeboat. One of our first visitors was the coastguard chief. He came to explain that they were waiting for new radio equipment and could not cover the area north west of the Butt in the meantime and could we help out. This was no problem; I always listened for distress calls in bad weather anyway. Twice we arranged for casualties to be taken off

North Rona

I heard a strange story from the men in Ness who kept sheep on North Rona. Crossing this stretch of water in their small boat had been too dangerous during the war. When they went back for the first time, a woman and her husband begged to be taken with them; they were ornithologists. The shepherds finally agreed, in spite of the couple's unpopular criticisms of the Sulasgeir guga hunters. When they reached North Rona they walked up together to a deserted cottage where they made a horrifying find: a dead German officer was sitting outside the door, still dressed in full uniform. By now he was just a skeleton. There were no clues as to how he came there and no aircraft wreckage to be seen. There was one theory that he was a Gestapo officer, abandoned by a submarine that was going to surrender. Many German vessels carried an agent to report on crew members and he could be a menace to the company if they capitulated; perhaps this man had been identified by others on board, put ashore and left to die. The body was taken to be buried in Stornoway, but the wife took the dead man's cap as a souvenir and refused to hand it back; an irreverence which annoyed the Ness shepherds.

Over the years we were asked to keep in radio contact with various groups visiting North Rona and Sulasgeir. They had no other way of communicating with the shore and I found this very interesting as they told me about their observations. North Rona had been uninhabited for about a hundred years, but 'a skiff their navy and a rock their wealth,' was said of its people at one time. Now it was home to sheep and wildlife, especially seals and seabirds. The seal population had increased since the Ness men gave up sealing expeditions to the island, causing the tenant of the day to complain that the seals' oily bodies damaged his pasture where they hauled out. A party from the Nature Conservancy went to examine the large colony. Afterwards they invited me to dinner at a Stornoway hotel, enlivening their stories with seal impersonations.

These verses were written by a naturalist friend, Malcolm Douglas, after his visits to the island:

Eilean nan Tuath Rona

Standing remote far out in the sea
An island recalled so vividly
With white-crested waves ringing her shore
Like the rise of the Phoenix of ancient lore

Isle of North Rona, isle of the seals
Of foam crested waves dancing wild reels
Of sheer towering cliffs where seabirds cry
As they float in the wind that rises high

For Rona protector and Saint Ronans cell
Under the stones of the cottages close to the well
The lazybed lines worked by earlier folk
That had lived and died on this windswept slope

ships, but one was foreign and I had language difficulties with her radio operator. We were also involved with lifeboat exercises and an occasional call-out. In time we would provide cover for various expeditions to North Rona and Sulasgeir, about 40 miles away.

Fortunately, Angus soon came on leave from the RAF; he had worked with the types of engines we had here and they all needed urgent attention. He overhauled the Stuart Turners for the beacon while I attended to the Kelvins that operated the foghorn. The powerful Kelvins had to be started by hand – a very heavy job – with the starting handle being two or three times as big as the old car cranks. We heaved this till the engine fired and had to step back quickly, as the recoil could break an arm. A barograph recorded the hours they were running for the monthly returns. Brass and copper fittings were kept polished. Coconut matting surrounded each on the floor of red and yellow tiles. As usual the engine room was large and warm; a good place to work.

There was no electricity during our early years at the station. The houses had Tilley lamps and coal-fired kitchen ranges. Mains water had not arrived though we had our own good supply from a nearby peaty well and all the houses had a WC. The surrounding peat was very deep. After we left we heard that an engineer, who was testing its depth, plunged a 14-foot pipe into the ground and it disappeared for good.

The Butt of Lewis was also a weather station. According to the Guinness Book of Records, it had once registered as the windiest spot in the United Kingdom. The anemometer showed us how windy it could be the day that our reading shot off the scale. Another time Angus was crossing the moor to the shop when he saw a lapwing being buffeted relentlessly by the wind. Suddenly, an almighty gust drove it into a telephone line and it dropped to the ground. He found the body in the heather and its severed head a few feet away.

There were 168 steps to the top of the tower. As at all stations, these steps were unlit, apart from a paraffin lamp in the lightroom where we completed the logs. Outside, its red brick walls showed up well from the sea, so it did not have to be lime washed. A paraffin autoform lamp had replaced the oil burner (the original fuel would have been fish or whale oil). This revolving light flashed white every five seconds. As well as winding up at regular intervals, we checked the gas pressure in the lamp every so often. The log was filled in, but there was little else to be done on a normal night watch. Scanning the sea from the balcony every 15 minutes brought blasts of air to the face and helped to keep you awake.

In spring the lighthouse painting started. Only the outside of windows and doors needed a coat, but the inside of the tower was repainted from top to bottom every three years, and the engine room and radio room were whitewashed every year. We each painted the inside of our houses – outside doors were green and window frames white.

To the west of the Butt lay a vast stretch of the Atlantic that foamed as it battered the rocks and stacks by the cliff. Only North Rona and Sulasgeir lay between us and the Faeroes. At spring tides there were strange rumbling noises at night as the sea washed into a deep cave under the tower. Once I climbed down the cliff to glance inside but saw nothing unusual. Some years after I left the Butt of Lewis, the keepers noticed that the rumblings were getting louder and reverberating right through the tower. Experts found that the sea cave underneath was beginning to collapse; no one was allowed upstairs, even to take a watch, until contractors filled the cavity with special cement.

I came across something unusual in the engine room shortly after I arrived – there was a group of complete strangers looking at the machinery. When I asked what they were doing, a man stepped forward.

'It is quite all right, Mr MacEachern, I am just showing my friends round the lighthouse,' he said.

'Who gave you permission to come in? And who are you?' I asked.

'I am the Free Church minister here and I don't need permission to go anywhere in Ness.'

I asked him to telephone before any future visits.

Very soon Peggy and I noticed another thing that puzzled us. Every Sunday afternoon a group of children ran round and round on top of the lighthouse boundary walls for hours at a time. One of my assistants said the children always did this while their parents were at church. At first I was too busy to do anything about it, but eventually I went out to them.

'Why do you keep running around the walls?' I asked.

'Because the old man chases us,' they giggled shyly.

'Well, I am the old man now and I won't chase you. Why don't you come to the house and meet my family.'

For the next six years the children visited every Sunday, bringing younger brothers and sisters with them. They all sat round our table with lemonade and biscuits, speaking English to us and lapsing into Gaelic among themselves. Sometimes they wanted to go up the tower and walk round the balcony. Now and again, on a weekday, we would find a bag of potatoes or turnips on our doorstep; occasionally a parcel of fish or a leg of mutton appeared. 'From a friend' was all that our enquiries revealed and we guessed these were gifts from the children's families.

Before long we felt very much at home and local folk often called to visit. The warmth of the islander's welcome was special; a cup of tea and a chat would 'make a wee ceilidh'. Peggy joined in church activities and country dancing and spent a lot of time knitting and sewing. A grocery van came weekly from a store owned by the local Justice of the Peace. He was good to the people in his village and gave us useful advice on local matters. At Port of Ness, Habost, Fivepenny, Eoropie, and Dell, most houses were on a croft of a few acres. At one we saw a litter of red cocker spaniel pups and Peggy took a fancy to one. He was named Rusty and was so tiny that I could carry him in the palm of my hand, but he soon proved easy to train and good on shooting trips.

Our meat was delivered by van. Donald 'Dolly' Mhor the butcher always brought our orders in the evening and stayed late to chat; he was full of humour and a keen fisherman. Sometimes I went with Dolly to collect meat from Stornoway abattoir. On the way back one afternoon he ran over a large rooster that was crossing the road. He picked it up and went to the door of the nearest croft, where a furious row erupted in Gaelic. To my surprise, he returned to the van still carrying the carcass: 'Och well, I could not waste it, could I? I gave her seven and sixpence.'

I was delighted to get to know the boat builder in Ness, the sailor who had been the hero of the *Iolaire* tragedy – he had saved many by his efforts in getting a line ashore. He was awarded a decoration at Buckingham Palace but, being a modest man, had been rather reluctant to step into the limelight.

After a year I had to change assistants. When the superintendent asked if I wanted anyone in particular to replace them, I remembered how well Malcolm had assisted me at the Flannan Isles light. He and his wife had a son, Calum, who was now a keeper at an Orkney light and I knew how much they missed him. A local man called Donald would be ideal too. He lived quite near the lighthouse and would be able to work his croft in his spare time. Also, Donald had been at sea, so the routine of night watches would be no problem for him.

The pressure of work began to ease with the appointment of Calum and Donald; both were conscientious workers. Once the new crew had settled down, we could actually enjoy the Butt of Lewis. We were able to take a day off every week and leave the station for a fortnight's summer holiday. Successive supernumeraries also helped. Sadly one of them drowned shortly after he left us for the next stage of his training. He and a companion were fishing lobster creels at Ailsa Craig when their boat capsized.

By 1955 my father was in his mid-80s. He had retired to Edinburgh where Kitty kept house and worked at Crawford's restaurant, repairing linen with fine invisible mending. One day Bobbie telephoned to say that Father's health was failing. The annual maintenance was just starting at the Butt and I was supposed to be in attendance. However, the superintendent told me to go; he would stay with the artificers for an extra week and take charge of the light. Father still knew me, but he died a few weeks later. We were fortunate that Bobbie's wife, Mary, was a district nurse and had helped Kitty to care for him. Usually our stores were unloaded at Stornoway and brought the rest of the way by road, but one year the *Pharos* came to the lighthouse landing instead, so Bobbie was able to spend an hour with us.

BIRDS AT THE BUTT

The Butt area was a birdwatcher's paradise, visited frequently by enthusiastic naturalists. Among these was Ludwig Koch – famous for his early recordings of birdsong as well as being an ornithologist – who came to the lighthouse on several occasions. He was also a keen geologist and told us much that was fascinating about the local rock formation – apparently it was some of the oldest in the world. We got to know him well and he was partial to Peggy's fruit scones with his cup of tea.

Professor Meiklejohn from the University of Glasgow came to the lighthouse several years in a row. Once, while recording bird numbers, he reported seeing 300 empty beer bottles in roadside ditches between Stornoway and the Butt!

Ken Williamson at London Zoo wanted numbers of geese in particular. During migration, the sky would be black with skeins – I saw approximately 3,000 on one occasion. I kept records of all species seen and corresponded with him. Only a few migrants flew to this light but one day an unusual thrush-like corpse below the lantern was identified by Ken as a white-cheeked thrush, a first sighting in Lewis. Black guillemots, known as 'tysties', nested on the cliff; puffins occupied the grassy slopes; while fulmars and gulls occupied ledges. A colony of guillemots had taken possession of the rock face near the Eye of the Butt. Starlings flocked during the autumn, fouling the lantern and grating which hads to be cleaned constantly.

When the Royal Yacht *Britannia* made a visit to Lewis, members of the royal family visited the lighthouse at Tiumpan Head. Peggy and I were invited there for the occasion but a last minute problem with the engines at the Butt prevented our going.

Two or three times the Ness people asked me to go to the peats when I had a day off – the cutting and gathering was a communal effort. By now peat was carried home by tractor and trailer but in Scalpay I had seen women with the heavy loads on their backs. The men still cut the dark slices with special spades to be propped on edge like houses of cards. The cutting was usually finished in June and the peats left to dry for a few weeks.

The first time, 20 or 30 of us went to the moors in a late summer spell of dry weather. A fire was lit before the work began. To start with, I was on the wrong side of the trailer as people threw on the dried chunks and dust began to fly. Everyone sang and kept busy as the tractor moved from heap to heap; soon tea was brewed and baking was handed round.

Gaelic banter was punctuated with peals of laughter and there was a gala atmosphere. People spoke to me in English as I only remembered a few words of Gaelic. When two of the men came to speak to me, one asked 'Your mother died in Stornoway hospital, did she not?' and I was made to feel very much at home.

A good peat reek from the fire filled the air and in the middle of the day a hot dinner was produced for everyone: fish or lamb chops and potatoes, followed by more scones, pancakes, and tea. Chatter and song kept us going until all was gathered and a neat stack could be built at each house.

The fishing on Lewis was wonderful – salmon, sea trout, and brown trout. Port of Ness people showed me how they collected bait for sea fishing too; we dug under the lugworm casts that covered the shore with a 'heuk' and dropped the lugs into tins on strings around our necks. Occasionally I caught pollock at the landing and plaice at Coundle.

We became very friendly with our Church of Scotland Minister, the Rev Malcolm – also known as Calum – and he and I often fished together. One day we arrived at a loch that was new to us and the ghillie asked us if we would mind sharing a boat with the Colonel, since his friend hadn't turned up. Before long a large man with a moustache appeared from the hut. 'Don't worry about rowing,' he said. 'I'll row all morning and you can take over in the afternoon.' He was expert at handling the boat. After a while Calum hooked a small fish, but he played it so long that the Colonel got restless and said:

'Stop farting about and pull the bloody thing in, man. It's only a tiddler anyway!'

'My friend is the Church of Scotland minister,' I told him quietly.

The Colonel was very put out: 'Oh my God! I am so sorry, Reverend!'

Calum just smiled and pulled in his fish, which was stone dead by now. Later we chatted as we lunched on the bank and the Colonel handed round his hip flask, addressing Calum as 'Reverend'. At the end of the day they parted the best of friends, with a few sea trout in the bag.

On another occasion Peggy and I were picnicking by a little bridge on our way to Harris. A man was fishing on the river and we saw a freshly caught sea trout sticking out of each of his pockets – clearly he was having a good day. I went to chat and asked if it was possible to get any fishing there. 'Yes, any time the water is in spate and it'll only cost you ten shillings a day,' he replied. He owned the fishing rights and after that he phoned me whenever conditions were good. From June it was a prolific river for salmon, but especially for sea trout. I took many a 'bar of silver' from the Scaladale.

Dolly Mhor had grouse shooting and fishing rights. He often asked me to the moorland lochs and to shoot with him. On the way, Rusty and Dolly Mhor's labrador, Prince, had to be tied in his van to prevent them fighting; though they ignored each other while they were busy retrieving. On several occasions we saw a handsome cock grouse, perched like a sentry, on the same peat hag. 'Pekk, pekk! Gbakk, gbakk, gbakk!' he called anxiously, to warn his family of danger.

'You're not going to shoot him, are you?' I said, the first time we passed.

'Och no! We'll never shoot the big man,' Dolly assured me.

We usually ate lunch by the Frying Pan Loch as we called it; beside the water was the ruin of a black house, with a blackened frying pan still hanging on a wall.

A thick mist engulfed us when we were making a long day after an early start. Treacherous peat bogs surrounded the expanse of moor, so rather than getting hopelessly lost, we decided to shelter. Dolly Mhor knew of a nearby hut where the door was left unlocked for anyone who might be caught out by the weather. Inside, there was a straw bed and a cupboard full of tinned food and bottles of lemonade; a notice on the door asked anyone using the tins to replace them later for others. Cooking utensils were provided and a stove – we could make tea. But we did not touch the hut supplies. Instead, we boiled some of the trout we had caught earlier – two for each of us and one for Prince. The mist showed no sign of lifting, so we were there for the night.

We awoke early to a beautiful, clear, sunny morning, and ate a breakfast of leftover sandwiches with tea before skirting the bog easily – bagging several grouse on the way – and arrived at Dolly Mhor's house about one o'clock. When we had not returned the previous night, his wife had reassured Peggy that we would have sheltered in the hut. She put a huge dinner in front of us, starting with a delicious plate of sheep's head broth. After that, the whole sheep's head was brought to the table, its boiled, staring eyes still in their sockets; I no longer felt hungry. The meat was tender, but I had not eaten sheep's head since Scalpay days. I did enjoy the tasty milk pudding with brown crunchy skin that followed though!

On a shooting trip a year or two later, we stayed in a shieling for several nights. A cluster of about five stone huts stood in a little green valley – crofters' wives used them in summer when they took their cows to the moor for a bite of fresh pasture. Each was thatched with heather and had a window, a fireplace and a chimney. One had a wide straw bed that was covered with old mailbags and quite comfortable. We were lucky to see a golden eagle with one young when we passed near a rocky eyrie. The grouse shooting was very good; the weather was fine. All the shielings were occupied for the first two days and we were asked to take evening meals with our neighbours. On the last night we ate alone and Dolly Mhor prepared a couple of our grouse. He presented them for me to cook, gutted and roughly plucked but still covered with down.

'We can't eat them like that!' I said.

'Och, they will be fine,' he insisted.

However, I singed off the soft fluff over a shovel of burning paper. They made a good enough meal with tea and bread, although they might have been improved by an onion.

On another occasion, I fished a loch on the moor with Angus. When the sun was beginning to go down, we turned for home. Soon we caught sight of the next loch ahead of us and saw someone fishing there. 'I don't think he's a local; he's using a split cane rod,' I commented. 'Let's ask what flies he has on.' We lost sight of the loch briefly, and when we reached the spot, no one was there. There were no footmarks in the soft peat beside the water, and nowhere anyone could be hidden in the flat treeless expanse. After searching for a while, we felt quite strange. 'Let's get away from this place, I don't like it,' said Angus. We were both glad when we reached Dolly Mhor's and spoke to his wife. 'Oh dear me!' she exclaimed. 'That's a bad place! A fisherman was drowned there two years ago.' She did not explain further. Neither Angus nor I were superstitious, but we never went back to that loch.

The sense of community was strong. Ceilidhs were always lively and welcoming affairs in Ness houses. Most of those present took part, singing or reciting in Gaelic, or playing the accordion, fiddle, and occasionally the pipes. I was at one where a man got up to sing and stood on the family cat; it howled like an accompaniment and nobody laughed. Wedding celebrations went on for days, though festivities stopped at midnight on a Saturday. I have never seen anything like the home-cooked food the island women provided; they were renowned for their hospitality. Beautifully set out in the village hall, ashets bearing chicken and lamb covered long tables, the trays of baking were out of this world, and whisky flowed like water. We danced late into the night.

Funerals were also big occasions. It was moving to see a long black procession snaking slowly across the machair or filling the little roads. Mourners gathered from villages and townships, joined by relations from all over the world. Relays of men bore the coffin on their shoulders to a cemetery, which was often near the sea and a very long way to walk. There were no licensed hotels or bars around Ness, but in some places there was a 'bothan', a hut where local men could gather for a drink and a chat. An outsider could only go if invited and no money changed hands.

We got to know our local doctor well when Kathleen became very ill. He was wonderful and visited her often during these worrying weeks. When she was well again, the doctor advised us that she should leave school. She decided to go to her granny's in Girvan and worked in the office of a grocery. A kind though rather eccentric man from Fraserburgh, the doctor was gruff and matter-of-fact. He was not a Gaelic speaker and we enjoyed our chats together about the Buchan Ness area. Not all the patients were happy with him, however. One elderly lady, dressed in black, went to his surgery on a cold day. She was complaining of a chest problem but did not want him to sound her chest and refused to take off any clothes. It was too much when she said she would rather come back another day. 'Strip, damn you! Strip!' was the response; she never did go back.

Although he held various surgeries throughout his scattered practice, people frequently stopped him on his rounds. One day he was exasperated when a woman waved down his car to ask for medical advice. 'Go to Eoropie, go to Port of Ness, or go to hell!' he yelled. Having his car chased by collies irritated the doctor intensely and he kept a supply of stones on the passenger seat. One day he smashed the window when he forgot to open it before aiming at a darting dog.

I bought our first car for £300. There was an advert in the paper: 'Wonderful Bargains for the Highlands and Islands!' I crossed to Kyle of Lochalsh where I had arranged to meet a Glasgow salesman. His car seemed just the ticket, but when I opened the driver's door an awful smell greeted me. I soon found out what it was on the test run: the brakes were faulty, and I nearly knocked a woman down. The deal was off.

Back in Stornoway that evening, I told the taxi man glumly about my wasted trip. Well, he had just the car for me at his garage, he said, and he took me to see it. Sure enough, the Ford Popular seemed ideal and was only one year old. I was delighted; I had enough money on me to pay for it in full, and I drove it straight home that night. The single-track roads were dead quiet, which was just as well as I had never taken a driving test. I did think the headlights were rather poor and discovered the next day that they had been dipped all the way. There was a lot to learn.

I failed my first driving test in Stornoway; the examiner nearly jumped out of his seat when I drove through a halt sign. I passed at the second attempt though, and from time to time I drove over to Breasclete to visit my old friends, Malcolm and his wife. You needed your wits about you on these unfenced roads – off-duty sheepdogs that appeared to be asleep on verges ran at the wheels of passing cars, and sheep, cows and hens wandered at will through the common grazings on either side.

We covered many miles in the Ford Popular and soon discovered the beautiful expanse of sand at Luskentyre in Harris. Between Stornoway and Ness the road crossed several burns. Often on Saturday evenings in summer, groups of boys and girls danced on the little bridges, a lovely sight. Sometimes an accordion or fiddle accompanied them and cars would have to wait for an eightsome reel to finish, though the occupants were happy to watch.

One winter we had hurricane-force winds that blew down the aerial for the radio beacon. We had to rig safety lines across the courtyard – a struggle in the persistent wind. The repair tided us over, albeit with a weaker signal, till artificers could come from Edinburgh.

Heavy blizzards followed the hurricane and left us isolated with no telephone for days on end. The foghorn sounded continuously, but thankfully the light functioned normally while snow fell thickly. After our lines were repaired I rang the snow plough driver to see when the road would be cleared – the snow was apparently too deep for the plough! Then an emergency arose. Calum became seriously ill with measles, and we had to call the doctor. On his way to the lighthouse his car skidded into a snowdrift. He continued his journey on foot, though he nearly walked over the edge of the cliff in a blinding blizzard. I went to meet him in the Popular; luckily its tyres were wide enough to catch a grip. However, by the time the doctor arrived, Calum was losing consciousness and his eyes were rolling back, showing only the whites. The doctor acted quickly to save him as there was no way we could get him to hospital.

Calum made a good recovery, but his health had been permanently affected during the Second World War when he was a prisoner of war in Germany. On the terrible death march through Poland, he and his companions were made to dig up and re-bury bodies of Polish officers massacred by the Germans. In time his group were rescued by the Allies, although their plane crashed on the way home and Calum was injured. In spite of this, he was an excellent assistant – always on time, and ready to do anything he was asked.

That proved to be an exceptionally hard winter. A helicopter dropped fodder to stranded livestock in 'Operation Snowdrop'.

Word came one summer that a Commissioners' visit was due shortly. Precise details would come through the grapevine and I had to make sure everything was ship-shape. I knew the traditional dodges, like wiping paintwork with white spirit to 'freshen it up'. Calum and Donald worked very hard, and on the day we appeared in our best uniforms with a tidy polished station and newly cut grass. I showed the Commissioners around and they were satisfied with what they saw. Even the coal cellars were open to inspection. The visit reminded me that when we were small, the Commissioners always brought sweeties for lighthouse children – each was given a wee white box with a tape tab to open the lid.

On one occasion, the general manager of the Board was aboard the *Pharos* while she was anchored in Stornoway Bay over the weekend. On the Sunday I had a telephone call to say the general manager's wife had died suddenly. I was asked to contact the ship immediately. We had no telephone link with the *Pharos* – radio messages were only accepted at pre-arranged times and emergency contact had to be made through the harbour office. After a long wait, my phone call was answered. 'We do not answer the phone on the Sabbath,' said the lady at the other end, and hung up before I could explain properly. As a last resort, I rang the police station. They relayed the message to the *Pharos* and she sailed immediately for Kyle.

As in so many island and seafaring communities, the Church played a particularly important role, with most of the Ness people belonging to the Free Church. Sabbath observance was very strict and no work at all was done that day. At the lighthouse we only carried out essential jobs unless there was an emergency. Sunday was for correspondence and bookwork; the NLB flag was raised and we dressed in full uniform. Services at the Church of Scotland were in Gaelic, apart from a monthly service in English for lighthouse families.

In spring and summer we received many visitors at the lighthouse. One sunny afternoon Calum was showing a party of ladies around outside while I took a family up the tower. As we reached the lightroom, a small boy announced that he was bursting.

Unfortunately, the bucket that was kept on the balcony for emergencies had been blown away and he had to pee through the balcony rail. 'My, that's surprising!' exclaimed a lady in Calum's group below. 'A few drops of rain, but the sky is clear blue.'

It was the custom every summer for a group of Ness men to sail 40 miles north to the gannet colony on Sulasgeir. They stayed on the rocky island for two or three weeks to harvest hundreds of gugas, the young gannets. One year I had a call from the Fishery Protection vessel to say that they could not make radio contact with the guga boat. I was asked to keep a look out and listen for any message, but we heard and saw nothing. As the days went by, anxiety mounted throughout Ness. Then a fishing boat, the *Wyre Monarch*, came on air to say that she was heading for Sulasgeir and would search the area. At long last, there was a delighted shout from Calum up in the lantern, who had spotted the little boat approaching. The men gave us a wave; we passed on the good news to Port of Ness, and jumped into the car to meet the boat at the harbour. 'We were fine. What would be wrong with us?' the guga men called to their folks who had gathered. These skilled seafarers were quite unconcerned that their radio had failed; everyone else breathed a sigh of relief. Elated people arrived by bicycle, car and on foot to line up for a share when the catch would be divided among the community.

The boat was loaded with greyish brown gugas, already gutted and split. Soon a big mound of the dried bodies, looking more like kippers than birds, covered the pier. Some would be packed in biscuit tins, the lids soldered in place, to be posted to relations in Canada, Australia, and New Zealand. I only ate guga once; it is an acquired taste, between fish and fowl. The dark meat was boiled until it was very tender and was relished by many in Lewis.

One day the Stornoway coastguard alerted me to say he was worried about a yacht, the *Mary Rose,* which had left North Rona in very bad conditions. I radioed repeatedly: '*Mary Rose; Mary Rose.* This is the Butt of Lewis lighthouse. Can you hear me? Please come in. Do you require assistance?' Eventually a girl's voice responded faintly, saying they did not require help at that stage but she begged me to keep in touch. Before long, conditions worsened and she feared they were going to sink. Then Bobbie called me from the *Pharos,* lying off Handa, in mountainous seas and a Force 10. He said the yacht would be in great danger now and if necessary the ship would divert to rescue the couple. I stayed on air with them all night; mercifully, they reached Broad Bay hours later. The next day they asked me to meet them in Stornoway, where they were resting with a very battered boat. I was delighted to see them, exhausted but safe. They gave me dinner and I told them that the *Pharos* had been standing by. Several times after that I covered them by radio around the Western Isles.

In the winter of 1959 we were involved with a lifeboat disaster on the east coast. I had tuned in to the distress frequency when I heard Fife Ness coastguard call: 'Broughty Ferry lifeboat! Broughty Ferry lifeboat!' There was no response from the lifeboat. When I spoke, the coastguard asked me to take turns at calling because our radio was so powerful. Soon another voice joined us: 'This is Wick Radio Station. I am standing by with you, to try and pick up the lifeboat.' Calum and Donald took all our watches that night.

It turned out that the North Carr lightship had broken adrift near the entrance to the Firth of Forth in a severe southeasterly gale. Broughty Ferry lifeboat, the *Mona*, had been called to her aid. I guessed that the *Pharos* would be going to assist. Bobbie was her chief officer now and I phoned Mary in Edinburgh – she said the ship had already left Granton. Soon I heard the *Pharos* tell the coastguard they had contacted the lightship; they had been heading towards rocks but had been able to check the drift with a spare anchor. Though the *Pharos* was standing by, the seas were so wild in shallow water that she could do nothing to help. Bobbie reported a helicopter hovering over the lightship; her crew cut down the mast to allow a winchman to land on deck, and he rescued the crew members one by one. The *Pharos* lay off in deeper water till the weather moderated and she could tow the lightship into port. All this time there had been no sight or sound of the *Mona*.

The silence from the lifeboat was never broken. The full horror dawned the next day, when she was found drifting, upside down and empty. Her crew of eight were all lost. 'Greater love hath no man than this, that a man lay down his life for his friends' was the text quoted at the inquiry into this tragedy.

Forty years later I was travelling from Inverness to Glasgow by bus; the man in the seat beside me had been visiting Wick. In the course of our chat, he said he had been the radio operator there when the Broughty Ferry lifeboat was lost; we had spoken to each other throughout that long night of searching.

I was informed in November 1960 that I was being transferred from the Butt of Lewis to Turnberry lighthouse. Folk had made us feel very much at home during our six years in Lewis; now we had to head for Ayrshire.

MORE FROM THE FLANNAN ISLES

On my last visit to Malcolm at Breasclete, he surprised me. 'There is something I want you to know. It is about the Flannan Isles...' he said quietly, as if to unburden himself.

He told me that soon after the lightkeepers vanished, the shore around Breasclete was strewn with wood and debris. They knew this came from a wrecked Norwegian sailing ship because her name was on one of the planks. When I asked if these finds had been reported, Malcolm said:

'No. The Receiver of Wrecks would have taken the wood from us. There were also some bodies.'

'What happened to them?' I asked.

'They were buried in the machair, Archie.'

I knew it had been customary around the coast for bodies from shipwrecks to be buried in machair land. Those of us in the Lighthouse Service knew only too well that worthwhile wood brought in by the sea should be put to good use.

Allowing for tide, wind and current, this corresponded roughly with the date of the disappearance from the lighthouse in December 1900. Malcolm's sombre account confirmed in my mind that the three men on the Flannan Isles drowned, but they were trying to avert a shipwreck, not the loss of ropes.

It was known from reports that hurricane force winds were blowing on 15th December. The island would have been shrouded in mist and spray. My theory is that one keeper, wearing his oilskins, had gone up the tower to fill in the log. He went on to the balcony to check the wind and caught sight of the topmast of a sailing ship that was being driven straight for the cliffs. It is likely that a second keeper was outside, also dressed for the weather. The third man was in the kitchen.

The ship was only visible from the balcony with furious spindrift obscuring the view from below. Clearly she was in imminent danger of foundering as she headed helplessly for the island. The keeper on the balcony would have run downstairs shouting, 'ship in trouble, lads! Come on! Quick!' The cook ran out to join the others, not waiting to put on waterproofs.

Their immediate reaction was to race to the aid of a ship. They knew that if they could get a line to the crew, there might be a chance of saving those on board. To reach them, they would need the crane on the upper platform. While they were kneeling to loosen its clips, a wall of water raced up the rock face, snatching them from above. As the cascade retreated, their bodies would be tossed into the sea. The ship would have broken up very quickly.

On 15th December 2000, an official press announcement from the Lighthouse Board commemorated their deaths with dignity. We read in the 'In Memoriam' column of *The Scotsman*:

> It was on this day in 1900 that the 3 lightkeepers at Flannan Isles wrote their last entry in the log. James Ducat, Thomas Marshall and Donald MacArthur were never seen again and lost their lives in the service of the Mariner. The Northern Lighthouse Board pays tribute to them and their families.

Having considered official reports, and my own and Father's experience of the Flannan Isles, I am left in no doubt: the three men were attempting to save other lives when they lost their own.

13

Turnberry

1960–1963

LIGHT ESTABLISHED 1873
WHITE TOWER, 24 METRES HIGH
ENGINEERS – DAVID AND THOMAS STEVENSON

The lighthouse stood beside the 9th hole on the golf course and could only be approached through a manned security gate. The course was owned by Turnberry Hotel who regulated this access. Peggy's father had been principal here some years earlier (where sadly he died suddenly), so she was familiar with our new house.

We were welcomed to the station by Harry, the outgoing principal and a distant relative of Peggy's. First of all the log was signed, and after tea it was down to business, which included buying Harry's twelve hens.

The light itself was identical to that at the Butt, though it revolved on rollers instead of a mercury bath and there were only 76 steps to climb instead of 168. Things here were in excellent condition. With no fog signal or radio, the duties were lighter, but as it was a two man station with only three hours between watches, sleep was generally scarce in winter. It was easier with three keepers, on the occasions when we had a supernumerary. It was simple for me to go on watch at night: an extra door from our bedroom opened directly on to the tower stairs and this saved crossing the courtyard in the early hours. Life was pleasant, though we missed our Lewis friends. We were more accessible at Turnberry for relations to visit us, with marvellous opportunities for golf – enjoyed by Bobbie especially – and Kathleen was in nearby Girvan with her grandmother.

After about six months my assistant, Donald, was transferred and replaced by another Calum, a Skye man with a fine sense of humour and a quiet manner. Calum was a very accomplished fly fisherman and we shared our enthusiasm for golf as well as fishing. The Turnberry course was first class; we were given free golf when no

Inside Turnberry lantern. (Duncan Baillie, from a colour painting on canvas)

tournament was in progress. In return, we were asked to keep an eye on our corner. We watched the big competitions in our spare time and it was easy to get a close view of play, though it was not always easy to access the lighthouse; twice Calum was refused permission to drive in. On both occasions he was wearing civvies and had difficulty convincing the security man that he was returning to his house and work – rather different from Lewis where we never locked our doors!

The lighthouse stood above the ruins of Robert the Bruce's castle, which had a dry grassy moat. Below was the cave where Bruce was said to have watched the inspiring spider. In the past, the nearby Bristo Rock had caused many shipwrecks. Naval ships passed often and cargo ships made for the Clyde; yachts tended to sail more to the north. Both Arran and Holy Isle were visible from Turnberry on clear days.

It saddened me to see so-called 'sportsmen' shoot everything that moved along this shore. I asked them to stop after I found the corpses of redshanks, turnstones, and ringed plovers lying where they had fallen. I wrote to George Waterston's widow for advice but there was nothing we could do about it.

Before long I decided to buy a 12-foot dinghy from a boat builder in Stranraer. I added an outboard and made six lobster creels in the winter. In spring I started setting the pots and a line for flounders and skate in Turnberry Bay; catches were good.

One afternoon a boy in his early teens – Duncan, son of the head greenkeeper on the course – came to the door and asked if he could see up the tower. After this, Duncan appeared often, eager to learn about the lighthouse and keenly interested in fishing. He soon became familiar with our routine and expert at winding up the machine; a happy addition to our number.

Duncan learnt how to cast and Calum took him to the river for his first proper attempt. One summer's evening Peggy and I were sitting at our tea when the door burst open and Duncan appeared. 'Look what I caught!' he announced excitedly, and a large slippery salmon was laid proudly on the tablecloth. He had cycled a long way with his first catch strapped to the handlebars. Later, he marked the occasion by painting a lovely watercolour of the lighthouse for us.

It was grand to have a boat again. As I was usually alone on board, I often thought of my father's guidance. He had learnt a lot skippering yachts on the west coast before he became a lightkeeper, and had passed this golden rule on to Bobbie and me: 'Never take anything for granted at sea.' 'Always keep one hand for yourself,' was another excellent piece of advice, especially when working creels singlehanded and handling ropes or sails. It was only too easy to fall overboard in these situations.

Duncan helped to make creels, including the one that we baited with Kit-e-Kat. Someone had recommended this tinned cat food for catching lobsters and the next day that pot was full of velvet crabs. Once when we released a large conger eel, it terrified Calum's little terrier, slithering at speed towards her.

An old fisherman once told me that April and May were the best months for lobsters. The time was right, he said, when the silvery trails of large black slugs could be seen on the ground in the morning, as that was when the lobsters came from deep water to change their shells, nearer the shore. The best catches could be made before they crawled into holes in rocks. A deep hole in the wall of our slipway made an ideal refuge for lobsters and a fisherman gave me a tip for a successful lure – a scrap of white rag dangled on a stick. As soon as a lobster grabbed this, I pulled it out of the water. Fissures in cliffs and in rocks on the beach usually extended underwater and we set our creels off these. We landed a regular supply; there was usually a lobster or a crab in at least one creel. By June it was not worth setting any for a month; after that we fished again till autumn, when the lobsters' new shells would have hardened and they headed back to the deep for winter.

It was important to know the state of the tide for working the creels. I set mine at low water because I could see them better. I had learnt as a boy that neap tides were slacker; the springs ran stronger, peaking at full moon. Also we always thought the weather was inclined to be better at full moon; the preferred time for reliefs at rocks.

I pondered on seafarers' words about weather. One day when I was a sailor on the *Pharos*, we were passing through the Pentland Firth when an experienced seaman looked at the sky and said:

'We're in for trouble today, Archie.'

'Why? It's a lovely morning!'

'You see that red patch up there? By the time we get to the Flannans, we'll be in a real snorter!'

Sure enough, the wind freshened as we left Cape Wrath and storm-force winds whipped up big seas off the Butt of Lewis. The captain decided that conditions were too bad for the Flannan Isles and we made for shelter in Loch Roag.

'You should always watch the horizon,' a fisherman at Boddam told me. 'If a dark line appears, wind or occasionally fog, will come very soon. Then a small boat should make for home.' A 'tooth' of rainbow on the horizon was also a warning of wind, according to a Moray Firth fisherman. Clouds against the wind might mean a lull before a storm. When it was very calm a 'cat's paw', or occasional ripple, troubling the surface was of no significance. A few feathery clouds in an otherwise clear blue sky showed there was high pressure and it would remain quiet. Blue skies mottled with white were a good sign, hence the saying: 'Mackerel skies and mares' tails let small ships carry tall sails.'

Though less exposed than the tip of Lewis, Turnberry could still be very windy. The hens were blown around at times, but they did not suffer any ill effects. They were good at negotiating the henhouse door by planing with outstretched wings on a strong gust. In winter I brought the boat inside the grounds. Even here it blew away once, becoming impaled on a metal rod and I had to replace a plank.

One summer afternoon a woman turned up with a very distressed wee boy. His beach ball had blown away from the sands at Ayr and they were told it would drift to Turnberry lighthouse. 'It's my birthday present!' he sobbed, pointing out to sea. Sure enough, we could see a row of balls bobbing on the water; I launched the boat and brought in six. 'That's mine!' he exclaimed, beaming, as he claimed one.

At the lighthouse there were two large, productive gardens enclosed by a wall. Generations of keepers had worked the ground and like them, we carted barrowloads of kelp from the beach. As well as the usual vegetables, we grew excellent carrots on a big scale, and I sold these to Coopers in Girvan. Our potatoes were poor though, and could not compete with locally grown Ayrshires.

Carrots were a favourite crop in many lighthouse gardens as they thrived in sandy soil. A story circulated about a keeper who was being shifted to a new station. When his boxes were being loaded on to the ship, someone asked why one was so heavy. It was filled with carrots packed in sand – too good to be left behind!

At one point, the Turnberry Hotel wanted to buy the gardens. Their plan was to extend the golf course and give us replacement plots in the castle moat. These would be a poor substitute though, and the moat would disappear. The Lighthouse Board asked my opinion and it was agreed that we should keep our fertile ground.

Our flock of hens increased to 40 and every morning Rusty came with me to feed them. He watched me collect the eggs and I always gave him one, which he carried to the house in his soft mouth before putting it carefully on the kitchen mat, never stealing or breaking any. Now and again Peggy rewarded him with an egg whisked in milk.

One day I was disturbed by a terrific squawking from the hens. I ran and found a Jack Russell Terrier attacking one. At the same time, a lady came flying over the garden wall and fell badly, not having seen the six foot drop on our side. She was upset, but not injured, and called frantically to the dog, which carried on killing the hen. I did not accept her offer to pay for it, though we appreciated her apologies.

Another time we were watching a party of golfers search for a lost ball when Rusty bustled past on his way to the kitchen. He dropped it on the mat and we returned it to the players. Now that I had no shooting, he became expert at retrieving balls instead of birds and, since he liked to be busy, often caught rats on the beach.

One afternoon I found a woman kneeling with her arms around Rusty's neck. 'My dog died before we came on holiday. Your dog looks just like him and I thought he had come back,' she explained. The next day she and her husband brought a beautiful lunch box from Turnberry Hotel made up with chicken bits and biscuits for Rusty, who was in clover. They returned several more times, welcomed warmly as soon as he saw the white box of goodies. They came in for tea and they wrote from their home in Cornwall afterwards, with a gift of Cornish cream.

These were just some of many visitors to Turnberry and its golf course. We watched many of the golfing greats in action at tournaments, and even saw Arnold Palmer in exhibition matches. Jack Nicklaus was the most friendly and well-liked by spectators; he chatted to us by the greens and once I saw him hit a hole-in-one. Calum and I took hour about to follow play, as one of us was always on watch. It did not take long to catch up as we knew the shortcuts.

One afternoon Calum was working in his garden when he was disturbed by two American bodyguards. 'Who the hell are you and what are you doing here?' they asked. They were not convinced by his explanation till I stepped in; precautions were extra tight because Eisenhower was playing. He was often in his buggy, which was a novelty at that time.

Several of the regular spectators became our friends. An old fisherman from Maidens used to walk along the seashore to watch from a hillock. Officious security men rushed up to arrest him one day – the poor chap got the fright of his life – but a local intervened. Then there was a kind elderly priest who had been a good player himself; his idol was Jack Nicklaus. He could not afford a spectator's ticket (supposedly because he gave so much to needy people), so we asked him to watch from the lighthouse and Peggy always gave him tea.

One day I met Archie MacPherson who was commentating for the BBC. To help him cover two games at once, we gave him the use of the lighthouse balcony for an overall view of the 'Ailsa' and 'Arran' courses.

This was Burns country and Burns Suppers were very popular. I was invited to attend one for which I was asked to wear uniform. A card in rhyming verse was placed at each table setting; mine said: 'Sit doon, MacEachern and tonight, Forget aboot yer bloody light!' At the end, I was piped out ceremonially.

Andy, one of Peggy's brothers, was principal at Ailsa Craig and our nearest lighthouse neighbour. The rock could be seen clearly though it was about 16 miles off the mainland, and we visited him on a boat trip. As we walked up to the lighthouse there were snakes wriggling through the grass around our feet; harmless slow worms. Back at Girvan harbour, we saw new curling stones from Ailsa Craig being unloaded.

On days off, we often drove from Turnberry to Stranraer, which had an interesting harbour. I still recall the words of a furious young mother that I heard while waiting in the street: 'Greetin' again! Ye're aye greetin' and if ye're no greetin', ye're fa'in' doon the bloody stair!' the woman wailed, towing a howling child along the pavement.

Bobbie was captain of the *Hesperus* now. I joined him in Troon to watch a ship being launched from a neighbouring berth. We had a good view of the large cargo vessel slipping into the water. Afterwards, on the *Hesperus*, we were served dinner at the captain's table by the steward, my old friend Jimmy. I half expected Jacko to steal a handful of pickles from under his nose!

After two and a half years at Turnberry, I had news of a shift to Barra Head. A Stranraer fish salesman came to ask if I would sell the Ford Popular. I explained that it had a high mileage and a hole in the floor that was covered with a piece of cardboard; this was before the days of MOT tests. 'I ken a' aboot that,' he said. But it was just what he needed for running between Stranraer and Girvan. He gave me £60 for the car and bought the boat as well.

14

Call of the Wild

Barra Head

1963–1966

LIGHT ESTABLISHED 1833
WHITE STONE TOWER 18 METRES HIGH
ENGINEER – ROBERT STEVENSON

Barra Head lighthouse marked the southern tip of the Outer Hebrides; it had been reclassified as a rock station and Oban was now its shore station. During my previous spell here I had lodged with the principal and his wife. But with no doctor or nurse on hand, the remote clifftop on Berneray was not a good place for families. The memorials in its tiny graveyard were sad reminders of keepers' children who 'died of the croup'. Accompanying one inscription to a two-year-old boy was the following: 'The Lord gave and the Lord hath taken away. Blessed be the name of the Lord'.

The families spoke daily from the Oban radio room to the men on the rocks – Skerryvore and Dhuheartach were housed here too. Our new home on Pulpit Hill overlooked the Sound of Kerrera and the Northern Lighthouse Board pier. Bobbie was now master of the *Fingal*, attending the west coast lights, and lived in Oban with Mary and their two young daughters. We always knew when he was ashore as we could see at a glance if the ship was at her berth. Above our house was open ground where Rusty was happy to hunt for rabbits instead of golf balls.

Soon we had settled in and were ready for the new routine. There was some exhilaration at the thought of returning to a wild place. The isolated lighthouse cliffs were over 600 feet high and on clear days I might be able to see the distant outline of St Kilda from the lantern. But I knew things there were not good. Some weeks earlier, at New Year, there had been a sudden death at the lighthouse and police were still investigating.

Captain Robert Maceachern (Bobbie) in middle. (NLB)

I was at the Oban ferry terminal by five in the morning, ready to cross to Barra on MacBrayne's ferry. Depending on the weather and tides, it was sometimes necessary to spend a night there before the lighthouse boat took me out to Berneray. As usual, quite a few people had gathered on the pier to meet the *Claymore* at Castlebay. This time though, a stranger staggered up to me. People shouted in Gaelic: 'You've got the wrong man!' as the drunk lunged forward and laid into me with his fists. He was hastily removed by bystanders and John MacNeil, the lighthouse boatman, walked over to greet me. 'Come on up for your tea, Archie. Margaret is expecting you,' he said, as if nothing had happened. Later he explained that it was a case of mistaken identity when I had stepped off the ferry in lighthouse uniform; the result of friction between an assistant keeper and some Castlebay people.

We left at six o'clock that evening on the lighthouse boat for the remaining 15 miles to Berneray. The *Barra Head* had the lines of a sturdy fishing boat and was very well equipped. At the lighthouse slip, stores, mail, and equipment were unloaded and empty boxes taken on board. John assured me he would come out to Barra Head whenever he was needed; he would set out from Castlebay as soon as I radioed. John and I had become friends years earlier when he lived aboard the *Pharos* with us for three weeks.

He had come to supervise the building of a new attending boat in Fife. As well as being our boatman, John ran a taxi business, made masts for boats, and kept a few sheep.

John did not know any details about the keeper's death. He had, however, taken police officers out to investigate as soon as it was reported, and brought the body back to Castlebay.

When we landed at the slip, the first assistant was ready to depart; there was only time for a brief word before he left for his fortnight ashore. The Land Rover was parked near the landing. 'Who's the driver?' I asked. But once again, neither of the remaining assistants here could drive. The steep track was in a poor state. Previously, the station had been in very good shape, but now it looked unkempt. The courtyard was a mess and covered in oil which someone had hoped would kill the weeds, and annoyingly, the kitchen needed a coat of paint. The atmosphere was tense – was it because I was the new boss? Something was worrying these two.

After I had set the watches, one of the assistants, Bruce, showed me round. A radio beacon had been installed and I found both the light and the beacon working perfectly. The cliff was so high that the light was often obscured by low cloud; there was no fog signal. An unopened half bottle of whisky lay on the window ledge of the radio room. It had been there since New Year, and inquiries showed that the Board's 'no alcohol' rule had been broken at Hogmanay. At the tea table he broke it to me that the station was £400 in debt. The keepers' rock victualling allowance had not been used for provisions, and money was owed to the general store in Castlebay and to several shops in Oban. It seemed likely that I would inherit the debt.

The next morning Bruce was talkative, though the second assistant was very reticent; he stayed in the kitchen as he was cook for the week. Both had been on duty when the third keeper died. While Bruce and I were cleaning the lens and preparing the light, I asked why he was so agitated. Not only had he been upset by the tragedy, but he was also particularly disturbed by the way their colleague's body had been handled while it was being transferred to the boat to be taken to Castlebay. It had not been secured well enough to the stretcher and it slipped into the sea; somebody had had to retrieve the dead man from the water. Later, Bruce added that he was afraid of the assistant who had gone ashore as I arrived.

One of my first jobs was to send the police the windowsill from the radio room and the half bottle of whisky. In the course of their initial investigations they had found a handprint in blood on the sill so they wanted to examine this and the bottle that had been sitting on it. Then I found a bloodstain on the ground outside the tower door. This was below the handrail and had escaped notice previously; so far enquiries had focussed on the house because the man had been found in his bed. In spite of persistent questioning by detectives, little information had emerged. The other two had clammed up.

When the first assistant returned to duty, he was quite plausible and eager to get on with his work. I asked him about the debt. He said it was nothing to do with him; it was the principal keeper's responsibility and the Lighthouse Board would pay it. I pointed out that no keeper who was new to a station should have to pay outstanding costs. 'Well, I'm not paying anything,' he replied. As I expected, the office would not clear it because the victualling allowance had already been paid for the period in question; it was to be my responsibility. Four hundred pounds was a daunting sum to produce out of the blue, and I had no idea how to find it in a hurry. As soon as I went ashore, I explained the situation to each of the shopkeepers and asked for time to settle. Most of them agreed reluctantly, but one was insistent and I paid him myself in full. The others promised not to cut off future supplies if we paid as we went along. They already knew Bobbie and he assured them I would make good the full amount as soon as possible.

At the same time, Peggy passed to me disturbing news of troublemaking by the first assistant at the shore station. It was causing havoc among the families and had to be dealt with as soon as possible.

The police telephoned the lighthouse as they pieced together various strands of evidence. It became increasingly obvious that the second assistant was very withdrawn, probably as a result of the tragic episode and police grilling. I suggested to the office that he might be better at a less remote station and he was transferred quite soon.

The new second assistant, Alastair, travelled out with me for his first turn of duty and we stayed overnight in Castlebay. That evening, several tough looking fishermen in heavy jerseys sat at tables in the hotel bar. They chatted among themselves in Gaelic and nodded silently as I walked up to the counter. The barman brought my beer and then disappeared. When he came back with my change, he set seven glasses of whisky in front of me:

'These are for you from the boys.'

'But I can't drink all that,' I said quietly.

'Just take a wee sip of each or they'll be offended,' he replied.

Not wishing to offend the boys, I said 'slainte bha!' and raised each glass in turn. I was pleased to have been accepted by the locals, especially after the earlier encounter on the pier; luckily Alastair arrived with a friend a few minutes later. 'Drink as many of these as you can,' I whispered.

Our occasional was coming off duty when we arrived at the landing the next day. He was a nice, helpful man, but that day his face was unusually red as he walked to the boat: 'That's it! That's it, I'm finished! I'm never coming back to this place.' He swore and pointed to the first assistant. 'That so-and-so's made my life hell.' We lost a good worker and no one from Castlebay would replace him as long as this assistant remained in the crew, so a supernumerary was sent to replace him. Things seemed to be going from bad to worse.

Some weeks later we heard from the police that the death at the lighthouse was being considered as accidental and they would take no further action. The conclusion was that all three keepers got drunk at Hogmanay, and in the early hours of the morning one had left the house and made his way towards the tower. When he got to the door he toppled backwards, hitting his head so hard on the iron handrail that it bled profusely and left a lasting stain on the ground. Then he went to the engine room where his bloody handprint marked the window ledge. He must have staggered back to the house and gone to bed, where the other two found him. Bruce said he felt so cold to the touch that they put a hot water bottle beside him. Only later had they realised that he was dead.

During the winter I thought hard about making a garden to reduce our food bills. Bruce and Alastair were enthusiastic about the plan and the area beside the landing would be ideal. I spoke to the consortium of shepherds who leased the grazing; they had no objection to our cultivating this plot by the shore if it was fenced in.

Wire and fence posts were bought on our next trips to Oban, and very soon the fencing was complete; the ground was dug and plenty of seaweed was added. Alastair was exceptionally good at digging, though breaking up the turf was hard work. Fortunately, we had good soil. It had probably been cultivated by crofters from the five or six houses that now lay in jumbled ruins beside the plot. We sowed potatoes, carrots, turnips, cabbages and rhubarb that first year.

In early summer we had an inspection from the superintendent, who agreed that much needed doing to bring the station up to standard. He was quite pleased that we were growing our own produce – keepers here had never had a garden. Our early turnips were delicious, and by the end of the first season we had dug two hundredweight of potatoes. Berneray's former inhabitants had certainly left a good strip of ground.

The rest of the summer passed very quickly; the outside of the tower and all the buildings and boundary walls were limewashed, and paintwork inside the house was tackled. Heavy casks of oil and diesel had to be manhandled and ferried from the landing by Land Rover.

During a spell ashore in the autumn, I realised that troublemaking among the families was imposing intolerable strain on the young keepers. On the way back in the boat, John glanced towards the landing. 'You're in trouble now!' he exclaimed. 'The Land Rover's just gone off the road!' When we landed, I found its wheels hanging over the edge and the vehicle in danger of rolling into the sea.

'What on earth happened?' I asked.

'Oh, I must have made a mistake!' the first assistant said, smirking as he boarded the boat.

I sent Bruce up straightaway to put in the light – it would soon be sunset – while Alastair and I got to work on the Land Rover. We took empty oil barrels from the store to build up a platform under the dangling wheel. In darkness, we eventually managed to rock the vehicle and the back wheel caught a grip; we were off. However, it was eleven o'clock when we reached the lighthouse with the stores and gear. Bruce had everything working perfectly, though he had missed tea to keep the watch. We made a huge pot of tea, fried masses of bacon and eggs, and Alastair took over from Bruce as soon as we had eaten.

When the first assistant returned from the shore station, I told him he would not be with us much longer. Keepers' disputes were normally settled among themselves, but I could do nothing to resolve this. My letter to the office went on the first boat; the reply came with a copy saying he would be transferred shortly and why.

'You little rat!' he shouted at Bruce. 'You reported me!'

I stepped in. 'Oh no! I reported you. Would you like to do anything about it?' He left the room instead.

Christmas and New Year passed peacefully enough, with heavy coats and watch-boots and no festivities. I was on duty with Alastair and the first assistant. He left early in January and with him went the turmoil. Donald, a Lewis man, arrived to take his place; he was an experienced rock keeper with a good reputation and a dry sense of humour.

For most of the winter we were battered by winds – the handrails kept us on our feet as we crossed the courtyard. Cloud covered us, and sleet followed rain on the short days, though snow did not usually lie.

Now I devised a plan to discharge the station debt in full – we would fish for lobsters off Berneray and sell the catches in Oban. I drew up a design for a small boat to be built in Troon; she was to be twelve and a half feet long and made of larch and oak. That winter I would make 24 lobster creels and in spring we would start to set them. I explained this to Donald and waited for him to say it was nothing to do with him. On the contrary, there was an enthusiastic response: 'That's a good idea. And the first time I'm ashore, I can drive down with the plans and get a price.' John offered to collect our lobsters at reliefs free of charge; the *Claymore* would take them to the pond in Oban, and a trustworthy fish salesman there agreed to buy the catches and pay the money straight into our new bank account.

Fishing commercially was against Lighthouse Board rules, but after months at Barra Head, this was the only solution I could find. The creditors had waited long enough, so I decided to take a chance.

We bought twine for the netting and special plastic that would bend easily for the frames, although we still needed a coil of lightweight rope, cork for lines, and red buoys to mark each creel. There was plenty of wood from the shore to make bases and scraps of lead at the lighthouse for weights. I already had net needles and fencing wire for the eyes.

Before long, Donald brought news that the boat was to be ready by the end of March. I knitted the netting, Donald fitted this over the hoops, and the new pots were soon completed. He collected the boat, Bobbie took her to Castlebay on the *Fingal*, and John delivered her to us. I was very pleased; she was beautifully built and exactly to the plans. She was ready for the water when we added the engine, oars, rowlocks and anchor. In further preparation for the lobster fishing, we made a big wooden box with holes in the bottom and sides to store our live catches. It was secured in deep water off the landing, with a heavy anchor. We fished for poddlies (little saithe) to bait the new pots.

The next time Donald arrived for duty he was smartly dressed in uniform and carrying a big box under one arm.

'What's in the box, Donald?' I asked, thinking it was something for lobster fishing.

'Well, it's a broody hen – I thought it might be useful – and a dozen eggs too. We can put them in the old henhouse,' he said.

'What a good idea!'

The arrival of the hen and eggs was a pleasant surprise and Donald insisted on paying for them. Household scraps would feed them well enough till we could get grain at the next relief. We made a nest for the hen in a wooden tea box by cutting a hollow in a turf and filling it with dried grass; all the eggs hatched. The original stone henhouse was ideal for the growing chicks once netting was added outside to deter murderous crows and black-backed gulls.

After that I took my gun out to the station to scare off the black-backs. They preyed on the sheep, picking out their eyes with wicked beaks when they were lambing or stranded. They also tormented young seabirds relentlessly, especially puffin chicks when they ventured onto the sea before they could fly. These young were pecked and harried and swallowed whole. The arrival of razorbills to nest high on the cliff always gave us the first hint of spring. The hundreds of puffins, flying in clouds to the west side would disappear into burrows on the edge, with beaks full of sand eels. Like solemn Members of Parliament, these comic figures were welcome and approachable neighbours for a few weeks.

Guillemots, kittiwakes, and more razorbills nested on lower rock faces while gulls nested in huge numbers on the ground. No gannets bred here, but we did see them diving; from our clifftop they looked so small when they reached the water I was delighted to find a small colony of storm petrels nesting in the crevices of a boat shelter near the landing. Big flocks of barnacle geese came to Berneray in the autumn and fed furiously on the grass in the lighthouse enclosures. When that was cropped short, they moved to graze by the landing for weeks.

Birds did not flock to the light at night and we seldom saw anything except seabirds from the lantern by day. Perhaps they were deterred by the frequent covering of cloud and the hordes of resident gulls probably chased most songbirds from their territory. I saw few migrants – apart from an occasional rock pipit – on the flat ground by the sea. However, we did get a surprise visit one day. 'There's an eagle sitting on the henhouse roof!' shouted Donald. Sure enough, there was a fully grown golden eagle. Maybe it had seen the hens before they scuttled hastily to safety under the netting. We enjoyed a wonderful view of the huge bird, which was in no hurry to leave its perch. Eventually though, it took off and disappeared slowly over Mingulay.

A long fine spell helped the garden to grow well. Without being asked, Alastair would nip down in the evenings to weed, or to hoe up potatoes. All the seeds came up this year, though lettuce was not as happy as hardier cabbage in this windy place. Beautiful pink shoots of rhubarb appeared again. 'Och yes! It grows in Lewis, so it'll do fine here,' commented Donald, who baked good rhubarb puddings.

One quiet afternoon we set a dozen creels at promising-looking locations, with another ten to be put out later and two being kept as spares. We went back eagerly the next afternoon. The first creel contained an enormous conger eel; no good to us, even as bait as lobsters will not go near them. There was a dogfish in the second – also useless. Donald began to look a bit depressed, but his face lit up when he hauled the third creel and found a lovely little lobster. He unlaced the door and held up the catch proudly. It flapped its tail energetically, and he swore and dropped it over the side.

'What on earth did you do that for?' I yelled. 'As soon as we catch one, you throw it back in the sea!'

'Well, I got a fright,' he muttered sheepishly. I do not think he had fished lobsters before; he never dropped another one though. There were six more that day and some crabs. Two of the lobsters we kept as a treat for tea.

The next day we set the rest of the creels, and by the end of a fortnight we had about 30 lobsters in the box for Oban. Two months later we had cleared a good deal of the debt, and the garden was helping to reduce our living costs. Things were looking up. After a break, while the lobsters changed their shells, we started again in earnest at the beginning of July

One calm evening Alastair was rowing slowly while I had two lines out for bait. 'Don't look now, but I think we're being followed!' he said suddenly. The enormous mouth of a basking shark gaped wide just four feet from our stern; this creature was longer than our boat.

'What do I do now?' asked Alastair.

'Just ease the boat gently into shallow water; they're afraid of grounding,' I said.

As soon as we could see shingle on the seabed, it swam away. These harmless sharks followed us quite often, probably sifting through morsels stirred up by our oars as they searched for plankton. Sometimes we thought they might upset a small boat accidentally because of their size.

By the end of that September, we had paid off the whole debt from the proceeds of our fishing. It was a huge relief, though the shopkeepers had been very patient. We eased off fishing once we recouped the cost of our outlay. From then on we could have a treat once or twice a week and share any remaining proceeds. The venture brought no repercussions from the Lighthouse Board.

Because the weather often changed without warning, we always towed our lobster boat to a shelter above the shingle. This had a tumbledown wall that we repaired roughly and storm petrels nested here. After Donald and I had both left Barra Head we heard that the boat was smashed up in a gale, having been left on the landing overnight, tied to the derrick. Only a piece of wood was left at the end of the rope and the creels ended up at the bottom of the sea.

When we stopped fishing, there was a big programme of lighthouse work to be completed before the winter. The road repair, started the previous summer, had not been finished as we had run out of materials. The ship had therefore brought more gravel and tar with the latest stores.

All this time Bruce, Alastair and Donald worked well together. However, Bruce had never entirely lost his air of unease and he took no part in the fishing. The strain of the past had taken its toll, and he soon resigned from the Lighthouse Service; we were sorry to see him go. He was replaced by Alex, from Lewis, another experienced keeper who fitted in well, often yarning in Gaelic with the other two. No new occasional had been appointed and we still had supernumeraries.

Every day after dinner the assistants would wash the dishes while I sat trying to doze. Whenever I was about to drop off, there was a clatter, a laugh, and Donald saying 'wake up, boss! We've got to work this afternoon.'

As well as a few wild goats that roamed the cliffs and sometimes sheltered by the lighthouse, Berneray was populated by hundreds of sheep. These were kept by a group of Barra shepherds, led by Neil. Several times a year, five or six men arrived with numerous collies in a big fishing boat. The dogs swarmed off the boat, desperate to lift a leg on the nearest object and race away to their flock. When it was time for a tea break, the men built a driftwood fire to boil water, until I said we would brew tea and bring it down in the Land Rover. After that we always joined them for a yarn and a cup; they were good company. Sometimes the shepherds gave us a lamb, already killed and skinned – they were so pleased with the teas we gave them.

We offered the shepherds crabmeat with their cups of tea (the crabs we caught were not saleable, but the claw meat gave us good eating) and Neil always said: 'I wouldn't mind a taste.' It was especially good for a sandwich when we came off watch at night, though eating too much of it sometimes brought us out in spots and we would have to give the rest to the hens.

In the course of these tea breaks, the shepherds recounted vividly their recollections of the SS *Politician*, the ship made famous in *Whisky Galore*. They said that numerous boats from Barra had crossed to the wreck off Eriskay, and hidden bottles from the cargo clinked in many a rabbit burrow around Castlebay. John MacNeil told me that one salvaging escapade had ended in the sacking of a lighthouse boatman who had loaded the attending boat with full crates of whisky but drank too much on the way home. By the time he reached Castlebay, he was incapable of mooring the boat and ran aground at Kisimul Castle.

One summer a contractor's gang arrived to chip and paint the tall radio mast. We fed and housed them for four weeks and they paid us the going rate for food. After their second week, I distributed our mail from the boat as usual; however, there were no wage packets for the painters. 'Right!' said the foreman. 'We're going on strike. No money, no work!' He and his men walked out of the room. Unfortunately, this was Saturday afternoon, and the boat was not due with mail for another two weeks. Donald shook his head in disgust. I radioed John and asked him to phone the Northern Lighthouse Board first thing on Monday and request the money immediately. 'I'm sorry to hear you're in trouble there, Archie. I'll do what you ask,' John said, and hung up. The workmen re-appeared for their tea and we tried to act normally as we sat together at the table. Early the next afternoon, Alastair shouted to us:

'The boat's coming.'

'What boat?'

'The *Barra Head*!'

'Nonsense! It's Sunday. She's not due for a fortnight. It'll be a fishing boat.'

'Come and look for yourself then,' he said.

Right enough, I saw the lighthouse boat butting her way round the end of Mingulay. As we arrived at the landing, John appeared from his wheelhouse with a smile and a large brown envelope with 'Five Hundred Pounds Enclosed' written on the outside.

'In the name of Goodness! How did you get all this money on a Sunday?' I asked.

'Och, I always keep a few pounds in a drawer. It comes in handy sometimes. Cheerio! I'll see you in a fortnight,' John said.

Here was another instance of Western Isles kindness. I called the foreman, who was lying on his bunk, and work started again.

Before long two radio engineers arrived to service the beacon, which meant there were nine of us staying at the lighthouse. It was cheerful having the extra company (it was lucky that Alastair and Donald were both good cooks), but by mid-September we were back to a three-man team.

We had finished repairing the mile of steep road by the end of October. When the weather closed in, the light took most of our time, and little outside work could be done. On fine afternoons we sometimes took the Land Rover down to the store and walked to the ruined houses or the bay at the end of the plain. Here we picked up any useful driftwood, though we did not need fuel as there was an electric fire in the house. In a windy spell we retrieved two beach balls, but they soon blew back out to sea when we were kicking them about. They might have floated over from Ireland; when it was very clear we could make out the Irish coast from the lantern.

It was good that we could move about the island freely in winter, though travel plans were changeable. On rough mornings, not many of the *Claymore*'s passengers appeared for breakfast and we would get two kippers each! Now and again the ferry could not call at Castlebay in severe weather and we were stranded on Barra, or we flew

Collies and Captains

On Macbrayne's ferries, sheepdogs were very much part of the scene as they accompanied the shepherds from various islands to the livestock sales in Oban. Afterwards they were frequently left to find their own way home while the men concluded the business of the day in the town's bars. The collies would run back to the harbour and up the gangplank to catch the *Claymore*. One of the crew would tie each of them to a rail on deck for the crossing; sometimes there was a row of dogs sitting patiently or curled up, even in the roughest weather. After we sailed he gave each dog a bowl of food; then it usually slept. I often sat beside them, though they had no time for anyone but their own boss or the sailor who fed them. Every one of these remarkable animals recognised its home port as the ship called at a succession of islands – it would waken and leave the ferry of its own accord.

I reflected on some of the stories I had heard of Macbrayne skippers on the island services. During my time on the west coast, I got to know a few. One in particular was Captain 'Squeaky' R. On one occasion in the war, his ferry was halfway between Barra and Tiree when he became aware of a man in civilian clothes coming on to his bridge.

'Get off my bridge, you …!' he spluttered.

The man was very agitated. 'But I must talk to you urgently, Captain. I am the vice-admiral in charge of the Northwestern Approaches and I think we are running into danger.'

'If that is so, you had better come down to my cabin, sir, and tell me all about it.'

'Do you have a chart, Captain?' he asked.

After searching in a drawer, he produced a very dusty chart. 'There you are, sir.'

Pointing to one area, the Admiral said: 'You see these little spots, Captain? They are, I think, our latest minefield.' Squeaky examined them carefully.

'If they're what I think they are, we'll be all right, sir.'

'And what is that?'

'I think they're fly shit.' Men like this captain knew their waters so well that they did not need to consult charts regularly. My father once heard a helmsman being told 'never mind the compass, keep your eye on the hills.'

from the Cockle Strand to Glasgow. But reliefs by the attending boat from Barra Head were never overdue; John MacNeil and his crew were expert in all conditions.

On wild days he took a more sheltered route to Berneray, motoring behind Mingulay and other little islands to save battling headfirst into the waves. Once I was due to go ashore in an easterly gale when it was too rough to use the landing so he put in to a little bay on the south west.

'I didn't expect you today, John,' I said.

'But I said I would always come for you,' he replied.

The next morning it was too stormy for the *Claymore* to complete the relief, so I flew to Glasgow in a Rapide that collected us from Barra's cockle sand beach.

After one of these flights Alastair and I were walking into Glasgow bus station, both wearing uniform and carrying kit bags. A wee man in a bonnet sidled up and muttered:

'If yous are lookin' for women, come wi' me.'

'Clear off!' I said.

Alastair threatened to punch him and he slunk away.

The day came when an extra collie appeared in the rush from the shepherds' boat. While the others settled and worked the sheep, a beautiful young dog ran behind Neil all day. As we drank our tea I commented on this. He just would not work, Neil said. His children had made such a pet of the animal that he was useless as a sheepdog. He

CASTLEBAY LIFEBOAT

Two stories about the Castlebay lifeboat tickled us. Neil, the shepherd, was the assistant coxswain. He had eight daughters but people thought he would still like to have a boy. One night the lifeboat was called out to a French trawler wrecked on the Monach Isles. After a long and tiring time without sleep, Neil was at the wheel on the way home while the others rested below. As they entered a narrow sound, the lifeboat hit a buoy with a crash that woke everyone. She bounced off without damage, and the coxswain shouted through the hatch: 'It's all right lads! Neilie's got a "buoy" at last!' In due course Neil's wife did have a ninth baby and it was a boy.

Following one lifeboat rescue, a reporter from a national newspaper phoned the coxswain. He was a retired Merchant Navy captain from Barra who had returned to spend his time fishing for lobsters.

'What do you do?' he was asked.

'I'm a lobster fisherman,' replied the cox in his strong Hebridean accent.

The report on the incident appeared with the headline: 'Obstetrician Saves Crew'. This caused hilarity in the Islands.

was going to put him in the sea and drown him on the way home. Horrified, I offered to buy the dog in case this was no empty threat. 'You can have him for nothing,' said Neil. After the men had sailed for home, Donald shouted:

'They've left one of their collies!'

'No, Donald, he's mine now. Neil's just given him to me.'

Donald grinned, picked up the dog unceremoniously, and put him in the back of the Land Rover.

From that day, the handsome black and white collie, Bob, was a member of the Barra Head crew. He was 18 months old and housetrained. He only made one 'mistake' and it was on that first evening – when some dogs barked on television he barked a reply and lifted his leg on the set.

One day a fishing boat brought a party of schoolchildren from Castlebay to visit the lighthouse. Bob was delighted when the teacher brought them to the kitchen for a cup of tea. Neil's younger children were there and a great fuss was made of the dog. He wanted to go back with them on the boat and looked quite dejected until Alastair gave him a big mutton bone.

He did not understand English at first, only Gaelic, but he learnt very quickly. The first English word that he recognised was 'boat'. As soon as anybody mentioned 'going to the boat', he was up and waiting at the door. Before we launched, Bob would jump aboard eagerly, and would stand on lookout in the bow with his ears cocked while we motored along, especially alert when he saw the seals. He got very excited when we hauled in a creel, head tilted to one side as he looked to see what we had caught. However, he took no chances with creatures from the deep; always frightened if a conger eel arrived, he would run up to the bow, grab a dogfish and shake it violently. A wary eye watched crabs and lobsters, which crawled and flapped menacingly. 'You're chicken, that's what you are!' Donald would say, and the tail wagged.

Bob followed me everywhere, even while I worked, and he slept beside my bed at night. The lads were good to him – he was well looked after while I was ashore. He loved the Land Rover and always wanted the middle front seat.

John delivered a regular order of poultry food. When the hens were in full lay, we had more than enough eggs at times and took some ashore. But suddenly the production rate fell dramatically – Bob had learnt how to squeeze into the henhouse and steal the eggs. We soon put an end to this by spreading mustard in an empty shell and replacing it in the nest box. On his next raid, he spat it out quickly and did not try that again.

One sunny afternoon in late spring I had been setting creels with Donald, who was always keen on exploring. 'Let's go in and look at this gulley,' he suggested. We passed through a deep cleft in a wall of rock and the water below us was as clear as glass. 'There's something white at the bottom of that cliff!' Donald shouted. I nosed the boat in and he jumped onto the tiny rocky beach to investigate. He came back carrying a very small lamb – it was only about a day old and had been standing forlornly beside its dead mother. How they had got there was a mystery. There was no way the ewe could have climbed down the sheer rock face, nor could she have walked from the shore, which was only accessible by boat. She must have fallen over the cliff and given birth before she died. Donald nursed the orphan all the way home, with Bob watching his every move.

When we reached the lighthouse we opened a tin of condensed milk and Donald tried to feed the lamb with drops on his finger. Bob helped by licking its face. We burned a hole in a cork to make a makeshift teat on a medicine bottle full of diluted condensed milk. The lamb drank the lot and we left him in Bob's care for the night, lying in a box lined with straw. Each man gave the lamb more milk as he came off watch and it was quite frisky in the morning. It was kept in the kitchen for a few days till it started jumping out of the box and had to go to an outhouse.

Soon the lamb was drinking so greedily I was afraid it might swallow the cork. I radioed John and asked for two baby's feeding bottles with teats at the next relief. He chortled: 'Oh! Who's had the baby then? I've heard many things about you men at Barra Head, but never that!' The bottles, teats, and more condensed milk arrived with our next supplies. John had asked an old shepherd for advice and told us the tins should be well diluted. In no time the lamb was eating grass as well as downing all the milk on offer. Bob regarded it as a friend, lying beside it while it grazed and licking its mouth after drinks of milk. When the orphan was big enough, we released it to roam with the other sheep.

Another afternoon Donald noticed a sheep cut off by the tide below a steep drop. He shinned 20 or 30 feet down a rope while I held the end. Beside me, Bob watched anxiously until he could stand it no longer and scrambled down to help. Once the sheep was cornered, Donald tied it on his back and I pulled them up, but poor Bob was left on the rocks with no way up and was in danger of being washed away. I went down the rope and tied him on my back with a length of the rope round his middle, and Donald hauled us up. Bob licked my ear all the way and his sharp claws gripped my shoulders.

A group of 12 students came to Berneray one summer on a research project; they camped on the plain for two weeks. We asked them to the lighthouse; bringing biscuits with them, they joined us every day for coffee and crabmeat. One lad had found a baby cormorant on the rocks and kept it as a pet. It was very young and very ugly. As soon as he brought it into the kitchen on his shoulder, I asked him to take it outside; it was set on the wing of the Land Rover in the garage while the boy was in the house. After a day or two, I noticed that Bob was annoyed at this bird sitting on his vehicle and bared his teeth, which was unusual for him. When the boy went back to collect the cormorant, it had disappeared, and he was very distressed. 'That's impossible, it can't get out of the garage,' I said; it was too young to fly anyway. The two of us searched but we could not see the bird anywhere. I detected a smug look on Bob's face – he must have killed it. 'Bob!' I seldom raised my voice to him, but now he slunk away looking guilty at the scolding tone. No trace was ever found, not even a beak. Perhaps Bob had buried the corpse while we drank our coffee.

The second mate on the *Fingal* was interested in burial grounds and told me about an old graveyard below the lighthouse. There were some headstones, a number toppled, and bones were visible where the grass had been cropped smooth. Whether these were sheep carcases or human remains exposed by colonising rabbits, we did not investigate. The Berneray folk would have needed every fertile inch of lower ground to grow crops but this slope was adequate for burial.

Occasionally we saw a Norwegian cruise ship landing tourists for a brief visit to Mingulay, where they explored the abandoned church and houses. It seemed to us that most of the headstones in the cemetery there marked the grave of a MacNeil. According to a legend, Noah had invited a MacNeil of Barra to sail in the ark with him; MacNeil had declined, saying that he had a good boat of his own.

Barra Head lighthouse still had no running water or bath and the chemical toilet was in an outhouse across the courtyard. It took the best part of a day every three or four weeks to bring water from the brackish well near the shore. We pumped it by hand into barrels, took these up by Land Rover, and hand-pumped the water again to the kitchen tap. When we found another well of sorts much nearer we thought it should be investigated. 'If the supply is adequate, you could bring piped water right up to the station,' the district superintendent said on his next visit. 'Clean out the well and let it fill with fresh water. I'll give you containers to take samples. You could put a bathroom, hot water tank, and flush toilet into the washhouse. If you are prepared to do the work, I'll provide the materials.'

A motor pump would be fitted at the newly discovered well to bring the water up to the house, though the ground was so rocky it would be impossible to dig trenches for the pipes. This meant that they would have to be laid on the surface. The main drain would go through the boundary wall and be taken 60 feet down the cliff; not a task for the fainthearted. It was very similar to the work I had watched as a boy when artificers laid pipes to remove engine room fumes on Scalpay.

We started by removing the layer of flat stones that covered the well. When we bailed out all the water we discovered a beautifully built circular stone lining. The bottom was hidden by thick black mud – Alastair went down a ladder and found this to be about six inches deep. For the rest of that day, we hauled up bucketfuls of sludge until we reached a floor of solid stone. The well was ten feet deep, and after a while we saw water trickling down the sides. Things were looking good. 'We'll cross to Mingulay on the first fine day and get four or five bags of clean shell sand to put in the bottom,' I suggested. 'We'll leave it to settle and see what happens.'

The next Sunday was very calm, so we took the boat over to a bay where we sank to our knees in the wet white sand. We returned with full bags, tipped them into the well, and covered it to stop inquisitive sheep falling in. After four or five days we were quite elated to find it three quarters full of lovely clear water. Samples sent to be analysed were found suitable for human consumption, albeit a little hard.

Plans were made the following winter, though we had no plumbing experience and no drawings for guidance. In April the *Pharos* brought everything we could possibly need that year, including thousands of gallons of paraffin and diesel, more tar and gravel for the road, and tons of extra supplies for the new project.

Soon we started on the concrete base for the sectional hut that would house a diesel-driven pump. The hut was attached to bolts in the base to stop it being blown away. Cement had to be mixed by hand as there was no mixer. The pipework from the well to the lighthouse took time as we had to thread and join each length.

Now the most difficult job had to be tackled: laying the drain down the west cliff to carry effluent to the sea. The rocky surface was so uneven that it had to be built up in places to support the pipe. At times, it seemed impossible to work down the cliff with the sheer drop to the sea; on windy days we could do nothing there at all. But there were plenty of other jobs to do if we were to be ready on time, and luckily the weather was mostly good that spring and early summer. Everything had to be completed before the superintendent and his team came in July. They would install the pump and other fittings, put finishing touches and inspect everything.

The washhouse was prepared as our new bathroom. We ripped out the boiler, fireplace and two washtubs (these had not been used since all the keepers' wives left the station); covered the floor with concrete and cut a hole in the wall for the pipe. One day when I was splitting a stone with a hammer, my eyes were filled with splinters. I got most of them out immediately and a doctor in Oban removed the rest a week later. Fortunately, that was the only mishap in the course of the operation.

While I was ashore that time, I left instructions for the others to build supporting pillars to carry the water tank. When I returned I found single pillars and not the double ones I had planned. To heave the tank into place we rigged up a tackle on the flat roof of the house. A rope was tied to the rear of the Land Rover and Donald drove away slowly; Alastair and I stood on ladders to position the tank onto its pillars outside the kitchen window.

Soon the pipeline was complete and ready for connecting to the toilet. Routine lighthouse work was up to date and things were going well. Or so we thought. In order to connect the water pipe for the kitchen sink, we had to lift one of the stone slabs in the pavement. Underneath, to our horror, we found a foul-smelling lake of dirty black water. Apparently there was no drain from the kitchen sink and over the years all the waste had collected below the house. Despair set in. We dug a trench in the grass to let the sludge run down the hill, but it left a long black stain and we had no idea how long it would take to dry up this mess or how we would carry away the waste. What's more, the kitchen sink could not be used till we found a solution. This was not part of the plan and the superintendent was due in five days.

Then we remembered some lengths of pipe that were left over from the main drain. Our next step was to lay these from the sink. Making a hole through the whinstone boundary wall was the hardest part and a trench had to be dug through the road, which had only been tarred the year before. But luck was with us now; the slime stopped running and we were ready just in time. 'What's that in aid of?' asked the superintendent when he saw the new pipework from the sink. Like us, he had assumed that a sink with a tap would have a waste pipe. I helped him set up the pump in the hut and we were delighted that it fitted the floor perfectly. The artificers installed the bath, wash-hand basin, toilet, and hot water tank in the washhouse. A light and an immersion heater were put in, with a power line from the generator.

The water in the well was at maximum level and beautifully clear on its bed of Mingulay sand. The pump was tested and the pipes connected. The great day had come at last; we were ready. Water gushed out of taps and everything worked perfectly. Thanks to a good crew and a far sighted superintendent, we had mod cons at last!

Three days later a severe gale blew up from the west. Alastair, who had been cleaning the lens, came down and announced: 'There's filth all over the lantern!' Blasts of wind from the sea were blowing the sewage back and scattering it wildly, though the pipe went well down the cliff. 'What on earth do we do now?' the superintendent said as we looked over the edge. Everyone was downcast, but we would not accept failure after all this work.

'We still have a few lengths of pipe left from the kitchen waste,' I remembered, and pointed further down the cliff. 'We could add them till the opening is sheltered by that big rock.' It was very dangerous extending the sewer. However, one of the tiffies (artificers) worked with me, and the boulder helped to protect us from the drop below. There were no further problems with waste which disappeared into the sea through this lengthened pipe.

Now that the plumbing worked well, it was time for the usual lighthouse maintenance and inspection. One evening, the superintendent asked me to show him our garden. But as we were getting into the Land Rover, Bob pushed past him and sat on the middle front seat. He flatly refused to move so I lifted him out, still clutching the cushion. The superintendent smiled and said: 'He seems to regard that as his seat. Just leave him to it and I'll sit on the outside.' So Bob sat, bolt upright and smug in his favourite place, whining with excitement at the rabbits we passed on the way down the hill.

In the meantime, however, things at home were not going well. Peggy became ill and had to have a major operation for cancer. It was difficult to leave her in hospital and return to the rock when my two weeks were up – my request for another week of leave had been turned down. Thankfully, Kathleen was living at home so I knew that Peggy was in good hands, and Donald brought first-hand news from his turns ashore. His flat was above ours and he called on her regularly now with offers of help, a smile or a joke. Support from family and colleagues was invaluable as she gradually improved.

Early that winter, the *Fingal* took me ashore with a stomach ulcer. Bobbie was on leave, so our friend Norman, the chief officer, was acting captain. I was off for about three weeks, though I was back at the lighthouse for Christmas and New Year.

That was a winter of bad weather with many travel problems, but John never failed to collect me from Barra Head. Once I was stranded in Castlebay for three days before the small plane could leave the Cockle Strand. Then our take off was so bumpy that the girl behind me fainted with fright. When we landed on Tiree to refuel, she said she would never set foot in a plane again. She recovered though, and the pilot took us up to blue skies with cotton wool clouds that cleared in time to reveal the Trossachs.

In early spring some little pockets of green appeared on cliff ledges, while most of the grass looked lifeless. From my bedroom window one morning I noticed three sheep on a minute ledge of the adjoining cliff. By the end of the week I realised they were trapped with nothing left to eat. There was no way we could reach this inaccessible spot so we tried to lasso them, but without success. The second week saw them eating the wool off each other's backs. I radioed Castlebay, and John said he would tell the shepherds, though he knew no one would come. I threatened to climb down with ropes.

'On no account,' he replied, knowing how dangerous this ledge was.

'Well, tell the men if they don't come in two days, I'll shoot the sheep.'

John could do no more and at nights I lay thinking how these starving animals were suffering. No one came and finally I shot them. If only the shepherds would put a little wire here and there to save their sheep from the cliffs! I gave them some coils from our supply and eventually they fenced the area where I had to put the creatures out of their misery.

That April Bobbie brought the *Fingal* to take me ashore as my ulcer was playing up again, worse than last time. Before long I had a letter to say that I was being transferred to Covesea Skerries at Lossiemouth. This would be a good move as Peggy could continue her medical treatment.

I returned for another six weeks, in which time I had to decide what to do with Bob.

A dog of the wild places, he was a much loved member of the lighthouse crew. Barra Head was his territory and I did not think he would be happy in urban surroundings. Rusty had always welcomed me home, but he would not like another dog on his patch. Bob was fond of my assistants, who were always good to him, and I decided that he should stay.

Donald remained at Barra Head for some time after my transfer, and he made sure the dog would be well cared for when he left. Bob lived until he was 16 and the keepers made a bonny little cement headstone with his name inscribed on it. Years later some visitors from the Lighthouse Board were flown out to Barra Head. They were asked by the helicopter pilot to take 'a bunch of flowers for the dog's grave'.

Bob the Barra Head dog in old age.

15

Winding Down

Covesea Skerries and Chanonry

1966–1975

Covesea Skerries

LIGHT ESTABLISHED 1846
WHITE TOWER 36 METRES HIGH
ENGINEER – ALAN STEVENSON

My transfer to Covesea Skerries on the Moray Firth signalled the end of the lonely years. It was a relatively easy station on the outskirts of Lossiemouth, a busy fishing town that was popular with tourists. Many of the personnel from the Lossiemouth and Kinloss air bases lived locally. Our immediate neighbour on one side was the Fleet Air Arm base, and it took a while to get used to the roar of aircraft by day and night. On our other side, a big caravan site was busy all summer and people often cut through our grounds to reach the huge sandy beach below the lighthouse. Beyond this fine expanse of sand lay the rocks called Covesea Skerries. Our new surroundings could not be more different from Barra Head.

Angus had been posted to RAF Kinloss, meaning he was close by. He played in the pipe band, which performed in full uniform outside the lighthouse for us one glorious summer afternoon – very exciting! Before long, Angus decided he wanted to go to sea and left the RAF to join the Merchant Navy. Kathleen and her husband, Tom, came to live in Lossiemouth with their baby daughter.

During a storm in 1826, 16 vessels had been lost in the Moray Firth, so in 1846 this flashing red and white signal was established. I found the lighthouse in good condition and the work easy in most respects. There was no foghorn, but as it was a two-man station, we were short of sleep in winter. My assistant was Syd, an excellent keeper. He and his wife came from the Isle of Man and were good company. The occasional was a retired fisherman from Hopeman. He always smoked his pipe as he cycled over for turns of duty at Covesea – it took three fills of tobacco from his house. When he was young, the fishing industry on the east coast had declined so he had 'emigrated to the west coast'. At one point their boat was dismasted in a storm. They were working off Barra Head and were driven north for days. After the wind eased, they put up a jury rig and made for Stornoway, but their catch of herring was past using by the time they reached port, and they returned home with no money.

Though the work was not hard, we had to remember that every morning the man extinguishing the light must lock the tower door as he left. Before our time a stranger had gone upstairs and climbed over the balcony rail. A keeper found his body on the quarter deck roof below.

Syd and I limewashed the tall, white tower during the long days of summer. It was quite a struggle for two of us – particularly since we had to allow an afternoon sleep for the man taking the first watch – and it took a full week. We still used a heavy wooden stage suspended on ropes, which we rigged on the pavement and hauled to the balcony, moving the stage round as we completed vertical strips of the tower. There was a knack to diluting the limewash (it was made up in a special bath by pouring water onto a lime block). If the mix was too thin then it would give a dirty effect; the correct consistency made a sparkling finish. Safety helmets and harnesses were not yet required, but a new rule forbade on safety grounds the painting of wooden ladders. At another station with a tall tower, a visitor came to ask if she could scatter her husband's ashes from the balcony. That day the keepers had just finished their limewashing and had left their newly painted ladders to dry at the foot of the tower. The following morning they found a coating of his ashes adhering to the paint.

From the lantern one night, the occasional saw red flares shooting into the sky and a torch flashing on the rocks. We called out the lifeboat which rescued a group of airmen whose boat engine failed while they were fishing.

On another occasion it was daylight and I was watching a passing helicopter from the lantern. Suddenly, the rotors stopped, and it dropped to the beach. I was relieved to see two men step out, unhurt. Then a race began against the tide to remove the damaged aircraft, with RAF equipment. There were sometimes minor air crashes locally that involved aircraft in training.

During my second summer at Covesea, the machine broke down – Syd and I kept the lens revolving by hand for two nights and it had to rotate at the correct speed. Each watch lasted for four hours so we were glad it happened while the nights were short. I approached a local engineering firm and they produced replacement parts in 48 hours.

Coincidentally, the director of the company rented a beat on the Spey and invited me to fish for salmon; a wonderful opportunity since Spey fishing was as scarce as hen's teeth. For most of my days off in the season I fished on the River Deveron.

One day the Spey was very high and coloured after heavy rain. A tantalising salmon kept jumping within reach of the line but refused to take any of my flies. After watching for a while, the ghillie waded out and handed me a large earthworm. 'Try that!' he said and it worked like a charm. A distinguished looking gentleman in a kilt and glengarry walked along; I took him to be the laird.

'I see you got a fish. Nice one too,' he commented as he saw the gleaming beauty on the bank.

'Yes, it's about eight pounds,' I said.

'What did you catch him on?'

'A Blackbird's Fancy,' I answered, hesitating as I knew this was a 'fly only' beat. He just snorted and walked on.

Prince Charles was still a senior pupil at nearby Gordonstoun, and he often walked past the lighthouse on his way to the beach. One day I asked his bodyguard – always in the vicinity – if the prince would like to cut through our grounds. We saw him quite often after that, but left him in peace.

When I had been at Covesea for nearly two years, the occasional was told by the Lighthouse Board that he must retire since he was 65. He was heartbroken and pleaded with me to be kept on, but I had to tell him that we could not change the regulations. He took to his bed and I visited often to sit with him, but he died within a short time.

The Lighthouse Board owned quite a big area of land that was mostly overgrown with whin bushes. To Rusty's delight it was infested with rabbits, though I decided to clear as much as possible. Syd and I hacked and burnt the undergrowth, greatly helped by the Fleet Air Arm who sent two men from the base and a fire engine on standby. Gradually the ground was returned to grass which we kept mown.

We enjoyed life here. Our social life was good, and we were in fairly frequent contact with the Lossiemouth base. At one time, Peggy and I were invited to a sumptuous dinner in the officers' mess, where a handsomely decorated salmon took pride of place on the table.

Every summer Peggy ran the shop on the caravan site and, as perks, we were given a free caravan to take on holiday each year. There was no shortage of entertainment on our doorstep in the holiday season. Live music and dances were organised every week for the caravan site. A large natural cave in the cliff beside the lighthouse made an ideal venue. Syd and I took turns as bouncers, judged competitions, and enjoyed many evenings at 'The Cave' with our families. One Saturday night a group of visiting singers went sea-fishing afterwards and had to swim ashore when their borrowed boat began to sink!

I could not believe my ears the day a man phoned the lighthouse and said he was going to kill me. He was coming to slit my throat, he said. I did not take it seriously, but Peggy rang the police. They arrested a man with a criminal record at the caravan site; I had chased him out of our garden the previous day when I caught him stealing vegetables.

A very different telephone call invited me to visit a local laird at his house. A chauffeur-driven car was sent to collect me, and I was shown into an astonishing room, with stuffed animal heads on every wall – the trophies of a family of big game hunters. During our conversation about shooting and fishing, my host wanted to know if partridges still nested in the lighthouse grounds. He brought me a big glass of whisky which I could not finish, so on the quiet I emptied the last drops into a handy plant pot.

After nearly four years at Covesea Skerries, we moved further round the Moray Firth to Chanonry; familiar ground for us. Before we left, however, I was amazed and very honoured to be awarded the British Empire Medal. Peggy and I went to London for this exciting event.

Chanonry

Light established 1846
White tower 13 metres high
Engineer – Alan Stevenson

Some referred to the Black Isle lights as 'MacEachern territory'. By this time my cousin, Finlay, was the keeper at Cromarty lighthouse and it was my turn now for Chanonry.

Chanonry Lighthouse (present day)

Years earlier Finlay's father, Claude, had served at Cromarty and my own father had retired from Chanonry. Here, Peggy's increasingly vital medical treatment was within easy reach, although her health was failing. I was thankful to be back on familiar ground when the family and I had to face the inevitable.

Angus came on leave from deep-sea trips with the Merchant Navy, and Kathleen and Tom had moved to just a few miles away with their children, Fiona and Calum. It was good to recognise faces in the village, including my old friend, Jock.

The lighthouse marked the narrows in the Firth between Chanonry Point and Fort George. Also known as the Ness, this flat spit of land juts into the Firth, with Fortrose and Rosemarkie on either side.

Popular as a pre-retirement station, Chanonry was easily run by one man. There were only 48 steps in the tower and no watches to be kept in the lightroom. There was no machine, so no winding up, and no foghorn. As usual, the single storey house had a flat roof and the tower had a flat quarter-deck over its lower area. It was not difficult to limewash the small tower and the adjacent house or tar these roofs on my own.

Originally Chanonry's fixed light had been manned by two keepers. After the First World War, the light was converted from oil to coal gas, which was delivered by the *Pharos* and stored in tanks. The Commissioners decided then that the lighthouse could be run efficiently by one keeper, as long as an alarm bell was fitted in his bedroom to rouse him if the light failed. An alarm bell in the bedroom still called me if there was a fault during the night, though the supply of gas in cylinders was delivered now by road. A time switch had been installed and it was no longer necessary to switch on at sunset and off at sunrise.

When the streets of Inverness were first lit by electricity, ships heading for Inverness found it difficult to see the Chanonry light against the bright lights of the town. It was decided then to change the character of the light from 'fixed' to 'occulting', and make it more conspicuous. One and a half seconds of darkness following four and a half of light made up the new cycle of six seconds.

Several lighted buoys warned ships of the many surrounding sandbanks. These had to be checked every night through binoculars. The station's long brass telescope was no longer used for this, but it still lived inside the door of the house on big hooks in the lobby. 'Navity Bank', 'East Riff', 'Skate Bank', 'Craig Mee', 'Meikle Mee', and 'Munlochy' were ticked on a log for the returns. A spare buoy lamp sat in working order on the workshop floor. Now and then I had to repair or replace one, though the ship still serviced buoys each year. It was lucky that any buoys that needed repair were fairly close and I was able to reach them easily in my second-hand wooden dinghy (named the *Fiona* after my granddaughter). To attend any that were more distant, the Inverness pilot would assist.

Chanonry was also a weather station. Returns for rainfall, temperature, wind speed, cloud cover and sunshine were sent to the Met Office every month. On the

Left to right: A lighthouse barometer, rock box and an ornamental piece of the Skerryvore balcony railing, retrieved after the fire.

Left to right: Brass name discs from canvas mail bags, commemmorative shield presented when the last Scottish lighthouse was automated in 1998 and commemorative shield presented to Archie when he retired finally in 1993 from the attendant's post at Chanonry.

Left to right: Copper lightroom shovel, uniform badges and buttons and a model ship in a bottle (a favourite hobby – Archie made this at Dhuheartach).

Left: Small folding table that Archie made at
Dhuheartach from driftwood found on an Erraid beach

Right: Standard issue at lighthouses – a General Order
Book and a Shiprewck Return Book

SHIPWRECK RETURN BOOK

I noticed in the shipwreck return book that eight vessels had run aground off Chanonry Point since 1881.

The last entry was in Father's handwriting, dated 1930:

> At 2.30 am of the 7th March the S.S. *James Tennant* of Newcastle went aground on Chanonry Point while outbound from Inverness to Invergordon. The alleged cause of the stranding was given by the master who said he mistook his distance off Chanonry light. At low water the vessel was dry but lay with her light cargo on an even keel two hundred yards from the lighthouse. She was floated off undamaged with the afternoon tide the next day and proceeded to Invergordon. Eight persons were saved and none lost.

The crew members had been taken to the lighthouse that night and Kitty gave them tea and food.

A sloop called *Victory* was driven on to Fort George Point by high winds in 1889.

In 1888 a schooner, the *Amalia*, was stranded with a load of coal. 'They could not see the land owing to the snow and darkness of the night,' the entry stated. Aground on sand to the east side of the lighthouse, she was 'expected to become a total wreck.' The principal of the day recorded that 'The crew came ashore in their own boat, and as they could not get lodgings near hand we had to accommodate them with beds.' Fortunately we did not have to house marooned seafarers at Chanonry now!

In 1881 a Norwegian schooner, the *Anne Marie*, valued at £100, ran aground here in a gale and snow. She had been bound for Wick with staves for making herring barrels. No one had drowned in any of the incidents.

Last entry in the Shipwreck Return Book at Chanonry, signed by Archie's father.

sun recorder, the rays shone through a solid glass ball and burnt a line on a measured strip of card. However, the ball was pinched so often by people trespassing through the grounds that sun records here were discontinued.

The Commissioners visited one summer and I hoisted the NLB flag to mark the occasion. They strolled around in yachting caps and plimsolls looking at everything of interest while the *Pharos* lay at anchor. When she headed round Chanonry Point for Cromarty I dipped the flag and the gentlemen waved from her deck in time-honoured fashion.

We needed the *Fiona* in an emergency that arose while Angus was on leave. A gale was blowing, when a holidaymaker and his two young children had headed for Eathie in an inadequate dinghy. Standing on the Point, his hysterical wife watched for them in mounting waves. Their trip very nearly ended in disaster and the *Fiona* was starting to fill with water when we reached them and took them to safety.

Having the *Fiona* meant I could cross Rosemarkie Bay to set creels, and these brought in good lobsters and crabs. This was when I had my closest encounters with dolphins – often they leapt beside me and plunged under the boat. During one month in particular, I had a unique experience of their company. I was going to the creels regularly, often at five in the morning to suit tides and lighthouse work, and a

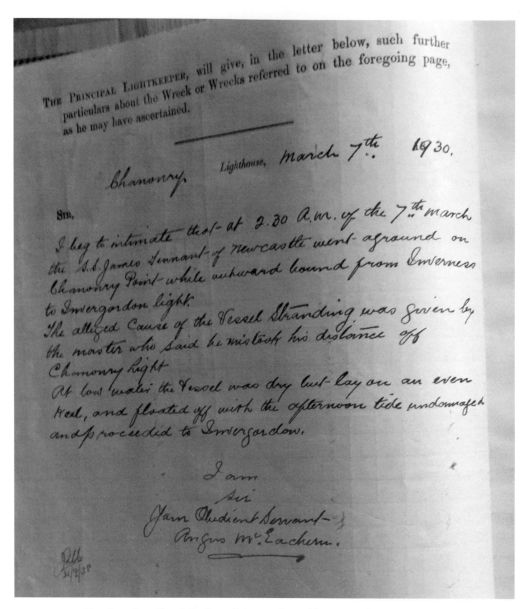

THE PRINCIPAL LIGHTKEEPER, will give, in the letter below, such further particulars about the Wreck or Wrecks referred to on the foregoing page, as he may have ascertained.

Chanonry, Lighthouse, March 7th 1930.

Sir,

I beg to intimate that at 2.30 a.m. of the 7th March the S.S. James Tennant of Newcastle went aground on Chanonry Point while outward bound from Inverness to Invergordon light.

The alleged cause of the Vessel Stranding was given by the master who said he mistook his distance off Chanonry Light.

At low water the Vessel was dry but lay on an even Keel, and floated off with the afternoon tide undamaged and proceeded to Invergordon.

I am
Sir
Your Obedient Servant
Angus McEachern.

Further details of the last shipwreck at Chanonry Point in 1930.

dolphin would join me halfway across the bay. Escorting the *Fiona*, it surfaced near me, sometimes to blow, and an eye gazed straight into mine. Seated at the tiller, I could probably have touched it. This was a big dolphin, as long as the boat. It would play about while I emptied and re-baited the creels, and then accompanied me back to the middle of the bay. We parted at the end of the season when I took in the creels.

Off the Point, large runs of fish were pursued by leaping dolphins. In displays of acrobatics, they played with their catches, throwing them into the air. Where the shingle shelved steeply, dolphins chased to the edge. We could see them from the pantry window while we washed our dishes. No longer referred to as 'louper dogs', only a few members of the public were taking an interest, in contrast to the widespread fascination that was to come. In spring and summer, salmon and sea trout ran right past our door. On a mild summer's evening I could wander down in my slippers and catch a sea trout on the fly. At one time the Lighthouse Board had owned the netting rights on this foreshore; some mornings 'One for the Pot' could still be seen on the flagstone floor of the workshop.

The numbers of other fish, such as cod, had fallen since I was a boy. I noticed changes in the bird life too, especially ducks; we no longer saw huge rafts of duck on the water in autumn. No partridge reared a brood in the lighthouse grounds, but terns and ringed plovers still nested in shingle scrapes at the top of the beach, and in harsh wintry spells, flocks of snow bunting flitted on the bent grass below the gate. After one gale, I found a dead storm petrel in the coal cellar; a rare sight here, it had probably been blown off course. At the end of summer gannets filed past, flying west from breeding grounds – many dived for little fish in the bay. Porpoises surfaced, in roly-poly rhythm, about September.

For days off, there was good salmon fishing on the rivers Conon and Alness and regular holidays on the lovely Deveron. At certain times, I had good catches of herring in my net when thick shoals came to this part of the Firth. One autumn there was a bigger influx than usual; fishing boats from far and wide filled Rosemarkie Bay and took great catches. Some worked very close to the lighthouse and we heard snatches of radio conversation in the air.

By 1975 it was time to retire and leave the lighthouse world for the first time. Or so I thought. Instead, I was asked to cover for a welfare officer who was ill. During the next six months I enjoyed visiting every lighthouse in the north of Scotland, Orkney, Shetland, and the Western Isles, and catching up with many colleagues. About two years later I was appointed occasional keeper at Chanonry, and after the station was automated in 1984, I became attendant there. However, there would always be time for my favourite hobby – fishing!

Postscript

A couple of pages from Tarbat Ness lighthouse records, dated May 1885, came to light recently: a monthly letter and lighting log. Both are written in copperplate handwriting and signed 'Arch'd MacEachern, Principal Lightkeeper' – Archie's grandfather.

The old log includes a column headed: 'A Keeper absent from the Lighthouse will here state the Period of his Absence and the Cause'. Among the reasons given are: 'At Church' and 'At Portmahomack taking delivery of coals from 5.30 am till 4 pm'. In the monthly letter we see that on the '29th the smack Union Jack delivered at Portmahomack, 20 tons of Scotch Coals for the use of the station'. The principal would have been at the harbour that day arranging for a horse and cart to transport the coal to the lighthouse. A registered letter was received on the 18th containing money to pay the quarterly accounts. On the 19th he was absent from the station for four hours paying accounts at Portmahomack.

Some interesting items appear on a lengthy list of the stores received, including a watch cloak for each keeper, 12 steel pens, and half a pint of ink. That year they were supplied with 3lbs umber, 3lbs ochre, 2lbs red lead, 3lbs black lead, 4lbs pearl ashes, 1lb rotten stone, 44 fathoms machinery rope, and 12 fathoms signal halyard. Items for maintaining the light include 6 doz Argand wicks, 4ozs reflector rouge, and ten chamois skins. After these, four aprons are listed –the white linen aprons that keepers wore for working on the lens, though more recently they were used by wives in their kitchens. Lighthouse window screen and a ball of cord for window screens are among the many other necessities listed. How things changed! From Tarbat Ness, the keepers were required to observe the light at Lossiemouth, and the monthly letter concludes with: 'Covesea Skerries Light seen every night this month.'

Large official books with imposing leather bindings were kept up to date at every lighthouse. Among earlier entries in these order books were many exhortations that would have been read by Archie's father and grandfather. Falling asleep on duty or failure to wind the machine on time resulted in instant dismissal, followed by naming and shaming in memos throughout the service. Other misdemeanours were punished by a fine of one guinea, and some with demotion. There were also mentions and rewards for 'meritorious conduct' and lifesaving. Orders and memos on all manner of topics were circulated and pasted into the station's books. Headings included: 'Regarding Misconduct', 'Regarding Negligence', 'Regarding Dismissal of Lightkeeper', and 'Regarding Want of Cleanliness'.

One memo in 1857 rejected a request for a pay increase, effectively telling keepers how well off they were:

> The Commissioners are satisfied that, taken as a class, lightkeepers enjoy greater privileges, combined with perfect security than any other class of the same grade in the kingdom. The Commissioners require and expect from lightkeepers the strictest integrity and unwearying zeal and vigilance in the discharge of their highly responsible duties. For this they are rewarded by being removed from all anxiety and care attendant on the maintenance of themselves and families.

Most aspects of life were covered. At remote stations, books were issued for the children's education. In 1848 'general directions for teaching' were included, stressing 'the necessity of exercising patience'. Even back in 1858, the Board was supplying periodicals to families. A principal keeper received the *Leisure Hour*, and assistants were sent the *Welcome Guest* and the *Family Herald*, with instructions to exchange these 'so that each Lightkeeper may have the perusal of all the Periodicals'.

In 1848 advice on the prevention of cholera stressed that clean living was the best safeguard:

> The first precautionary advice given by all medical men is to avoid intoxication or excess in the use of spirits. The Commissioners trust that it is unnecessary for them to repeat such a caution to any lightkeeper in their service [...] it is by no means uncommon for a fit of intoxication to pass into an attack of Cholera [...] The lightkeeper should be aware that persons living apart from the general population, in comfort and cleanliness, and without indulgence in dissipated habits, are extremely little subject to be attacked by malignant Cholera in this country [...]

Directions for treating cholera 'where medical aid cannot be obtained' included giving opium, cardamom, and camphor. 'Mustard blistering on the belly' was recommended, and if that failed:

> [...] a blister on the belly with boiling water applied by means of a soaked and folded towel for a few seconds at a time. In a stage of fever the head should be shaved and a common blister applied over it.

If the patient survived all of this as well as the cholera and regained their appetite 'the lightest food only should be given, such as sago or bread and tea.'

In 1873 an order was issued 'Regarding Bed Curtains':

> On a recent tour of inspection by Commissioners several of the lightkeepers and their wives stated that they found these bed curtains to be unwholesome, as preventing their obtaining pure air while sleeping [...]
>
> The Board have directed this General Order to be issued, recommending their lightkeepers to cease using curtains on their beds; but at the same time where bedrooms at lighthouses are much exposed to draughts, this recommendation need not be acted on.

Fair Isle South 1998. Attending the ceremony to mark automation of the last Scottish lighthouse. Archie 2nd left.

More recently, an order in 1941 regarding the annual requisitions for medicines stated:

It is observed, almost without exception, the whole of the pint of Brandy is shown as being consumed each year [...] its use must be restricted to its necessary use in an emergency. I have to instruct you that in future, on each occasion when Brandy is used, the name of the person to whom it is given, the date, the amount used, and the reason for giving the Brandy is to be entered in your quarterly Medical Return.

Bad news for Christmas puddings!

In 1998, we were honoured to be invited to Fair Isle South for the official ceremony marking the automation of the last manned lighthouse in Scotland and the Isle of Man. The other (more recently) retired keepers who had been invited wore uniform as requested. Archie no longer had his full uniform, so he put on his uniform cap with his suit. It was a splendid occasion and the first time that he had been to Fair Isle since 1939. Some changes could be seen on the island. Stewart and Annie drove us to Fair Isle North lighthouse where the housing block had been demolished. 'The Rock' stood firm in the sea nearby and hosted many fulmars and of course Sheep Rock still dominated one side of the island's landscape. There was a warm Fair Isle welcome at an evening party in the hall and much to make the visit memorable.

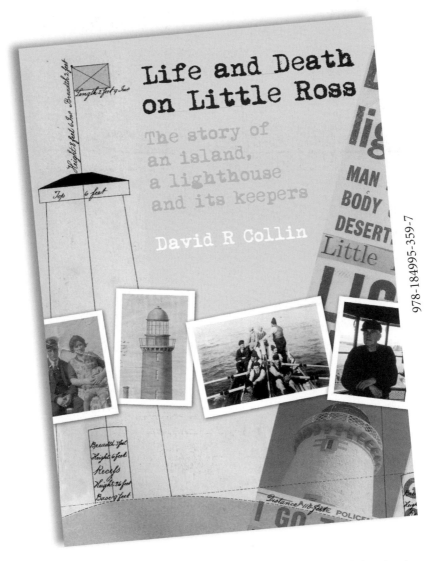

978-184995-359-7

Collin has written a broad-ranging human and natural history of the island, its keepers, and their families. ... writes with great knowledge and affection for the island... ...we are fortunate that Collin has set down the history of a small island lighthouse that might have otherwise faded into obscurity. **The Lightkeeper**

Without doubt this is a valuable social document. **FLASH, The Trinity House Journal**

...this extraordinarily detailed book. Collin goes to great effort to provide the reader with every detail imagined about the island and its lighthouse. ...Life and Death on Little Ross is a comprehensive and thoroughly researched history of the island and its lighthouse. ...the book is very well written and a tribute to a bygone way of life. **World Lighthouse Society**

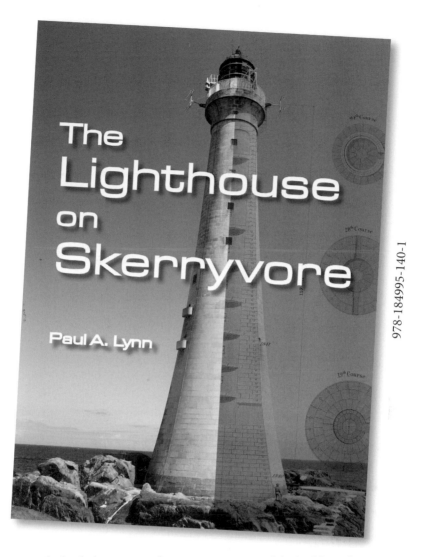

…a gem of a book that is more than just an account of the building of a massive stone tower on a treacherous ledge. …Lynn blends art and science, distilling the story of Skerryvore into a highly readable, engrossing chronicle. **The Lightkeeper**

…a thorough account of the building of the lighthouse as well as a discussion of Stevenson's personal background and the personality behind this remarkable Victorian engineer. … I would recommend this book to anyone with an interest in lighthouses, maritime history and historical accounts of engineering achievements. **World Lighthouse Society Newsletter**

…this publication is important. … I congratulate Paul Lynn on his articulate and skilful narration… …I found it a great read and have no hesitation in recommending it to the lighthouse aficionado as well as the casual reader! You will not be disappointed. **www.bellrock.org.uk**

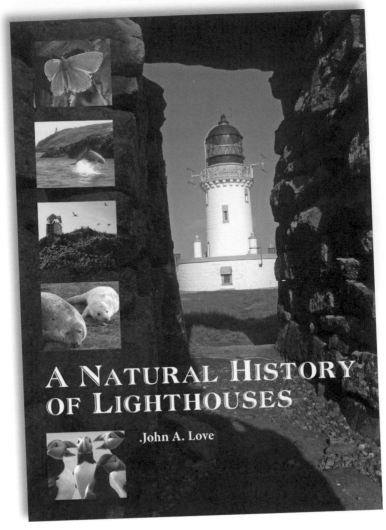

...a collection of great stories about the life of the keepers, as well as references to the work of lightships and their crew. ...there are plenty of marvellous stories here. This well-produced book also contains some terrific photography... **Nautilus Telegraph**

...an in-depth look at lightkeepers and their contributions to the study of natural history. ...a valuable account of those keepers who kept detailed records of bird sightings, weather, and other natural phenomena. **The Lightkeeper**

The author writes from a wealth of experience and the book is profusely illustrated. ...a very readable work, interspersed with many anecdotes. I can recommend this book, especially if, like me, you have a penchant for visiting lighthouses. **Scottish Birds**

To order books please visit our website, www.whittlespublishing.com
or call us on +44(0)1593 73133. We look forward to hearing from you.